Voodoo

Voodoo

The History of a Racial Slur

DANIELLE N. BOAZ

OXFORD
UNIVERSITY PRESS

Oxford University Press is a department of the University of Oxford. It furthers
the University's objective of excellence in research, scholarship, and education
by publishing worldwide. Oxford is a registered trade mark of Oxford University
Press in the UK and certain other countries.

Published in the United States of America by Oxford University Press
198 Madison Avenue, New York, NY 10016, United States of America.

© Oxford University Press 2023

All rights reserved. No part of this publication may be reproduced, stored in
a retrieval system, or transmitted, in any form or by any means, without the
prior permission in writing of Oxford University Press, or as expressly permitted
by law, by license, or under terms agreed with the appropriate reproduction
rights organization. Inquiries concerning reproduction outside the scope of the
above should be sent to the Rights Department, Oxford University Press, at the
address above.

You must not circulate this work in any other form
and you must impose this same condition on any acquirer.

Library of Congress Control Number: 2023939252

ISBN 978-0-19-768941-7 (pbk.)
ISBN 978-0-19-768940-0 (hbk.)

DOI: 10.1093/oso/9780197689400.001.0001

Paperback printed by Marquis Book Printing, Canada
Hardback printed by Bridgeport National Bindery, Inc., United States of America

Contents

Introduction vii

1. Emancipation, Civil Rights, and the Origins of "Voodoo" in the 1850s–1880s 1
2. "Voodoo" and U.S. Imperialism in Cuba in the 1890s–1920s 27
3. Love Cults and "White Slaves" in the 1920s 55
4. Human Sacrifice and African American Muslims in the 1930s 77
5. "Sacrifices at Sea" and Haitian Refugees in the 1980s 97
6. Sex Trafficking and Sacred Oaths in the 1990s to the Present 117
   Conclusion: Voodoo, Obeah, and Macumba 135

Notes 145
Bibliography 179
Index 187

Introduction

In January 2010, a 7.0-magnitude earthquake hit Haiti, displacing more than a million people and killing more than 200,000.[1] In the months that followed, some people—both in Haiti and abroad—claimed that the devastating quake was God's retribution for the widespread practice of "voodoo," which many equated with devil worship.[2] Some Christian missionaries and churches, who received a vast portion of the aid that went to Haiti, refused to give food or other necessities to people who practiced "voodoo."[3] Furthermore, as Vodou (a more respectful name for Haitian "voodoo") priests gathered to honor the dead and pray for the living, Christian extremists attacked them—throwing rocks, destroying their shrines, and urinating on their sacred objects.[4]

Approximately nine months later, in the middle of October, the world's largest cholera outbreak began sweeping through Haiti.[5] In just two months, cholera killed approximately 2,600 people,[6] hospitalized more than 60,000, and infected more than 120,000.[7] Before the decline of the outbreak in 2015, more than 9,000 would die and hundreds of thousands would be infected.[8] Some Haitians believed that the cholera outbreak was a result of Vodou adherents poisoning the water supply with a substance known as *poud kolera*, or cholera powder.[9] In November 2010, mobs began to murder Vodou devotees in the streets, frequently burning their victims alive. By late December, at least forty-five Vodou adherents had been killed in the Department of Grand Anse alone.[10]

A few months later, in April 2011, United Nations human rights experts urged the Haitian government to investigate these murders and ensure that such vigilante attacks were not permitted.[11] In its subsequent reports to the United Nations in July 2011 and January 2013, the Haitian government assured the United Nations that they had taken measures to protect Vodou devotees and punish the attackers.[12] In the latter report, they even went so far as to claim that all religions were free to practice their faith in Haiti and that "[t]here is no discrimination against the practicants [*sic*] of Vodou."[13] Seemingly unconvinced by the government's response, in April 2014, the U.N. Human Rights Committee asked Haiti to specify how many people they had arrested, how the perpetrators had been punished, what measures they had taken to prevent future attacks, and what assistance had given to the victims.[14] It appears that the Haitian government never responded.

Such attacks on African diaspora religious communities are becoming very common in the twenty-first century. For instance, in 2019, an Evangelical church in Santiago de Cuba recorded its leader destroying Afro-Cuban (Santería-Lucumi) shrines during a church service, while singing that "idols" have no power compared to the blood of Jesus. That same year, Evangelical drug traffickers invaded at least 200 Candomblé and Umbanda temples in Rio de Janeiro, Brazil, threatening devotees, destroying sacred objects, and, sometimes, burning the places of worship to the ground.[15]

In my first book, *Banning Black Gods: Law and Religions of the African Diaspora*, I document the systematic attacks on African-derived religions that are coming from multiple fronts. In addition to physical assaults on devotees, government officials have restricted the practice of these religions. Courts and lawmakers have limited devotees' rights to wear religious attire and hairstyles in schools, courtrooms, and other public spaces. Judges have questioned devotees' fitness to raise children and have revoked their custody rights. Police have pretended to be priests of these religions and have performed fake rituals to coerce adepts into confessing to crimes. In much of the Anglophone Caribbean, legislators continue to criminalize African diaspora religions through laws prohibiting "Obeah." The reason for the frequency of these legal and physical attacks is very simple. Discrimination against African-derived religions is one of the most pervasive and least questioned forms of racism in the Western Hemisphere today.

In recent years, there has been a growing movement to eliminate language and images that glorify slavery and colonialism or reinforce discriminatory stereotypes from these eras. For example, consider the rebranding efforts of companies like Aunt Jemima's, Uncle Ben's, and Mrs. Butterworth's, or the movement to rename places and remove monuments that honor slave owners, confederate soldiers, and colonial officials. Several popular music groups have even removed words like "Dixie" and "Antebellum" from their names to avoid being perceived as racist. Despite the widespread reevaluation of racially charged terms and images, there has been no backlash against the sale of "voodoo dolls" or Hollywood tropes about "voodoo" cannibalism and human sacrifice in movies and television shows. No one hesitates to denounce beliefs and practices that they wish to discriminate against as "voodoo." Nevertheless, as this book explores, the term of "voodoo" has extremely racist origins and has been used to denigrate people of African descent and their spiritual practices since its inception.

Defining "Voodoo"

What is "voodoo"? As the chapters of this book demonstrate, the meaning of "voodoo" has varied greatly over time and has shifted to encompass different religious communities, distinct practices, and evolving perceptions about people of African descent. When referring to this spelling and pronunciation, the term "voodoo" originated in the United States and, throughout most of its nearly 200-year history, has been deployed largely by people in the United States to refer to the alleged spiritual practices of people of African descent in North America or abroad. Since the term "voodoo" emerged in the nineteenth century, it has been a mechanism for racist individuals to invoke all their anxieties and stereotypes about people of African descent—to call them uncivilized, superstitious, hypersexual, violent, and cannibalistic, by merely uttering this single word. For this reason, I argue that "voodoo" has operated primarily as a racial slur—a term used to denigrate the spiritual beliefs and practices of Black people. However, language is dynamic and ever-changing, and it's possible that someday, African-diaspora religious communities might reclaim the term as their own.

Virtually every country in the Americas has its own version of the word "voodoo." As Europeans tried to identify (and often prohibit) the religions of the enslaved Africans in their colonial territories, they typically came up with terms that they used to refer to these belief systems. Although enslaved persons came from many parts of the African continent and had diverse religious backgrounds, Europeans often used just one or two labels to refer to the wide range of beliefs and practices that developed in their colonies. In Cuba, this term was "Santería." In British colonies, it was "Obeah." In French colonies such as St. Domingue, the term was "vaudoux." Eventually, as explored in Chapter 1, "vaudoux" evolved into "voodoo" in North American English.

In some cases, these labels developed from Europeans' perceptions of African religions. For example, "Santería" means "worship of saints." Spanish colonists used this term for devotees of African religions who disguised the worship of their own divinities (orishas) with the honoring of Catholic saints. In other circumstances, such as "Obeah," scholars have argued that these European labels were developed from words of African origin.[16]

"Vaudoux" is also likely a word of West African origin; it probably originated from the Dahomean word "vodu" or "vudu," meaning "spirit."[17] The French had adopted this term by the 1790s, when Martiniquean lawyer Mederic Louis Elie Moreau de Saint Mery published his now well-known description of "vaudoux" as an extremely dangerous weapon that could be cultivated by African priests.[18]

Such terror of African spirituality was extremely common in the Americas during the eighteenth and nineteenth centuries. Nearly every slave uprising during this period was organized by religious leaders, was held on a religious holiday, and/or incorporated religious ceremonies or talismans. As a result, in many colonies, African spiritual practices were restricted by law. Religious leaders were blamed for coercing supposedly "superstitious" Africans into rebellions; colonial authorities captured, convicted, and publicly executed them to undermine their spiritual power.

In the case of "vaudoux," two such uprisings stand out. First, in 1758, a maroon (runaway slave) leader named Francois Makandal organized an uprising in northern St. Domingue (modern-day Haiti) that involved poisoning the local water supply.[19] Makandal, who was rumored to be a Vodou ("vaudoux") priest, was captured before the plot could be carried out. He was promptly burned at the stake. After Makandal's execution, colonial authorities prohibited enslaved people from possessing talismans, which became known as "makandals."[20]

A few decades later, in 1791, a much more famous incident may have taken place. In August of that year, a large-scale slave rebellion began in the northern part of St. Domingue that would change the course of history. After more than twelve years of political maneuvering and warfare, in 1804, St. Domingue became Haiti—the first independent Black nation in the Western Hemisphere. Legend says that this rebellion, which has become known as the Haitian revolution, began with a Vodou ceremony in an area called Bois Caiman (Caiman Woods). Religious leaders allegedly offered prayers and sacrificed a pig to their spirits/divinities, seeking guidance and protection for the insurrection, as well as securing unity and loyalty among the rebels.[21]

These are just two examples of the dozens of large-scale insurrections that were carried out under the guidance and spiritual protection of religious leaders. If one adds everyday acts of empowerment and rebellion that enslaved persons performed through spiritual practice—creating charms to protect themselves, herbal remedies to heal, divination to find direction and purpose, and so on—it becomes clear why Europeans often regarded these religions in a negative light. Religion offered alternative sources of authority and knowledge to enslaved people, and this threatened the stability of the plantation system.

After emancipation, outsider perceptions of African-derived religions did not improve. In virtually every region of the Americas, plantation owners and others who had relied on enslaved labor sought new ways to coerce free or cheap labor out of people of African descent. In many cases, this meant the development of new laws governing "vagrancy" that barred certain activities like gambling, living in an unoccupied dwelling, begging for charitable contributions, or deserting one's family. These vagrancy laws frequently included bans on certain types of spiritual practices. For instance, in the British Caribbean, vagrancy statutes prohibited the practice of "Obeah."[22] As many of the people convicted of violating these laws were sentenced to perform manual labor as part of their punishment, these statutes served the dual purpose of suppressing African-based religions and forcing practitioners of these religions to work in areas that colonial authorities regarded as productive or fitting for Black people.

Additionally, as discussed further in Chapters 1, 2, and 5, people of European descent voiced serious concerns about the role of people of African descent in the Americas after emancipation. Several countries with large populations of Black people restricted or completely prohibited non-white immigration after emancipation to stop white populations from being outnumbered. Many places also attempted to control formerly enslaved people through regulations on their ability to vote, hold government office, and otherwise govern themselves. Many countries or colonies also adopted new restrictions on African-derived religions in an effort to culturally whiten their societies and to eliminate a powerful force of Black resistance. Policymakers frequently justified these restrictions by arguing that priests of these religions were charlatans and that they promoted superstitions and barbaric practices.

Therefore, even where scholars have been able to determine possible African origins of terms like "vaudoux" and "Obeah," people of European descent have been largely responsible for shaping the public meaning of these new labels for African-derived religions.[23] Because they feared and misunderstood these religions, the terms that Europeans used to describe African religions typically developed a very negative connotation. They came to mean all the things that Europeans viewed as the antithesis of religion—magic, sorcery, devil worship, vagrancy, fetish worship, charlatanism, and even human sacrifice.

These racist stereotypes persist until the present day, in part because popular culture has consistently repeated them. Leslie Desmangles explains, "Thanks to Hollywood and the film industry, what average persons conjure up in their minds when they think of Voodoo is a picture of witches and sorcerers who, filled with hatred, attempt to inflict diseases or even death on other persons by making wax or wooden representations of them, and perforating them with pins."[24] This is certainly true. Virtually every television series about policing and crime that has run for more than one or two seasons has featured at least one episode about "voodoo."[25] In these episodes, the criminal investigative teams (who are usually white) interact with someone who "superstitiously" believes that they are the subject of a "curse," and they race to unravel the truth before the "voodoo doctor" uses physical violence to prove the power of the threatened curse. These episodes frequently feature nighttime scenes with blood, bones, pentagrams, candles, and, sometimes, shrunken heads.

Movies also frequently center on plots about evil "voodoo" practitioners or adepts of other African-diaspora religions like Santería. These are typically horror films where the protagonist must escape from hexes, ghosts, poisons, and zombies.[26] However, even children's movies are not above reinforcing such negative stereotypes of African-diaspora religions. In Disney's first movie featuring a Black princess, *The Princess and the Frog* (2009), the story is set in New Orleans and the villain is an evil "voodoo doctor."[27] With skulls, shrunken heads, snakes, and voodoo dolls dancing across the screen, the villain tells the prince that his "friends on the other side" will help the prince achieve his wildest dreams. These film and television representations reinforce harmful, racist stereotypes of African-derived religions and provide fuel for the discrimination and violence against adepts of these religions in the twenty-first century.

Common Themes

Although the term "voodoo" has been used to attribute many heinous acts to people of African descent, there are a few characteristics of these alleged "superstitions" that have been relatively consistent over time. First, there has often been a gendered element to descriptions of ceremonies that are labeled as "voodoo." From the nineteenth century to the present day, women have been depicted frequently as falling victim to coercive "superstitions" and being manipulated by a cunning "voodoo doctor" or "voodoo queen" into participating in activities that would have been considered immoral or deviant at the time. It is important to understand these aspects of public depictions of "voodoo" as deeply connected to evolving gender norms, including fearmongering about the breakup of (white) families, and the desire to control women using claims about their vulnerability and purported fears of their abuse. They are also connected to long-standing post-emancipation claims about the sexual threat of Black men and the promiscuity of Black women.

Second, since the late nineteenth century, Black persons accused of human sacrifice or cannibalism have often been described as "voodoo" practitioners. One should not view the frequency of such claims as evidence that people of African descent practice ritual murder or engage in the consumption of human flesh as part of their religious practices. Rather, accusations of human sacrifice and cannibalism are ways of "othering" populations that have been common throughout history in every region of the world. They are ways of denouncing strangers, especially rivals, as primitive and barbaric, and justifying conquest, enslavement, and other brutalities against them. Perhaps the best-studied example is the long-standing myth of "blood libel"—the allegation that Jewish people ritually murder Christian children. This claim has supported centuries of anti-Semitism, including being used by the Nazi regime during the Holocaust.[28]

Typically, these claims are based exclusively on rumors or on suspicious purported eyewitness accounts. The cases discussed in this book are no exception. In each region, rumors of "voodoo" sacrifices and cannibalism began based on the actions of a person who was later adjudged legally insane or following a strange death or disappearance that was presumed to be the work of Black "voodoo doctors." Racist stereotypes about Black communities led to the assumption that these practices were prevalent among the entire population.

Third, slavery is intricately tied to the term "voodoo." As one will see in Chapter 1, the anglicized term emerged during the U.S. Civil War and initially referred to gatherings of people in New Orleans that allegedly violated laws prohibiting certain interactions between enslaved and free people. Over subsequent years, in the United States, Cuba, Haiti, and likely other places, purported "voodoo" practices were used as evidence that Black people were unprepared for emancipation and citizenship. Ironically, in later periods, "voodoo doctors" have been accused of using spiritual practices to abuse and enslave others, including during the "white slavery" panic of the early twentieth century and in human trafficking cases in the present day.

These themes—gender, sexuality, human sacrifice, and slavery—reappear again and again in the cases and time periods discussed in this book. By remembering these tropes, we can see larger biases about Black people reflected and reinforced in the usages of "voodoo."

Relationship to Other Terms

To better explain the development of the term "voodoo," it is important to briefly explore its relationship to other terminology used for Africana spiritual beliefs. First and foremost, in the following chapters, I discuss how the U.S. media, travelogues, and other texts sometimes referred to other African diaspora religions such as Obeah or Santería/Lucumi as "voodoo." It is essential not to think of "voodoo" as synonymous with Obeah, Santería, or other labels that were used to describe Africana religions in different parts of the Americas. The conflation of these religions with "voodoo" was inconsistent and, as in the examples discussed in this book, typically only became common when a major incident occurred to bring international attention to these other religions. Additionally, before the mid-twentieth century, the United States usually had an imperial interest in any colony or country where the U.S. media proclaimed that "voodoo" practitioners resided. In other time periods or in places where there was no potential political or economic gain from accusing Black populations of backwardness and "superstition," these religions were rarely mentioned by U.S. and other Anglophone sources and were less likely to be conflated with "voodoo."

During the times when the U.S. media and other outsider publications were referring to other African-diaspora religions as "voodoo," this terminology does not seem to have been picked up by local news or authorities in the country or colony where the alleged "voodoo" was taking place. For example, Chapter 2 discusses U.S. imperialism in Cuba and how the U.S. media used the term "voodoo" to describe allegations that Afro-Cuban "priests" were kidnapping and sacrificing children in the early twentieth century. While people in the United States interpreted these events as "voodoo,"

Cuban newspapers and authorities used local terms such as "brujos," "brujeria," and "nanigos."

As this example illustrates, one should not regard the usage or interpretation of "voodoo" as universal during most of the periods discussed in this book. Rather, it is a term that developed in the United States and that the United States has continued to mold and shape in subsequent decades. Over time, "voodoo" has become commonly used outside the United States; however, it continues to be most frequently employed in the Anglophone world, especially in North America and parts of Europe. One must recall that many other countries have their own terms—"macumba," "Obeah," "brujeria," and so on—that are somewhat comparable to "voodoo" and that described what the authorities viewed as illegitimate African spiritual practices. Most of these terms remain in use in non-English-speaking countries in the Americas and are frequently preferred over "voodoo."

Additionally, even within the United States, "voodoo" was not the only term used to describe African American spirituality. There were also other words, such as "conjure," "root work," and "hoodoo," that were common during various periods and in different regions of the country. The relationship between these terms and "voodoo" is and was, at best, very murky.

Yvonne Chireau explains that "[c]onjure is a magical tradition in which spiritual power is invoked for various purposes, such as healing, protection, and self defense."[29] In most cases, scholars seem to agree that "conjure" and "hoodoo" are very closely related terms that might be considered interchangeable.[30] Root work is also considered very similar to "conjure" and "hoodoo," but refers to an element of these practices that involves herbal remedies.[31]

Scholars frequently contend that "voodoo" is closely related to these terms but that it has a slightly distinct meaning, particularly among African Americans. For instance, Jeffrey Anderson argues that "conjure" "properly defined, falls between the two extremes of religion proper and low-level supernaturalism."[32] Anderson specifically distinguishes conjure from religions that "honor the gods and spirits" like "nineteenth-century Louisianian Voodoo and modern Cuban Santería."[33] Chireau observes that when "voodoo" is used to refer to practices within the United States, it would be distinct from other terms like "conjure" or "hoodoo" because it "connotes an illicit form of spirituality" and that "[s]upernatural harming is usually called Voodoo."[34]

Although scholars argue that African American communities, at times, distinguished between "voodoo" and other terms like "hoodoo" or "conjure," it was not common for people of African descent to openly debate about the appropriateness of the use of the word "voodoo" in the incidents that I discuss in this book. This was likely because, with the exception of the oaths and rituals discussed in Chapter 6, the alleged "voodoo practitioners" were not engaged in any kind of Africana spiritual practice. Instead, they were accused of slavery, cannibalism, human sacrifice, and other atrocities. Denying these practices entirely would have been a better defense tactic for both African American communities in general and for the specific targets of the allegation than to seek the recognition of "voodoo" as a legitimate religion or to argue using nuances (i.e., that they practiced "hoodoo" not "voodoo") that outsiders would have been unlikely to understand.

Additionally, many African Americans, particularly members of the middle and upper classes, may have agreed with public narratives about "superstition" in Black communities. For instance, Jeffrey Anderson argues that, in the period following the U.S. Civil War (when narratives about "voodoo" first became more widespread), it was not just white people who referred to African American religions as evidence of the inferiority or backwardness of the race. African Americans likewise denounced conjurers and argued that such "superstitions" were an unfortunately common feature of Black society.[35] Anderson explains, "As members of the small but growing middle class [of African Americans] became educated and quickly adopted the scientific outlook and social Darwinism of the larger American society, they confidently expected conjure to disappear. In fact, according to many blacks' ideology of racial uplift, such backward features of black society would have to give way before the race could hope to advance."[36]

According to Anderson, even the Civil Rights movement in the United States did not lend itself to a vindication of African American beliefs in "hoodoo" or conjure because the leaders of the movement were middle class and were from the segment of the population that had long rejected these beliefs as barbaric.[37] Furthermore, among Black Christians of the time, who played a key role in the movement, publicly embracing African-derived rituals (whether practiced behind closed doors or not) would not have been a key element of their vision of the uplift of the race. When coupled with the fact that "conjure," "hoodoo," and other spiritual practices had become much less prevalent topics in the media by the 1940s, it becomes easy to imagine why African Americans did not have a clearer voice in shaping the public narratives about "voodoo" discussed in this book.[38]

By contrast, after the end of the U.S. occupation of Haiti (1915–1934), Haitian intellectuals like Jean Price Mars led a movement that sought to defend the nation's African roots, including Vodou. Around this same period, devotees of Candomblé and Umbanda in Brazil engaged in campaigns against the criminalization of Afro-Brazilian religions. One of the tactics that they employed was distinguishing their religions from "macumba," which came to signify a "lower" level of African-derived spirituality that devotees of Candomblé and Umbanda agreed could be criminalized.

These different attitudes toward African diaspora religions in the mid-to-late twentieth century may explain why, unlike nearly every other term that outsiders have used to describe African diaspora religions, there has been little effort (except perhaps in New Orleans) to reclaim and reframe the term "voodoo" in the twenty-first century. In my work as a researcher and legal advocate for African diaspora religious communities, I have often heard friends and colleagues say other terms that are sometimes used to denigrate devotees. Among my contacts, it seems that devotees of Afro-Cuban religions use the term "Santería" at least as often, if not more frequently, than the less offensive "Regla de Ocha" or "Lucumi." Some members of Candomblé communities in Brazil informally refer to themselves as "macumbeiros" or their ritual gatherings as "macumba." Black women devotees of many African diaspora religions will occasionally refer to themselves as "witches" or "brujas," and their rituals as "witchcraft" or "brujeria" (particularly when speaking to one another).

With "voodoo," on the other hand, scholars have often cautioned that devotees would not recognize or use this moniker. Instead, they might avoid naming their practices at all and simply reference "serving the spirits." Alternatively, in the case of devotees of African diaspora religion in Haiti, they might use the more accepted spelling and pronunciation "Vodou."

In recognition of devotees' preferred terminology, scholars and devotees recently undertook a collaborative project to get the Library of Congress to change the spelling of its entry from "voodooism" to Vodou.[39] In a roundtable discussion in 2018, prominent Haitian studies scholars denounced Anglophone presses' continued use of "voodoo" as a "translation" for Haitian Vodou following this change. Kaiama L. Glover wrote that "voodoo" "represents a dangerous reification of the stereotypes that allow for the persistent inhumanity with which people in the US think, talk, write about, and treat Haitians."[40] Kate Ramsey adds that "[b]eyond journalistic ignorance and/or laziness, there is likely a profit motive operative in such choices. That is because 'voodoo' sells, and imagined in these ways, has long done so."[41] Carolyn Shread describes the use of the term "voodoo" as "the four fascinated holes of ignorance—oo oo" and argues that the prejudices that fuel the misspelling of Vodou are connected to "an outdated, self-interested depreciation of a culture by the forces of empire and white supremacy."[42] This study of the history of "voodoo" as a racial slur reinforces these arguments, illustrating why devotees and scholars distance themselves from this term.

Research Methods

The purpose of this project is to explore the public perceptions of "voodoo" from the development of the term until the present day, with an emphasis on the intricate connection between stereotypes of "voodoo" and debates about race and human rights. Therefore, the research for this project has consisted of examining historical texts published for public consumption such as newspapers, travelogues, magazines, and books. Occasionally, where a more official record of a situation helps reveal useful context, I have included information drawn from laws, court cases, and other similar documents.

Historical texts have been compiled from a variety of different databases, such as America's Historical Newspapers, Google Books, JSTOR, Proquest Historical Newspapers, newspaperarchive.com, 19th Century British Library Newspapers, Nineteenth Century Collections Online, and the Times Digital Archive. The newspapers cited in this book vary substantially in terms of circulation numbers, publication location, and intended audience. In the nineteenth century, where these distinctions often dictated how the author described "voodoo," available details about the publication are discussed. However, by the early twentieth century, U.S. news outlets demonstrated little variation in their reporting on "voodoo" across regions and in papers with different political bents. This was particularly true when discussing "voodoo" that took place abroad and incidents that garnered national attention. In fact, most stories about "voodoo" were reprinted in dozens of newspapers with little or no modifications. However, because databases of historical newspapers have incomplete collections, it is impossible to be sure in most cases whether certain types of newspapers or certain regions of the United States were more likely to reprint these stories than others. In the few instances where there do seem to be clear and significant discrepancies in reporting among different types of papers or regions of the country, these are discussed in the book.

In cases where it is important to identify the first mention of a term or the frequency of the discussion of an issue, I have tried to exhaust available resources to provide an accurate history of the evolving public discussions. However, it is impossible to prove that something was not discussed or did not occur. Another source or archive is always out there, waiting to be discovered or digitized, eventually challenging the historical narrative. Nevertheless, this book is not meant to track every moment in the evolution of the term "voodoo." Rather, through the discussion of several major themes and eras, it is designed to illustrate the broader connections between perceptions about "voodoo rites" and the civil or human rights of people of African descent.

Structure of the Book

This book is divided into six chapters. The first chapter examines the origins of the term "voodoo" as it splits off from the French word "vaudoux." It roots the concept of "voodoo" in the U.S. Civil War and the idea that Black Americans held certain "superstitions" that allegedly proved that they were unprepared for freedom, the right to vote, and the ability to hold public office. It also explores how stereotypes about Haitian "voodoo" emerged in the latter half of the nineteenth century and came into dialogue with existing narratives about "voodoo" in North America.

Chapter 2 explores the extension of these stereotypes about Black religions to Cuba, a newly "independent" nation which spent much of the early twentieth century either under U.S. occupation or with fear of imminent return of U.S. forces. This chapter situates the expansion of popular understandings of "voodoo" within U.S. imperialism in the Caribbean, adding to the well-known story about "voodoo" influencing the U.S. occupation of Haiti.

Chapter 3 returns to the United States, interrogating how media reports of the arrest of "voodoo doctors" illustrated fears about "white slavery," "race wars," and all-Black towns in the 1910s and 1920s. Chapter 4 continues this emphasis on the United States, discussing the founding of the Moorish Science Temple and the Nation of Islam, and the denunciation of these two Black Muslim organizations as "voodoo cults" in the 1930s.

The book skips over the 1940s–1970s because I did not uncover any major incidents that were widely reported connecting "voodoo" and human rights during this period. Although the word "voodoo" never entirely left the media or faded from public imagination, it seems to have temporarily lost some of its political power. This seems to be a natural consequence of Black people in the Americas securing the right to vote and hold office, U.S. colonial forces leaving Cuba and Haiti, fearmongering about white slavery quieting, and rumors of human sacrifice among Black Muslims dying down. Furthermore, this period corresponds with the decriminalization of African diaspora religions in much of the Americas (or at least the temporary end of widespread persecution and prosecution) and, as mentioned previously, the rise of several intellectual movements which sought to redeem public perceptions of African spiritual and cultural practices. The mid-to-late twentieth century was a brief respite for devotees of African diaspora religions from public scrutiny and discrimination.

All of this changed in the late 1970s and 1980s, when Haitians once again become the primary target of rumors and myths about "voodoo" practices. Chapter 5 examines the relationship between allegations of "voodoo sacrifices" at sea and U.S. policies toward Haitian immigrants. The final chapter continues to interrogate the use of the term "voodoo" in immigration controversies, but it returns to a more international scope and to the relationship between "voodoo" and slavery. It explores twenty-first-century rituals to bind Nigerian women to the human traffickers who transport them to Europe. Authorities, scholars, and the media have labeled these rituals as "voodoo."

1
Emancipation, Civil Rights, and the Origins of "Voodoo" in the 1850s–1880s

Voodooism, with its heathenism rites, holds its place among them, though scarcely known among the colored population of other states. They are to a great extent utterly unfit for the exercise of the voting power and *the ballot in their hands becomes a mockery.*[1]

This chapter examines the development of the term "voodoo" in the nineteenth century, when the French word "vaudoux" merged with the Anglophone term "voodoo" in the media. It studies the meaning of "vaudoux" and "voodoo" in the United States, where the latter appears to have first originated. Through this examination of the development and fusion of these terms in English-language newspapers and books during the mid-nineteenth century, it explores how claims about the belief in and practice of "voodoo," first in New Orleans and then in Haiti, were used to oppose African American freedom and political participation in the post-emancipation United States.

The Emergence of Domestic "Voodoo" in the Nineteenth Century

Based on an extensive examination of nineteenth-century books, articles, and newspapers, I contend that although the United States purchased the Louisiana territory in 1803 and scholars believe that "voodoo" practices in New Orleans can be traced at least back to the 1820s,[2] mentions of the words "vaudoux," "vaudou," or any other form of the word "voodoo" were *extremely* rare in English-language presses in the United States in the first half of the nineteenth century.[3] References to "voodoo" practices became more frequent in the 1860s and throughout critical periods of the restructuring of civil

Voodoo. Danielle N. Boaz, Oxford University Press. © Oxford University Press 2023.
DOI: 10.1093/oso/9780197689400.003.0001

rights in the United States, such as the introduction and ratification of the Fourteenth and Fifteenth Amendments. Tales of Black "voodoo" practices were commonly employed as narratives opposing emancipation and the extension of citizenship and voting rights to people of African descent.

It is not unexpected that "voodoo" would emerge during the Civil War and center on discourse about race, emancipation, and political participation; African religion (or supposed lack thereof) was one of the key arguments used in an attempt to justify slavery in the Americas. Europeans claimed that Africans had no real concept of religion, and that they only practiced "fetish" worship and engaged in other "superstitions." Therefore, Europeans argued, slavery was beneficial to Africans because it placed them in close proximity to Europeans, from whom they could gain an understanding of religion and become Christians. In support of this argument, many colonies in the Americas had laws that required enslaved people to be baptized and/or prohibited the practice of any non-Christian religions.

This trope of slavery saving African people from their supposedly barbaric "superstitions" even persists to the present day. For instance, in 2018, Florida State Representative Kimberly Daniels sponsored a bill that would require public schools to conspicuously display the state motto "In God We Trust." While Daniels was arguing about the necessity of this bill, reports emerged that she had publicly expressed gratitude for the enslavement of her ancestors because "if it wasn't for slavery," she declared, "I might be somewhere in Africa worshipping a tree."[4] To understand the origins of the term "voodoo," one should keep in mind this long-standing connection between racism, slavery, and popular stereotypes about African religions.

Voodoo and Slavery in New Orleans (1850s)

Over the years, the term "voodoo" has become synonymous with the city of New Orleans, Louisiana. Therefore, it should come as no surprise that in the United States, the earliest mention of "voodoo" in any orthographic form in English-language presses appears to have been in New Orleans newspapers. These references were extremely rare before 1850, when the *Times Picayune* began to publish accounts of "voudou" practitioners' legal woes in that city. These stories reveal that slaveholders and their supporters in New Orleans regarded "voodoo" ceremonies as a dangerous practice that brought people of different races together, creating the opportunity for abolitionist activities and for people of African descent to draw white women into "unsavory" practices. However, even these stories were uncommon and rarely circulated outside New Orleans.

In July 1850, New Orleans newspapers printed at least five articles describing two separate incidents of the arrest of "voudou" practitioners. The first two articles, published on July 6 and 7, were mere blurbs in the City Intelligence column, which provided brief descriptions of all significant local news, but typically emphasized legal affairs such as the passage of new legislation and important or unusual arrests. In the middle of this column, under the subtitle "insulting an officer" and situated between two other stories about assault, the newspaper printed a one-sentence report indicating that a "voudou woman" named Adele Catharine alias Victoire Pellebon had been arrested for assaulting and abusing an officer.[5]

The second set of articles were of a different character than the first; they were featured stories and editorials about the arrest of several "coloured" women in relation to "voudou" ceremonies. These arrests were connected to regulations about "unlawful assembly"—laws that prohibited enslaved persons from gathering in certain conditions, such as without authorization from their owners or the supervision of a white person. Starting in or before 1850, police regularly raided a popular "voodoo" festival that occurred each June on St. John's Eve.

In this case, Betsy Toledano, a "voudou" woman who claimed that she had been taught certain "mysteries" and "rites" by her African-born grandmother, was arrested on charges of holding unlawful assemblies because authorities found two enslaved persons with her at the "voudou" ceremony.[6] The author of the article describing these arrests contended that these unlawful assemblies were very damaging to the slave society in New Orleans because they brought enslaved people into contact with "disorderly free negroes and mischievous whites." That this contact occurred under the guise of a spiritual gathering was particularly concerning to the author because they believed Black people were prone to "excitement" and once affected by "superstition," they would become "helpless and useless."[7] A newspaper in Alexandria, Virginia, reprinted the story of Toledano's arrest a few weeks later in a story titled "Rites of Voudou," including details of the items confiscated from the ceremony and Toledano's assertions that she could control the weather, but omitting the narratives about the purported threat that such ceremonies posed to slavery in New Orleans.[8] Otherwise,

U.S. newspapers outside New Orleans appear to have typically ignored these "voudou" stories in 1850.

Reports of the arrest of "voudou" practitioners, presumably at the St. John's ceremony, resurfaced in New Orleans in the *Times-Picayune* in July 1851. Eleven free Black women were once again charged with violating ordinances against unlawful assembly because an enslaved woman was in attendance. The participants were fined $10 each.[9] Like the initial reports in 1850, stories of these "voudou ceremonies" were featured in the City Intelligence column, sandwiched between a lengthy description of changes to the wharfage laws and stories about arrests for disorderly conduct, battery, and stealing chairs. They were subtitled "the Voudous," and referenced the "rites and mysteries" of these "superstitious" individuals. After these two consecutive years of reports about the arrest of "voudou" practitioners, adherents and their annual festivals appear to have gone completely unreported in New Orleans newspapers or other U.S. presses until the 1860s, other than a brief subsection in the City Intelligence column of the *Times-Picayune* titled "Voudrous" on November 3, 1854.[10]

It is not difficult to imagine the motivation behind such reports of unlawful "voudou" assemblies in the 1850s. While New Orleans newspapers seemed uniquely fixated on the interaction of people of different races, the denigration of African-derived religious ceremonies and the fear that they would be used as an organizing space for slave rebellions was nothing new. For instance, since 1760, Jamaican law had prohibited the practice of "Obeah," the British catchall term for African spiritual practices. The decision to ban Obeah stemmed from its use in a large-scale rebellion earlier that year during which African priests performed rituals to protect the insurgents from detection and from harm. The Obeah law was part of a series of new statutes designed to prevent slave rebellions, and it vilified Obeah using stereotypes about "sorcery" and "devil worship"— imagery that would become familiar tropes about African diaspora religions over the centuries. This is just one example of dozens of religious rituals and ceremonies that were used to plan slave rebellions and protect the insurgents, and the strict laws that often followed to prevent these religions and gatherings from stirring further uprisings.

The Civil War and New Orleans (1863)

Early in the Civil War, in April 1862, New Orleans was captured by Union forces. This was a moment of critical importance, as New Orleans was the largest city in the South, an economic hub, and—due to its location at the mouth of the Mississippi River—a region of great geographic and military significance. Realizing that the Union takeover represented their chance for freedom, over the following months, enslaved people began abandoning their plantations and seeking refuge with the Union forces. Thousands of these men eventually became soldiers for the Union army.

By the middle of the following year, reports of "voudou" practices in the city became a regular feature of New Orleans newspapers. From 1863 until 1900, not a single year passed without some commentary about "voudou" or "voodoo" practices in the city. For the first time, newspapers outside New Orleans also regularly began to reprint stories about "voodoo." The sudden fixation on Black spiritual practices was no accident; one should recall that one of the arguments used to attempt to justify slavery was that Africans had no religion and Europeans needed to convert them to Christianity. These accounts were meant to show how quickly Black people would supposedly revert to African "barbarism" if freed from white rule.

The first post-occupation reports in the *Times-Picayune* shared some superficial similarities to those from 1850 and 1851; however, they were both more detailed and more judgmental than previous articles. When the *Times-Picayune* published an account of the arrest of voudou practitioners in 1863, presumably during the St. John's ceremonies, the story was no longer buried in the middle of the City Intelligence column, nor downplayed with a short recount or vague subtitle; it was the first paragraph in the column and was the lengthiest story.[11] Initial reports indicated that 38 "colored" and two Black women—all of whom were naked—had been discovered when a voudou meeting was broken up. Perhaps most significantly, the author reported that the women were "performing the rites and incantations pertaining to that ancient African superstition [illegible] Voudooism." Although one story from 1850 included Betsy Toledano's claims to have been trained by African ancestors and referenced the tendency of "negroes" to get "excited" by "superstition," this 1863 article signified the beginning of a period when reporters examining New Orleans "voudou" would regularly discuss the predominantly African origins of these "superstitious" practices.

This story was also the first about New Orleans "voudou" to circulate widely in newspapers across the United States.[12] Over the course of approximately two months, various presses in all regions of the United States not only reprinted but also reinterpreted accounts of these 1863 arrests. Most featured sensational titles such as "American Pagans of African Descent," "Heathenism in New Orleans,"[13] and "Superstition in New Orleans."[14] Virtually all versions of the story contained an introduction that seemed to be explaining "voodoo" to an audience who would be unfamiliar with the term. For instance, the author claimed that the women were engaged in "the fetish rites *known as* the Voudou mysteries" and explained, "These rites are very curious, borrowed from the idolatries of the fetish or serpent worshippers of Africa."[15] The author suggested that these beliefs were fervently held, asserting that some New Orleanians placed great stock in these "African mysteries" or "idolatries," believing them to "hold in their hands the lives and fortunes of all men."[16] Following the Union takeover of New Orleans, these stories about African "superstitions" would have almost certainly played a role in public debates about whether enslaved people should be joining the Union army and whether they were prepared for emancipation.

Although all versions of this article introduced "voudou" to the reader, there were some significant differences in how different newspapers reported on the race of these "voudou" adherents. The *Daily Milwaukee* and *San Francisco Bulletin* emphasized the interracial nature of the gathering, reporting that while the women arrested were mostly "colored," two "demure looking white women" were among them. These reprinted stories highlighted the complicity of white adherents at least four times in the two-paragraph story, referring to the voudou practitioners as "dusky skinned nymphs and their white allies." The *Daily Milwaukee* added, "A large mob of negroes and white folks assembled in the vicinity of the court house this morning, blocking up every avenue of approach and creating such a disturbance that the court was forced to order their dispersal."[17] The reprint in the *San Francisco Bulletin* continued, "It is surprising the number of white women, some calling themselves ladies, who it is said take part in these unseemly mysteries. They are made proselytes to the faith by the Fetish queens, who induce them to believe they can furnish them with potent love charms, and other agencies of an unnatural character. The peace of more than one family in this city has been destroyed through the arts of these old witches."[18]

Two newspapers from Connecticut, the *Norwich Aurora* and the *Columbian Register and True Republican*, drastically altered the characterization of the race of the "voudou" adherents to make it appear that only Black women were involved. The *Norwich Aurora* introduced the story by explaining it "presents the following picture of a strange phase of *negro* life in the Crescent City." The editors reprinted the entire story from the original source, the *New Orleans Era*, except for the section about the "demure looking white women" being arrested alongside "colored" women. The editors also added the word "negro" to the first sentence of the story so it read "a lot of negro women were engaged in practising the fetish rites known as the Voudou mysteries" rather than just "a lot of women. . . ." They did not print the sections about the interracial mob gathering outside the courthouse nor the "surprising number" of white women involved in voudou that the *Daily Milwaukee* and the *San Francisco Bulletin* included.

Whereas other titles had spoken generally of "heathenism" and "superstition" in New Orleans, the *Columbian Register and True Republican* titled their version, "American Pagans of African Descent." They also printed a much shorter version of the story (only one paragraph) that omitted any mention of white participants, reporting that "about thirty negresses were arrested on Marias street for engaging in one of the rites of Africa."[19] As opposed to other newspapers that had claimed that both Black and white people in New Orleans had a "great interest" in voudou, this version averred that "the entire negro population are said to fear the vengeance of the Queen of the Voudous." Another New England newspaper, the *Patriot*, referenced this incident again almost two months later and likewise discussed only the "superstitions practiced by the negroes of New Orleans" and that "a number of negroes, almost naked" had been arrested at the house of a Voudou queen.[20]

Although the sheer number of modifications in these New England newspapers suggest that the omission of white participants was intentional, it is difficult to be certain about the editors' rationale. They clearly believed that stories about "superstitions" thriving among Black populations in Union-controlled New Orleans would be of interest to their readers (who would have been predominantly based in Union territory); however, it appears that they thought that the involvement of white women made the narrative objectionable. Perhaps the editors worried that the original version of the story would undermine the Union's commitment to ending slavery by suggesting that free Black people would lead white women astray— enticing them to participate in their "unseemly" rites and worship their "fetish" gods.

Ultimately, the *Times-Picayune*'s follow-up story about the disposition of this case painted a very distinct picture of the function and format of the "Voudou rites" from any of the prior reports. Rather than a performance of "African barbarism" that emerged because of the supposed new freedoms experienced by Black people under the Union occupation, witness testimony suggests that the "Voudou ceremonies" were only attended by white and "colored" women, and that they were designed to restore the Confederacy, not celebrate its demise.

Like the defendants in the early 1850s, these alleged Voudou adherents had been arrested for unlawful assembly; however, the court dismissed the charges against these women because witnesses testified that there were no enslaved women present, only free women of color and a few white "visitors." Enslaved Black women and girls appear to have provided much of the evidence against the Voudou women, testifying about what they saw and heard in the ceremony that they had witnessed from a distance but had not participated in. The defense discredited these witnesses, describing the gathering as "a private social reunion, that it had been grossly misrepresented by some ignorant slave women."[21] The prosecuting attorney asked one of the witnesses whether she had overheard one of the accused women talking about the Confederacy. When defense counsel objected to the question, the prosecuting attorney told the court that "he was well assured that the object of the meeting was to produce spells and incantations which would restore the Confederates to power here, so that the slaves might no longer be on an equality [sic] with them—the free people of color."[22]

Reconstruction (1860s–1870s)

Although reprints of the 1863 article gave conflicting reports about the racial composition of practitioners, later descriptions of "Voudou" ceremonies and rituals in New Orleans and in other regions of the United States would focus on the emancipation of enslaved people as a turning point that had allowed "voudooism" to flourish throughout the country. For instance, in 1864, the *Times-Picayune* published a story about the desecration of a local graveyard, where coffins had been destroyed and bones had been scattered or removed. The author said there was no doubt that Black people were behind this vandalism because they had never "lost the barbarous tastes of their ancestors, nor forsaken their heathenish rites; but who now, freed from all constraint, are relapsing into the worship of the gods of cruelty and diabolism...."[23] The *Daily Ohio Statesman* (Columbus, Ohio) republished this story with the title "Shocking Recital. Freed Negroes Returning to the Barbarous Bites of Voudouism."[24]

As the Civil War ended and Reconstruction spread to other parts of the U.S. South, allegations that Black people had returned to barbarism, including "voodoo" practices, became a common feature in the U.S. media. They intensified as Congress took the first steps to restore the rights stripped from African Americans in the *Dred Scott* decision, with the passage of the Civil Rights Act of 1866, and leading up to the ratification of the Fourteenth Amendment to the U.S. Constitution in 1868. During this period, as reporters began to argue that "superstitions" were common among Black people outside Louisiana, the spelling transitioned from "voudou" to "voodoo."

For instance, in 1866, newspapers in Pennsylvania, Maine, Ohio, and Georgia reprinted a story that was originally published in a Memphis newspaper called *Appeal* under the titles "Voodooism. The Native African Paganism Rife Among the Freedmen," or "African Superstitions in America: The Negro Marching Back." Each newspaper included introductory remarks from a writer for the *Nashville Union and American* who had first reprinted the story.[25] The author of the *Appeal* story characterized "voodoo" as a "barbaric religion" that was practiced by many "Americanized negroes" but was most prevalent in Louisiana, where adherents had been purportedly discovered dancing naked around cauldrons filled with charmed snakes and human remains. They claimed that "voodooism" was "beginning to take hold among the negroes" and that African Americans had given themselves up to "baser passions," now that they were "free from the check which was once held over them." The editor of the *Nashville Union and American* version of this story referenced similar tales about "voodooism" that the paper had previously reprinted from Georgia and Mississippi, explaining that Black people in these states were "afflicted with the most grotesque and absurd religious superstitions."

These articles often depicted Southerners as the victims of Reconstruction—struggling under Union-imposed legislation and overrun by "voodoo" practitioners. In 1867, the *Crisis* of Columbus, Ohio, published one such article titled "The Black Cloud in the South." This article described efforts to register Black voters, which the author referred to as the "Congressional design to mongrelize the country" and "a burlesque on justice and an outrage upon decency."[26] The author continued, "While the miserable negroes, fresh from their Voodoo and Fetish worship, were being driven in crowds to the registers, the white men, the legitimate voters and citizens of the States, were kept away by the intimidation and insolence of the military mountebanks." They also asserted that if Black people were registered to vote, these "heathens who have no conception of what a law is" would take over the legislatures and the South would be "at the mercy of a race of pagans."[27]

In 1869, Congress proposed the Fifteenth Amendment to the Constitution, guaranteeing the right to vote regardless of race or color, and in 1870, it was ratified. In newspapers throughout the country, debates about the wisdom of African Americans being granted voting rights and other forms of political participation played out, in part, in narratives about "voodooism" among African Americans. For example, the author of an article published in the *Crisis* in March 1869 proclaimed that it was "impossible to conceive of anything worse" than the Fifteenth Amendment, which "encourages and enfranchises" all races "and places them upon an equality with American citizens of Caucassian [sic] descent" and would permit Asians, Native Americans, and Africans "to have their influence in the Government in proportion to their numbers."[28] The author predicted that due to "the pious fraud known as the fifteenth amendment," coupled with the freedom of religion guaranteed by the First Amendment, the United States would now "witness the burlesque—under the name of religion—of a pig-tailed Chinaman alternately worshiping and smashing his clay god; a Walrussian Esquimaux paying his devotions to a frozen toad or the tooth of a whale; an amiable Haytien drinking the blood of his murdered victim; or one of the swamp demons of Florida or Louisiana performing his pious Voodoo rites by devouring the corpses of his relatives."[29]

Perhaps the most explicit article about the relationship between voting and "voodoo" appeared in the *Defiance Democrat* in 1873.[30] The author argued that Louisiana (once a prosperous state) was becoming bankrupt and slipping into anarchy, in part because the Black population, other than the people of New Orleans, was composed of "mostly pure negroes, black, ignorant and superstitious."[31] The author asserted that "Voodooism, with its heathenism rites, holds its place among them, though scarcely known among the colored population of other states. They are to a great extent utterly unfit for the exercise of the voting power and *the ballot in their hands becomes a mockery.*"[32]

In addition to predicting the collapse or destruction of the South because of African American voters, Democrats characterized Republican politicians as tenuously holding office due to the support of "superstitious" Black people. For instance, in 1869, the *Mountain Democrat* published a sarcastic article about James Harlan of Iowa, who proposed a sixteenth amendment to the Constitution requiring the recognition of Jesus Christ as the supreme authority and the United States as a Christian nation.[33] The paper quoted a sister publication, the *Peoria Democrat*, as saying that this was "unkind" and "impolite" since it was coming "so soon after the nice little arrangement by which four millions of negroes are made into citizens, about half of whom are worshippers of the Voudou order."[34] The author argued, presumably tongue in cheek, that one must seriously consider whether the proposed sixteenth amendment would infringe of the "rights and consciences of these newly baptized Republicans."[35] The author cautioned Harlan, a republican, against proposing an amendment "so repugnant" to the "sooty Africans" who his party had just enfranchised unless his intention was "to legislate them into the Christian church."[36]

In addition to commenting on Black voters, many newspapers featured stories that connected "voodoo" and newly elected Black lawmakers. For example, in 1870, John C. Fisher, the editor and proprietor of the *Coshocton Democrat*, wrote a front-page editorial for his own paper, discussing the appointment of the first Black senator, Hiriam Revels, to the U.S. Congress.[37] Fisher claimed, "It is reported that the Republican Senators were consistent enough to congratulate him upon this triumph of their creed, but the Democratic Senators did not participate in the Voodoo worship of the [illegible] Sumner and his mongrel gang."[38]

An analogous narrative was published in an editorial circulated through numerous U.S. newspapers in 1883, titled "How Wade Hampton Saved His State."[39] This article referenced the hotly contested South Carolina gubernatorial election of 1876, during which President Grant sent federal troops to supervise the election process and quell the outbreaks of violence. When both Daniel Chamberlain, the Republican candidate, and Wade Hampton, the Democratic candidate, declared victory in this close race, President Grant permitted Chamberlain to send those federal troops to the State House to prevent the Democrats from forcibly taking office. The author contended that while the story of this election might be well-known, it was unlikely that Northerners were aware that after the election, ex-Confederate troops had gathered in South Carolina and were preparing for battle with the federal soldiers stationed in front of the State House. The author argued that these troops were only dispersed because General Wade Hampton came out of the State House and told them that the Democrats had won the state election and he advised the soldiers to go home, saying that the federal troops would see that "justice was done" (presumably that these Democratic candidates would be able to take office). The author contended that the former Confederate troops would have "annihilated" the federal troops if the battle had happened, and thereby sparked violent reprisals from the Northern and Western states. Thus, according to the author, by dispersing the Confederate soldiers, General Hampton "saved his state from this day being a wilderness, with African barbarians weirdly dancing and howling Voodoo among the ruins of her cities."[40]

In addition to these specific references drawing correlations between purported "voodoo" practices and African Americans' supposed unfitness for citizenship and political participation, there was also generally a stark surge in media interest in domestic "voodoo" practices during the postwar decades. One will recall that articles about "voodoo" in English-language presses were rare before 1863 and were typically confined to reports on purported spiritual practices in New Orleans. These stories were not often republished by presses outside the city. However, from the Union occupation of New Orleans in 1862 to the end of that decade, "voodoo" articles steadily increased. Accounts of voodoo in New Orleans newspapers more than doubled in 1869 and 1870, around the ratification of the Fifteenth Amendment. Nationwide, articles about voodoo seem to have quadrupled in 1869 and 1870 compared to the previous two years. These presses, many of which were Democrat-owned, made national news out of mundane events, recirculating tales of "voodoo" rituals, focusing on stories related to poisons, arrests, and charms.

After the early 1880s, the tone of media references to "voodoo" began to change. Stories about "voodoo" in the Southern United States continued to increase throughout the late nineteenth century. Nevertheless, unlike previous years, these articles did not specifically refer to Black political figures or the right to vote. Racially charged political commentary about the "voodoo" practices of the Black population of the United States continued during the 1880s and 1890s, but instead of directly opposing legislative and political changes like the Civil Rights Acts and the postwar constitutional amendments, many newspaper articles addressed the perceived problem of how African Americans could be shaped into productive citizens. This slight shift in the tone of articles about "voodoo" within the United States relates to the emergence of media coverage about "voodoo" practices in Haiti. Journalists began to compare the U.S. South to Haiti, and they used Haiti as an example of what might happen if Black people were not educated and "civilized" by whites.

The Emergence of Haitian "Voodoo" in the Late Nineteenth Century

In 1791, enslaved persons in the colony of St. Domingue did the unthinkable—they began a lengthy and violent rebellion that, in 1804, would lead to the establishment of the independent Black nation of Haiti. Displaced French plantation owners and their slaves scattered throughout the Caribbean, with large numbers arriving in nearby territories such as Cuba and New Orleans. This rebellion, which has become known as the Haitian revolution, changed the history of the Americas and the rest of the Atlantic world. In particular, it caused other slaveholding nations enormous anxiety, leading them to speculate about what had caused the uprising in St. Domingue and how plantation owners could prevent a similar occurrence.

As mentioned in the Introduction, years after the start of the rebellion, French colonists asserted that the uprising had begun with a Vodou ceremony at a region in the North known as Bois Caiman (Bwa Kayiman). Vodou priests allegedly led the insurgents in a series of prayers and rituals to their divinities (the *lwa*). They asked for support and guidance in the forthcoming insurrection. While it is unclear whether this ceremony actually took place, it was certainly a part of the nineteenth-century mythology surrounding the causes of the revolution, and it has become a component of the national folklore about the origins of the independent country of Haiti.

Because the founding of Haiti basically coincided with the Louisiana Purchase and because the specter of the Haitian revolution loomed large in all slaveholding territories, one would assume that the emergence of discussions about "voodoo" in the United States immediately incorporated references to the first independent Black nation in the Americas. This would be a particularly reasonable assumption because of the flow of "refugees" from the Haitian revolution into New Orleans. However, my research suggests that until the late nineteenth century, the term "voodoo" was not commonly used in reference to Haiti, and in the rare occasions that this term was employed, Haitian "voodoo" was understood as a slightly different phenomenon than in New Orleans or other North American societies.

Before the 1880s, U.S. media coverage of "voodoo" in Haiti was very limited. The earliest references to Haitian "voodoo" emerged in the late 1840s and early 1850s, during approximately the same period as the first articles about New Orleans "voudou" were printed in English-language presses. However, these publications employed a distinct spelling for Haitian "voodoo." They described it as "vaudoux," the same spelling that was commonly used by the French and British in their reports about purported ritual practices in Haiti. It would not be until the 1880s, when English-language texts about Haitian "voodoo" became more common, that these ritual practices in the first Black republic were described using the same spelling as those in New Orleans and the rest of the U.S. South. It is also during this period when stories about Haitian "voodoo" regularly began to be used to demonstrate the purported heathenism and barbarism that would be rampant among free persons of African descent.

After searching hundreds of U.S. newspapers using archival databases, I did not find a single reference to Haitian "voodoo" before the mid-1840s.[41] Reports on Haitian "voodoo" began in the second half of the 1840s and consisted of a few sporadic stories using the spelling "vaudoux" that were moderately circulated in U.S. presses. The earliest of these articles may have been in 1846, when the *Southern Patriot* published a story stating that the current president of Haiti, Jean Baptiste Riche, had declined to enter the city of Cap Haytian through a ceremonial arch erected for the procession because he feared that former President Jean Louis Pierrot, who had been the "reputed chief" of the "vaudoux" for many years, had bewitched it.[42] The author provided a description of "vaudoux," stating that it was a "superstition" from Africa, similar to Jamaican Obeah. The author's belief that it was necessary to define Haitian "vaudoux" in this article reinforces the idea that it was not a commonly used term in the United States at this time.

Riche died in 1847 and was replaced by Faustin Soulouque, who served as president, then emperor of Haiti from 1847 to 1859; scholars have argued that Haitian Vodou received unprecedented official acceptance during his reign and that this became a topic of international discussion.[43] Although this period does represent the first in-depth discussions of Haitian "voodoo" in the U.S. media, these references were far from common. At least one article marked Soulouque's transition from president to emperor in 1849, in which the author referred to Soulouque as superstitious, ignorant, and illiterate, stated that he was heavily influenced by "vaudau" practitioners, and that human sacrifice was practiced during his reign.[44] Several more articles emerged as Souloque's reign declined in 1858 and around the time of his abdication in 1859. Journalists described Soulouque as the king or high priest of the "vaudoux," which they claimed was a secret practice involving fetish worship and the veneration of a green snake that had thrived during Souloque's rule.[45]

After the 1850s, and notwithstanding the growing fixation on New Orleans "voudou" during this period, Haitian "voodoo" virtually disappeared from the U.S. media until the late 1870s.[46] This is particularly significant for two reasons. First and foremost, as previously discussed, "voudou" or "voodoo" in New Orleans and the U.S. South became a regularly featured story from 1863 onward. The lack of media references to Haitian "vaudoux" or "voodoo" at this time demonstrates that New Orleans "voodoo" was viewed as the epitome of Black "superstition" during the Civil War and the Reconstruction era, and that Haitian "superstitions" were typically regarded as something distinct from those in New Orleans. The scarcity of stories about Haitian "voodoo" in the U.S. media in the 1860s is also notable because of two events that brought Haitian "voodoo" to the attention of other foreign nations.

First, in 1862, Edward Underhill, secretary of the Baptist Missionary Society, wrote a book about his missionary tour in the British Caribbean titled *The West Indies: Their Social and Religious Condition*. This book contained several pages about Emperor Souloque's reign and the "superstitions" to which he had allegedly fallen prey. As many would later do, Underhill depicted Haitian "vaudoux" as characterized by serpent worship, drunken orgies, and the consumption of animal blood.[47] However, Underhill suggested that these barbarities were unique to Soulouque, claiming that "in all companies a sense of relief was expressed to me, at the extinction of this nightmare reign of sorcery and blood."[48] He gave a favorable description of Souloque's successor and asserted that if Haiti was uncivilized, it was directly connected to the "legacy of evil, vice, superstition, and ignorance, slavery left them."[49] Underhill believed that Haiti was likely to become "a bright example of African culture."[50]

Underhill's book received considerable attention in the media in the United Kingdom. Sections from his pages about "vaudoux" were printed in several newspapers under the title, "Soulouque, King of Hayti, and the

Snake Worshippers."[51] However, newspaper editors did not add extensive commentary to the reprints of his stories about voodoo; Underhill's book was merely featured in the literary sections alongside segments of other books, without remark about the broader implications of the practices that Underhill describes. When one considers the status of Britain's Caribbean colonies at this time, it is easy to understand the willingness of Underhill to accept that these alleged barbaric practices were just a fluke and the ease with which English newspaper editors reprinted his work without remark. As Britain had abolished slavery in the 1830s, there was no need to use the independent Black nation of Haiti to reflect on the wisdom of emancipation.

One can see the contrast in the sole U.S. newspaper that I found that referenced Underhill's popular book. In 1863, in the midst of the U.S. Civil War, the *Wisconsin Daily Patriot* published an article titled "The Logic of History," which opposed the abolition of slavery in the United States by listing examples of emancipation's purported negative effect on other parts of the Americas. The author focused on an economic argument, asserting that Haiti and the British Caribbean, especially Jamaica, had suffered drastic financial decline since emancipation due to "the worthless indolence of the negro" and that Black people would "seldom ever go voluntarily into the field to work" in Africa. Under a subsection titled "Negroes Relapsing into Barbarism," the author quoted sections of Underhill's descriptions of "vaudoux," asking, "Can it be possible that the advocates of emancipation find in such lamentable evidences of retrogression, encouragement for continued zeal in a cause that suffers debasement without a remedy?" After adding a quote from Mr. Webley, a missionary who published an editorial in the *London Missionary Herald* in 1850 in which he compared "vaudoux" to witchcraft, the author concluded, "History furnishes us no example on this planet where the negro race, with every advantage at their commend [sic], have shown their ability for colonization and self-government, even approximating that of the white race."[52]

The second incident that drew international attention to Haitian religion was the "Bizoton affair," sometimes referred to as the "Pelle case," in 1864, when several alleged "voodoo" practitioners were convicted of murdering a young girl as a human sacrifice. Several scholars have argued that this incident greatly increased the international notoriety of Haitian "voodoo," and fueled the negative stereotypes of this country that persist until today.[53] Historian Kate Ramsey has documented the extensive efforts of the Haitian government to prohibit "superstitious practices" in an effort to rehabilitate Haiti's image to international communities who had begun to use "voodoo" as a symbol of Haiti's regression.[54] However, out of hundreds of U.S. newspapers in the archival databases searched for this project, I found only six newspapers that referenced this story in the 1860s.[55] Other Anglophone countries, namely England, reported this event with just slightly greater frequency. The story appeared in at least nine English newspapers about a month after it was published in Haitian presses and about two months after the convictions allegedly took place.[56]

Even more illuminating than the volume of reports on the Bizoton affair is the language utilized in these accounts. Although by the 1870s British authors would be some of the most vocal in asserting that Haitian "vaudoux" was deeply ingrained in the entire population and received the support of the Haitian government, the primary article about the Bizoton affair (which was copied in 8 of the 9 presses) blamed the rise of "vaudoux" and human sacrifice on a single corrupt regime—that of Emperor Soulouque. Similar to Underhill's remarks the year before, the author depicted the Haitian government as firmly in control of these practices, claiming that except for the period of Soulouque's reign, "vaudoux" had been repressed successfully since Haitian independence and, with the introduction of a new president, would probably disappear again.[57]

Additionally, although Britain was also wrestling with questions about the ability of persons of African descent to handle emancipation and self-governance in their Caribbean colonies, the author did not make any judgmental references about how these events demonstrated the descent of Black people into barbarism. At least one author emphasized that the Haitian people were elated with the new regime's swift and harsh response toward the cannibals, declaring that the streets leading up to the place of execution were lined with people shouting, "long live civilization."[58] The others reported that the "immense crowd" attending the execution "were only restrained by the military from tearing the wretches to pieces."[59]

The few U.S. articles about the Bizoton affair had a completely different character from those in other places. First, unlike presses in Britain and Cuba, most authors did not refer to this alleged act of cannibalism and human sacrifice as a component of "vaudoux" or "voodoo," but rather as a form of "Obeah worship" that had been established by Emperor Soulouque.[60] The language of "Obeah" is interesting for several reasons. In addition to being different from the terminology used in other presses, it was not a phrase that was typically used in the United States at all. Rather, as mentioned previously,

"Obeah" was the term that the British generally used to refer to African spiritual practices in their Caribbean colonies. It had been outlawed after it was used to protect insurgents in slave rebellions.

The first article printed about the Bizoton affair in the United States was a purported letter to the editor of the *New York News* from a correspondent in Port-au-Prince who called herself/himself "Carribee." Featured under the title "Canniabalism [sic] in Hayti—Negroes Shot for Eating Children—Human Sacrifices," Carribee painted a grim picture of the Bizoton affair.[61] They wrote that the accused individuals "went to the place of execution shouting laughing and dancing, and defying the soldiers to shoot them; for they insisted that Obeah priests would protect them against the balls."

In addition to the bizarre characterization of this incident as an act of Obeah worship, Carribee's letter also differed greatly from the British reports in its depiction of the response of the Haitian people. Whereas both Underhill and the British articles about the Bizoton affair had characterized it as a barbarous trend begun by Emperor Soulouque and suppressed by the subsequent president, Carribee described these "loathsome mysteries" as a religious order "inaugurated" by Soulouque which continued to be "celebrated in secret," and asserted that "most of the horrors that are perpetrated never come to light."[62] Additionally, while the British newspapers declared that the Haitian population could barely be restrained from tearing the defendants apart and predicted that the government would swiftly stamp out these practices, Carribee asserted that "the population, incited by the Obeah priests, threaten to prevent the execution by violence."[63] Carribee described the government as "very unstable," and claimed "you may expect to hear of revolution at any time."[64] Reprints of this letter appeared in several other newspapers, often reflecting on the supposedly inevitability of such practices occurring in the United States following emancipation.[65]

Perhaps the most illuminating introduction to this letter was the one printed in the New Orleans *Times-Picayune*. The editor clearly meant to send a message about the dangers of abolition when it titled the article, "Canibalism [sic] Revived Among the *Free Negroes* of Haiti."[66] However, even in this article, the editor maintained the language of "Obeah" from the original letter and clearly distinguished the "Obeah" practiced in Haiti from the "superstitions" in New Orleans with an introduction that asserted "though the negroes of this country have never yet reached canibalism [sic], they show much disposition to relapse into heathenism practices, as is proven by their voudou practices and incantations."

The article in the *Delphi Times* that paraphrased Carribee's letter was even less veiled about the connection to the U.S. Civil War and the debate about the abolition of slavery. The author referred to this incident as "the most horrible human practice known to the calendar of crime."[67] They blamed the Bizoton affair on "Negro self-government," explaining that "it demonstrates the aptness of negroes to desend [sic] into the lowest depths of barbarism, into which the whole Affrican [sic] race will be irretrieveably [sic] plunged, if the emancipation policy becomes fully carried out."[68] As many others would assert from the 1880s onward, the author proclaimed that Haiti would soon provide proof of "the utter incapacity of negroes to govern themselves."[69]

One does not have to look very far to find the motive for telling these stories in this manner. All three of these were Democratic newspapers. On the front page—the same page where this story of cannibalism was featured—*Dawson's Fort Wayne Weekly* printed a plea to all Democrats to organize themselves for the next election. In the columns to the left of the story about Haitian cannibalism, it featured an article titled "The Popularity of the War," which referred to "[t]he negro worshippers and their allies" who were spreading "delusions" about the popularity of the Civil War.[70] In the *Sullivan Democrat*, the story about the Bizoton affair appeared next to a column titled "A Capital Hit—The Lincoln Catechism—Questions and Answers." Among other inflammatory things, the author referred to the president as "Abraham Africanus the First" and posed the question "What is an army?" with the response "A Provost Guard, to arrest white men and set negroes free."[71]

While the U.S. media typically appeared to use the few reports of the Bizoton affair to underscore the dangers of abolition without referring to Haitian "vaudoux," there was one exception. In September 1864, approximately six months following the initial reports in England and the United States, two newspapers in Indiana printed the same letter with the same title—"Voudou Superstition."[72] In perhaps one of the earliest moments when "voodoo" and "vaudoux" began to merge for the American public, the editors introduced the letter about the Bizoton affair with the statement "Remnants of the Fetish religion of native Africans, still exist among the negroes of Louisiana Cuba and Hayti, under the name of Voudouism." While the letter focuses on the brutality of the alleged sacrifice, describing it in graphic detail, it paradoxically concludes the same as the British stories about the Bizoton affair—with the claim that the Haitian population praised their president and cried "Long live civilization" at the execution.

Annexation (1870s)

Aside from the few articles that characterized the Bizoton affair as "voudou," discussions of Haitian "voodoo" were virtually nonexistent in the U.S. media in the 1860s. When they returned in 1870, it was in the context of debates about the possibility that the United States would annex Haiti. The author of one article stated that Haiti had been independent nearly as long as the United States; however, the country had deteriorated under Black rule and was run by lazy voodoo worshipers.[73] A similar article appeared in the *New York Herald* in 1871, again discussing the possibility of the U.S. annexation of Haiti. The author described his trip to Haiti and stated that former President Geffrard told him that he had tried to suppress "voodoo" during his reign but had not been successful and that he had shot eight "voodoo" practitioners whom he had found in the midst of cannibalism.[74]

There are two interesting and somewhat paradoxical things about these commentaries from the early 1870s. The first is a shift in orthography. Unlike prior articles from the 1840s and 1850s, which had referenced Haitian "vaudoux" or "vaudau," these articles used the spelling "voodoo" which, along with the increasingly less common "voudou," was used at this time to describe Black "superstitions" in New Orleans and the rest of the Southern United States. However, despite this merging of spellings ("vaudoux" was never again regularly used in the U.S. media), these articles made no comparisons between Haitian "voodoo" to "voodoo" in the United States, nor did the authors reflect on the correlation between the supposed deterioration of Haiti and the condition of newly freed Black people in the United States.

As the 1870s progressed, articles about Haitian "voodoo" continued to be relatively rare. In fact, during this decade, there were far more articles published about "voodoo" in New Orleans *each year* than there were published about "voodoo" in Haiti in *every year prior* to 1880 combined. The interest in Haitian "voodoo" slowly began to expand in the late 1870s as more French travelogues about Haiti were translated to English and more travelers from the Anglophone world wrote about their journeys to Haiti. These new accounts not only increased the volume of media attention on Haitian "voodoo," but also seem to have shifted the tone of dialogue about "voodoo" in the United States. From the late 1870s to the beginning of the twentieth century, Haiti slowly replaced Louisiana in U.S. newspapers as the home of the most infamous "voodoo" worshippers. Journalists who had once cited

Southern "voodoo" beliefs and practices as evidence that the Black population of the United States was unprepared for voting rights and other forms of political participation began to deploy stories about Haiti to illustrate the importance of maintaining white control over the Black population to prevent them from returning to "voodooism" and other kinds of "African barbarism."

One of the first important comparisons between domestic and Haitian "voodoo" was in 1877, when a monthly publication called *The Catholic World* featured an article titled "Nagualism, Voodooism, and Other Forms of Crytopaganism in the United States." In the introduction to this article, the author argued that Caribbean "vaudoux" and U.S. "voodoo" were one and the same—"the secret pagan religion of the negro and mixed races."[75] The author contended that cannibalism, human sacrifice, and devil worship had been brought to Haiti by enslaved Africans and that when the French owned both Haiti (St. Domingue) and Louisiana, "voodoo" was transported between them and spread across the Southern United States. They asserted that African Americans had recently been given more opportunities for education and prosperity, but the change in their circumstances had not decreased the influence of "voodooism"; rather, it had driven it further into hiding and had caused African Americans to deny their belief in it.[76] The author argued that the best example of the continuing influence of "voodoo" among Black people in North America was that an African American member of the Louisiana legislature had allegedly undergone a ritual to remove a spell that had been placed on him by a "voodoo priestess."[77] They contended that this legislator's actions exemplified the current conundrum in the United States; since Black people were now independent, they were becoming more "superstitious." Although "voodoo" practices in the U.S. South had not yet reached the "frightful enormities" of those in Haiti, the author argued that, with this degree of African American political control and independence, "voodoo power cannot but increase and all vestiges of Christianity disappear."[78]

Spenser St. John (1880s)

This narrative about "voodoo" as evidence of the possibility of African Americans descending into a state of African barbarism was intensified by a book published in 1884 by Sir Spenser St. John, former British consul to Haiti, about the condition of the Haitian state since its independence from France.[79] St. John introduced his book by arguing that Haiti was "in a state of rapid decadence ... unless influenced by some higher civilization."[80] He referred to the mulatto population of Haiti as the "civilizing element," but despite their presence, "there is a distinct tendency to sink into the state of an African tribe."[81] St. John asserted that, based on his experiences in Haiti, he would have to protest against Black political participation in Britain's Caribbean colonies. He said, "I know what the black man is and I have no hesitation in declaring that he is incapable of the art of government, and that to entrust him with framing and working the laws for our islands is to condemn them to inevitable ruin."[82]

To demonstrate this "fact," St. John included a lengthy chapter about voodoo and cannibalism.[83] He asserted that the practices of voodoo and cannibalism were widespread, permeating all classes of people, including government officials.[84] He discussed the sacrifice of the "goat without horns," a phrase referring to a human sacrifice, which would be repeated for decades thereafter in newspapers, books, and articles describing voodoo in Haiti.[85] To "prove" his claims, he included two stories that had been recounted to him about a French priest and an American correspondent who had allegedly witnessed voodoo ceremonies that included human sacrifice.[86] He also described the Bizoton affair in graphic detail.[87] He assured the reader that his accounts were based on the most reliable sources and that as he was writing this book, cannibalism was still very prevalent because "[a] black Government dares not greatly interfere, as its power is founded on the goodwill of the masses, ignorant and deeply tainted with fetish-worship."[88]

Scholars have emphasized the significance of this book, which placed Haitian "voodoo" at the center of debates about the rights and freedoms of persons of African descent. Alasdair Pettinger argues that St. John's "influence was enormous. Henceforth, travel accounts became obsessed with vaudoux, now considered the key to understanding Haiti, which was increasingly figured as dense and impenetrable, where before it was anomalous but fully open to inspection. Distrusting its thin civilized veneer, foreign visitors now attuned their readers to the sound of distant drums, booming from the interior after nightfall."[89] Paul Farmer noted that *Hayti or the Black Republic* became a bestseller in France, England, and the United States.[90] Due to this international acclaim, St. John declared that he would write a second edition of his book, which would include additional information on "voodoo" because he believed he had "underrated its fearful manifestations."[91]

During the year or two after its initial release, the U.S. media was flooded with articles discussing St. John's book.[92] In April 1885, an author claimed that Spanish-American newspapers reported that the "horrible cult" of "voodoo" had developed in Haiti to "an alarming extent" and included several documented incidents of parents murdering their own children and eating them.[93] They referenced St. John's description of one such incident, stating that he reports that "the people in the interior of the island are falling back to the condition of an aboriginal African tribe." Similarly, a man who claimed to have met St. John published an article titled "Demoralized Hayti. A Land of Cannibalism and Barbarous Voodoo Worship" in December 1885.[94] He referred to St. John as an authority on the history of Haiti and argued that St. John had evidence of cannibalism in Haiti from "credible witnesses." The author summarized St. John's book by explaining that he opined that Haitians are politically hopeless and that they have no moral nature. The author also reprinted St. John's assertion that Haitians dislike monkeys because they know there is little difference between themselves and these animals.[95]

More importantly, beyond the mere descriptions of the content of St. John's book, many articles discussed how the condition of Haiti had implications for the United States. For instance, in April 1885, one author argued that St. John had "carefully studied the problems of race and government" in Haiti and "[h]is conclusions are important."[96] The author summarized St. John's conclusions as follows: "He now believes that the negro is incapable of holding an independent position. As long as he is influenced by contact with the white man, as in our southern states, he gets on very well. But away from such influence, as in Hayti, he falls back to savage customs." A few months later, in June 1885, an article titled "Negro rule in Haiti" included the following passage: "At this time, when the negro race in the United States is unconsciously working out the answer to the vexed question of its capacity to advance in the line of civilization, anything that will give a forecast of the result or the difficulties to be met is of the highest value not only to the negro himself, but to the whites among whom he dwells and with whose future that of the negro is inextricably involved."[97] The author said that Haiti was the best measure for Black people's "power of self-development" because Black people had lived in Haiti "practically free from the presence of the white man" for nearly a century. The author lauded St. John as "a credible and impartial witness" about this topic and, among many other things, recounted St. John's claims about the spread of voodoo worship, human sacrifice, and cannibalism, as well as the unwillingness of the government to intervene. The article closed by quoting St. John's statement that despite the best education, Black people remain inferior and have proven themselves incapable of self-government or any measure of progress.[98]

Unable to Rule Themselves (1880s–1900s)

In the years following the U.S. Civil War, Congress had passed a series of Civil Rights Acts that either preceded or reinforced constitutional amendments granting all citizens the right to vote, hold public office, and enjoy public accommodations regardless of race or previous condition of servitude. The Civil Rights Acts, largely responding to violence carried out by the Ku Klux Klan and like-minded individuals, attempted to criminalize interference with such rights. However, in 1883, the Supreme Court determined that some of the Civil Rights Acts and the Fourteenth Amendment only protected against government discrimination and did not/could not criminalize racial discrimination carried out by private citizens. Meanwhile, more places were implementing grandfather clauses, poll taxes, and other regulations to prevent Black people from voting. Over time, such policies and court decisions rapidly eroded African Americans' newly guaranteed rights.

Perhaps because of the success of other attacks on African American political participation, within a few years, reporters became less focused on the implications of Haitian "voodoo" for domestic policy about African Americans and more preoccupied with what these practices generally suggested about the ability of Black people to self-govern. In 1889, *The Times Picayune* of New Orleans published a story titled "Orgies in Hayti: A Story of Voudou Horrors That [Illegible] Belief," which was a reprinted tale from a *New York World* Port-au-Prince correspondent.[99] The correspondent claimed to have "disguised and blackened" himself, and then attended a "voodoo" performance in Jacmel with a well-paid local guide. He asserted that he witnessed the sacrifice of a white goat at this ceremony, but his guide allegedly informed him that the previous year, a female child was drugged, then the participants drank her blood and ripped her body apart limb by limb. He concluded "[t]his seems incredible, but well authenticated, cases where recently buried bodies have been exhumed, cooked and devoured by the almost completely barbarous inhabitants of the southern department—the brutalized descendants of the lowest tribes of Africans—have been heard of."

In 1892, an article was published in the *Newark Daily Advocate* called "A Southern View of It," analyzing a publication by Thomas Nelson Page in *The North American Review*.[100] Page discussed the "negro question," or the issue of what would be done with Black people in the Southern United States. The author of the article agreed with Page that Black people were "not capable of receiving the white man's civilization."[101] He quoted Page's assertion that "in countries of their own," Black people seemed to be moving backward; that in Liberia, they were "lapsing into the condition of the barbarians around them," and in Santo Domingo "voodoo worship is springing up."[102]

On January 4, 1895, the *Times-Picayune* featured an article titled "Where the Colored Man Hath Sway; The Retrogression of Hayti Under Negro Domination; The Heathen Rites of Voudouism as Now Practiced"; the article claimed that a former U.S. consul to Haiti was advising others not to travel to the country, or take the risk of falling victim to its "dirt-engendered diseases and the perils of perpetual revolutions."[103] He purportedly had asserted that "every desirable element of civilization is almost wiped out in the decadence of the island under negro rule, and that the vast majority of the swarming black population are sunk in barbarism deeper than that of the aboriginal tribes of Central Africa." The author explained that Haiti, after "almost a century of negro rule" was "not encouraging to the advocates of the theory that all men are created equal," in part because "voudousim" is widely practiced, which the author described as African practices "mingled with the wildest superstitions and the celebration of fetish rites to propitiate evil spirits, of which cannibalism is the outgrowth." The author asserted "this is the only country in the western hemisphere where the negroes are the rulers, legislators, judges, generals, authors, arts—and where the white man is indebted to the black for liberty to live."

Perhaps one of the most conclusive reflections on this issue was British traveler Hesketh Prichard's turn-of-the-century book describing his experiences in Haiti, titled *Where Black Rules White*. In this travelogue, Prichard devoted an entire chapter to "Vaudoux Worship and Sacrifice."[104] Prichard described "vaudoux" as "evil" and "widespread."[105] He wrote, "The Government has, at all times, been too unstable to care to take the risk of seriously opposing so powerful a combination. The sect is universally feared, hence they carry on their rites and their orgies with practical impunity."[106] Prichard ends his book with a chapter titled, "Can the Negro Rule Himself?" He conclusion was this: "He has had his opportunity. That opportunity has lasted for a hundred years in a splendid land which he found ready prepared for him. . . . Certainly he has existed through one hundred years of internecine strife but he has never for six consecutive months governed himself in any accepted sense of the word. To-day, and as matters stand, he certainly cannot rule himself" (284).

Conclusion

Prichard's conclusion that the "negro" simply "cannot rule himself" illustrates the significance of the rhetoric of "voodooism" in the forty years after its first consistent uses in English-language presses. Beginning in earnest during the Union occupation of New Orleans during the Civil War, "voodoo" became a marker of the potential progress of African Americans and, as scientific racism grew, a yardstick for the development of the entire race. For these reasons, the rise of public interest in "voodoo," both in the United States and then in Haiti, was intricately tied to debates about the extension of citizenship and voting rights to African Americans. These (often made up or exaggerated) descriptions of Black spiritual practices served as purported evidence that persons of African descent needed to be firmly controlled by whites, even after the chains of slavery had been lifted. This general argument would slightly shift but never disappear.

News stories about the fear that Black people in the United States would deteriorate into some form of voodoo-practicing, cannibalistic barbarism decreased significantly after the turn of the twentieth century. Newspaper articles about "voodoo" practices among African Americans continued to be popular, but they did not contain the same political remarks that they did in the 1860s through the 1880s. Instead, media accounts that connected voodooism and an inability to self-govern turned toward the Caribbean and supported U.S. imperialism in both Cuba and Haiti.

2
"Voodoo" and U.S. Imperialism in Cuba in the 1890s–1920s

While civilization stands aghast at such deeds, done almost at the door of the American Republic, the hideous practices appear to be going on unchecked.[1]

As discussed in the previous chapter, in the last three decades of the nineteenth century, the focus of "voodoo" practices in U.S. newspapers, books, and pamphlets transitioned from New Orleans and the U.S. South to the Caribbean. This commenced with the publication of English-language accounts of the purportedly abysmal conditions of Haiti after nearly a century of independence from France. As numerous scholars have previously documented, this obsession with "voodoo" in Haiti and the purported disintegration of Haiti into "African barbarism" accelerated greatly in the early twentieth century. They have described how accounts like St. John's were used to illustrate that without white rulers, Black people would return to supposedly African practices of cannibalism and human sacrifice.[2] U.S. newspapers sent correspondents to Haiti to report about how this flailing empire was on the verge of collapse.[3] These reports were then critical propaganda tools to promote the U.S. occupation of Haiti from 1915 to 1934.

In this chapter, I examine an underexplored aspect of how tales of "voodooism" were used in U.S. imperialism in the Caribbean, by analyzing late nineteenth-century and early twentieth-century reports of "voodoo" in Cuba. The United States intervened in the government of Cuba several times during this period by sending troops and government officials. During the years when the United States "occupied" Cuba, tales of child sacrifice, orgies, and other forms of "voodoo" practices in Cuba were prevalent in U.S. newspapers and were used to defend North American presence on the island. I argue that these mini-occupations, most of which preceded the U.S. occupation of Haiti, laid the foundations for the relationship between U.S. intervention and "voodooism," and created patterns that would

Voodoo. Danielle N. Boaz, Oxford University Press. © Oxford University Press 2023.
DOI: 10.1093/oso/9780197689400.003.0002

be repeated in the U.S. occupation of Haiti. In fact, before the occupation of Haiti, the media often linked "voodoo" practices in the two nations—arguing that Cuba needed immediate intervention before it became another Haiti.

This chapter builds upon a rich body of literature that has explored race relations in the early years of the Republic of Cuba, including the impact of the rampant allegations of Black ritual cannibalism and human sacrifice and the significance of the constant threat of U.S. occupation.[4] While this literature has taught us much about Cuban intellectual and racial history, this chapter emphasizes the corresponding U.S. perspectives from this time and interrogates what can be gleaned from the media's coverage of Cuban "voodoo." Because of this focus on U.S. imperialism and outsider perspectives of Cuba, this chapter must oversimplify and even ignore complex political and intellectual discourses and events within Cuba, if they were not the subject of analysis and debate in the United States.

The Earliest Accounts of "Voodoo" in Cuba (1890s)

The second half of the nineteenth century was marked by tensions between Spain and its colonists in Cuba, with the latter pushing for independence following growing frustrations over taxation and other aspects of metropolitan governance. This led to the Ten Years' War between Spain and Cuba from 1868 to 1878; however, the colonists did not manage to secure their independence at that time. Twenty years later, in 1895, a second war for independence began. It is at the outset of this war that references to Cuban "voodoo" began to appear in the U.S. media.

An archival search of hundreds of U.S. newspapers revealed only one reference to "voodoo" in Cuba prior to 1896. In the latter part of the Ten Years' War, in 1876, an article circulated in at least two U.S. newspapers that described a festival in Havana where 150 "nanigos" (referring to the Abakuá, an all-male secret society in Cuba) were arrested while performing an animal sacrifice.[5] The author said that the beliefs and ceremonies of the "nanigos" resemble that of the "voodoos" but the author did not claim that it actually was a form of "voodoo." In fact, nearly 20 years later, in 1894, an article published in the *Olean Democrat* asserted that there were only three places where voodooism was practiced in the Americas: Haiti, San Domingo (now the Dominican Republic), and Jamaica.[6] There was no mention of voodoo practices in Cuba at that time.

Descriptions of Cuba began to change in 1896, shortly after the start of the second war of independence, when an article appeared in several U.S. newspapers titled "For Good Luck in War: Voodoo Incantations Invoked by Cuban Insurgents."[7] The author stated that a New York newspaper's correspondent in Cuba had reported some "curious intelligence that some of the insurgent bands, composed mostly of liberated slaves, are accompanied by voodoo women...." The author claimed that whenever the troops had to make a big decision, "the voodoo and her snake are consulted."

The article was full of subtle commentary on the spread of "voodooism" and efforts to contain its influence. The author described "voodoo" as having its origins in Africa, where it had been practiced for an unknown period prior to the arrival of Europeans, and from whence it spread to Haiti and then to Puerto Rico, Jamaica, Cuba, and Louisiana. They asserted that "voodooism" had not flourished in Louisiana because the French had "rigorously suppressed" the practice during the colonial period. In Haiti and Santo Domingo, by contrast, rulers had recently assumed power by "enlisting on his side a number of leading voodoos, who thereupon pronounced him invincible and warned all their hearers of the peril of opposing him."

Around six months later, a correspondent for the *New York Herald* published another letter describing life in "battle scarred Cuba" that again mentioned the role of "voodoo" among Afro-Cuban soldiers.[8] The correspondent devoted several paragraphs to describing the bleak conditions of Cuba's "cruel, bitter, relentless war" with Spain. They averred that the troops were weary, starving, and longing for the comforts of their wives and mothers. While generally praising the soldiers, the correspondent complained intensely about people of African descent who were working as servants or cooks in the camps. They averred that Black Cubans were prone to emitting an "abominable" "wail or chant" and "beating with their hands on rude wooden drums." While the Afro-Cubans referred to these vocalizations as singing, the correspondent claimed that to their ears, it sounded "like voodooism, cannibalism and every other disagreeable Africanism."

These, perhaps the earliest English-language references to "voodoo" in Cuba,[9] were loaded with meaning. During this time, the United States had started taking a more strategic interest in Cuba. By mid-1896, Cuban plantation owners and other elites had begun petitioning the United States to intervene in their war with Spain to assist them in gaining independence and perhaps to create a protectorate over the island.[10] For the United States, however, the possibility of their intervention in Cuba's war for independence was never a desire to merely liberate Cuba from Spain. Rather, the United States wanted to prevent Cuba from being acquired by another nation or from becoming independent under a regime that would oppose U.S. interests. Therefore, U.S. correspondents and officials argued that Cuba was completely unprepared for self-government.[11] These discussions of "voodoo" must be seen as part and parcel of this belief.

Both of these war correspondents who reflected upon the role of African "voodooism" in the Cuban insurgent camps wrote as if it were a widespread practice that was normal to the Cuban soldiers but "curious" or undesirable to observers from the United States. These reflections on the interactions between white and Black insurgents in Cuba would have signified how integration could impact all races. These narratives would have been particularly significant in the United States, where the Supreme Court's decision in *Plessy v. Ferguson* that same year had solidified the legality of racial segregation. Certainly, readers would have realized how the United States and Cuba were moving in opposite directions on the issue of racial mixing[12] and considered that integration in army camps had led to white Cubans' tacit acceptance of the pervasive sounds of voodoo songs, and the powerful influence of "voodoo" diviners who purportedly advised their followers by consulting with snakes.

In February 1898, a U.S. ship exploded in the harbor of Havana. A little more than two months later, the United States declared war against Spain. This war was short-lived; the United States and Cuba signed a treaty on December 10 of that year in which Spain relinquished its control over Cuba and ceded Guam, Puerto Rico, and the Philippines to the United States. A few weeks later, the United States installed a military government in Cuba, establishing its first occupation of the island.

As one might expect, in the earliest years of the first U.S. occupation of Cuba, North American publications began to refer more frequently to "voodoo" practices in Cuba. For instance, in 1899, George Clark Musgrave published an account of his experiences in the Spanish-American War.[13] Musgrave claimed that the Spanish had warned him that the Cuban rebels were cannibals and would eat him.[14] While Musgrave reported this with a tone of disbelief, referring to the Spanish as "ignorant," he observed in a footnote that some Africans living in the mountains of Haiti and Cuba maintained the "voodoo" practices of their ancestors. He asserted that in

Haiti "fetish medicine" was made of virgin's blood and herbs, but that in Cuba, they only murdered "for plunder."[15]

Also in 1899, an article titled "Fetish Worship in Cuba" circulated in several U.S. newspapers. The author asserted that "advanced civilization" had yet to eliminate "fanatical tendencies and customs among the black population of the island..." and that "fetishism" was more prevalent among Black people in Cuba than in most places.[16] This article featured a drawing of a man standing in front of the ruins of building, which the caption referred to as a "voodoo temple."[17]

In 1902, U.S. forces departed from Cuba, ending the first occupation and the first wave of U.S. publications referencing "voodoo" in Cuba. However, in the last year of the occupation, the United States and Cuba implemented a policy that would significantly impact relations between the two countries. In February 1901, the United States passed a law known as the Platt Amendment which contained a clause allowing the United States "to intervene for the preservation of Cuban independence, the maintenances of government adequate for the protection of life, property, and individual liberty, and for discharging the obligations with respect to Cuba imposed by the Treaty of Paris on the United States [referring to Cuba's debts to Spain that the United States assumed in 1898]."[18] In June of that year, Cubans reluctantly "accepted the Platt Amendment as an appendix to the new 1901 constitution."[19] This clause would hang over Cuba's head for decades to come, as a legal basis through which the United States could, and did, re-occupy the country.

Ritual Murder and The Second Occupation of Cuba (1904–1909)

The second intervention in Cuba began after two different political parties solicited U.S. support to oust their competitors. In 1904 and 1905, incumbent president Tomas Estrada Palma and the Moderate Party allegedly engaged in coercion and fraud to maintain control of the government—physically assaulting the members of the "scrutiny boards" who were responsible for the counting of ballots and the registration of voters.[20] In September 1905, Liberal Party leader José Miguel Gómez fled to the United States and began denouncing Palma's electoral abuses, asking for U.S. intervention.[21] By late November, certain liberals had begun to arm themselves and attack private rural properties.²² Some scholars contend that the Liberals planned targeted strikes against the outskirts of the city and the countryside so that they could pull the rural guard away from the capital and gain control of the government.²³ Others argue that when the United States ignored their request for intervention, the Liberals tried to force its hand by staging a rebellion that threatened property owned by U.S. investors.²⁴

Either way, over the following months, the Liberal rebellion grew. The Moderates used images of all-Black regiments killing white members of the rural guard to depict the revolution as "racial disorder, cultural savagery, and political anarchy."²⁵ On September 8, 1906, President Palma asked President Roosevelt to send troops to end the rebellion, stating that "the Government is unable to protect life and property," referencing the terms of the Platt Amendment. Shortly thereafter, Roosevelt declared himself the Provisional Governor of Cuba and sent thousands of soldiers and marines to the island.²⁶ U.S. forces would remain in Cuba for two and a half years, until February 1909. As word of the fraudulent elections and subsequent rebellion reached the United States and pleas for intervention began, the U.S media's interest in "voodoo" practices in Cuba once again increased. However, this surge in stories about Cuban "voodoo" was at least as influenced by a criminal trial in Cuba as it was by the broader political turmoil in the country.

The Niña Zoila Case (1904)

In November 1904, a 20-month-old child named Zoila disappeared from her home. Although no evidence ever surfaced about what happened to Zoila, after another girl was found with her body mutilated a short time later, it was assumed that she had been taken so that Black Cuban males could use her blood and body parts for their potions and rituals.²⁷ Eleven people, including Africans and Afro-Cubans, were arrested and sentenced to execution or lengthy terms of imprisonment.²⁸

Aline Helg has argued that elite Cubans used Zoila's case and others like it as a justification to suppress Black voting rights and political participation in Cuba, and that it was a mechanism for dividing working-class and elite Afro-Cubans.²⁹ This case and those that followed also laid the groundwork for intense intellectual debates about the cause of crime/criminality and its relationship to race.³⁰ While scholars have discussed the internal politics of this case and its implications for the status of people of African descent in post-independence Cuba, it is important to understand how discussions of this case as a form of "voodoo" figured into Cuba's relationship with the United States and the series of additional "occupations" that would follow.

In the year leading up to the second occupation, the Niña Zoila case was heavily publicized in U.S. newspapers. The first set of articles, which surfaced at the start of the trial, featured sensational titles such as "Ate White Child's Heart: Voodoo Doctor on Trial in Cuba for Murder" and "Negro Savagery in Cuba Equals Darkest Africa."[31] The authors of these stories averred that while many had known that "voudooism" was still practiced in Cuba, Zoila's death had illustrated the "most revolting character" of the practices that continued in the interior of the island and had been previously thought to be "harmless" compared to those "brought from Africa centuries ago."[32] A common theme among these media stories was that the people of Cuba, especially those of African descent, were so fearful of "voodoo doctors" that they refused to testify against the accused individuals.[33] One version of the story, written by the special correspondent to the *New York Herald* and circulated in several other papers, went so far as to allege that due to the dread of their knowledge of poisons, "voodoo doctors" were able to "maintain an almost supreme control over their people."[34] This suggestion that the people of Cuba were so "superstitious" or fearful of "voodoo doctors" that they dared not convict cannibals was the beginning of a common narrative that would continue to mark U.S. interventions in Cuba—that the U.S.'s "civilizing" presence was necessary to protect the inhabitants of the country.

To be sure, Cuban newspapers and presses throughout Latin America and the Caribbean were likewise following the story. However, they used Spanish terms like "brujos" ("witches") and "brujeria" ("witchcraft") or local terminology used in Cuba ("nanigos") to describe the alleged perpetrators. The conflation of these ritual murders with "voodoo" was a trend that was led by the United States and that supported U.S. interests in the fledgling nation. The use of the term "voodoo" allowed journalists, travel writers, and others to compare purported "ritual murder" in Haiti and Cuba.

One of the first such comparisons appeared in an article that began circulating in U.S. newspapers in May 1905, following the purported execution of two "voodoo doctors" in Haiti. The first and most sensational article was a special Sunday supplement to the *News Magazine* of Galveston, Texas, titled "Voodooism in the West Indies: Negroes in Cuba and Haiti Condemned to Death for Sacrificing Infants in Their Horrid Devil Worship,"[35] which was later republished in several other newspapers.[36] The author alleged that a Frenchman had blackened his face and snuck into a "voodoo" ceremony in Haiti, where he supposedly witnessed the sacrifice of a child followed by the drinking of the child's blood. The Frenchman reported the crime and "forced the authorities to act," leading to the arrest and execution of a Haitian man and woman. Although most of the article focused on voodoo in Haiti, under a subtitle "Convictions Not Popular," the author stated that Cubans had recently experienced similar problems with "voodoo." The author asserted that the case of Zoila had brought to light that cannibalism was still practiced in remote areas of the island. In both Haiti and Cuba, the author claimed, it was difficult to obtain convictions for these human sacrifices, because ceremonies occurred at night and because witnesses were so afraid of the vengeance of the "voodoo" practitioners that they were unwilling to offer evidence against them. The author presented the recent trial of the "voodoo" cannibals in Haiti and the Zoila case in Cuba as aberrations from this norm.

These comparisons continued in an article appearing in the *Daily Herald* the following month, published under the title, "Voodoo Mysteries: Haytians Returning to the Black Arts of Africa" with the subtitle "In Cuba Also the Voodoo Priest and Priestess Are Believed in and Their Services in Requisition."[37] The author, Henry Whitehouse, explained that "voodooism" is usually associated with "darkest Africa, with slave days in Louisiana, with the un-Americanized negro, with the past," but it still exists among "more or less civilized darkies" in places like Haiti and Cuba. Whitehouse, like many other reporters of that time, averred that high-level officials in Haiti ignored the practice of voodoo and that the president even participated in it. Whitehouse reminded the reader that "where but a century ago French civilization had no small influence, there one finds a reversion to barbarism." He observed "it seems pretty near home for this sort of thing to be going on unmolested."

These comparisons to Haiti, narratives about relapsing into an African state, and discussions about barbaric "voodoo" rituals would have helped lay the groundwork for Cuban politicians to convince the United States to return to the island, and for the United States to justify its second military intervention to the world. As Lillian Guerra notes, President Palma's invocation of the Platt Amendment "could not have come at a worse possible time" because President Roosevelt was trying to "improv[e] the United States' declining image as a 'democratic' leader abroad" following its war in the Philippines and acquisition of the Panama Canal zone.[38] It was necessary, Guerra argues, for the United States to appear "reluctant" and "benevolent."[39] It is likely that the U.S. public reflected on these accounts of the purported prevalence of "voodoo cannibals" in Cuba as they considered their acquiescence to Cuban Moderates' calls for intervention.

One must also recall that the Moderate Party had alleged that Black insurgents were slaughtering white members of the rural guard in a manner similar to the Haitian revolution. Claims that Black people in Cuba were "relapsing" into sacrificial practices like those in Haiti would have reinforced the notion that the United States had a responsibility to provide some "stability" to the nation. Indeed, a wealthy tobacco planter made such a suggestion to a U.S. journalist at the beginning of the second occupation. He warned that without intervention, Cuba would have been "in danger of becoming another Hayti," because the country was home to "many thousands of negroes not one step higher in civilization than those you find in the African jungles."[40]

The St. Lucia Cases (1870s–1900s)

The U.S. coverage of the purported outbreaks of "voodoo"-related human sacrifice in the Caribbean in the early twentieth century is as notable for its omissions as for its content. In the first three decades of the twentieth century, St. Lucia became a rumored site of ritual murder among Black communities. While numerous articles fixated on purported cases of ritual murder in the independent nations of Haiti and Cuba, I found very few U.S. newspapers or other North American publications covering the analogous allegations in St. Lucia that surfaced at the same time. Those that did mention these rumors described them as "Obeah" (as they would have been originally labeled in the British Caribbean) rather than translating them to "voodoo" (as they did with discussions of "brujeria" in Cuba).

The first incident that could have sparked widespread concerns about ritual murder in St. Lucia occurred in 1903, when Sir William Des Voeux published a memoir about his experiences as a colonial officer in various parts of the British Empire.[41] Des Voeux reported that in 1876, he had served on the Executive Council which reviewed death sentences issued by the Supreme Court in St. Lucia. Des Voeux described the case of Adolphe la Croix, a "dangerous Obeahman" who was convicted of murdering a small child to use his body parts for "Obeah" purposes. Des Voeux claimed that Sir John Pope Hennessey, governor of Barbados and the Windward Islands, generally opposed capital punishment and had pressured Des Voeux to reduce La Croix's sentence to life imprisonment. However, Des Voeux asserted that he was concerned that nothing less than death would deter other Obeah practitioners from committing similar crimes. Therefore, he neglected to tell the Executive Council of the governor's reservations and they unanimously voted to confirm the execution.[42]

Court records confirm the existence of such a case. Adolphe La Croix was prosecuted for the murder of a child in 1876 in St. Lucia. No motive was given at trial; however, officials assumed that the murder was for purposes of Obeah, noting, "The body was found mutilated in various ways—as is done, it is said, by Obeahmen for the purposes of their magic."[43] The court also mentioned that La Croix had allegedly killed his own child and that another neighborhood child had gone missing, implying that La Croix had killed that child as well. La Croix was convicted and sentenced to execution, never confessing to the crime nor claiming his innocence.[44]

Unlike St. John's 1888 description of a decades-old prosecution of Haitian "voodoo" practitioners for cannibalism, Des Voeux's account of the La Croix case does not appear to have launched his book onto the bestseller list, nor sparked widespread speculation about the need to suppress African-derived spiritual practices on the island. This is significant because, like St. John, Des Voeux stressed how widespread such "barbaric" practices were and how likely they were to continue. His description of Governor Hennessey's efforts to convince him to commute the sentence to life imprisonment also resembled St. John's account in the sense that it suggested a reluctance on the part of the government to take decisive action to ensure that similar incidents did not occur in the future. However, this tale of ritual "Obeah" murder did not spark the same kind of interest or analysis of governance of this British-controlled island that purported ritual murder in the free Black nation of Haiti had.

This single publication could easily be dismissed as too insignificant to have generated widespread concerns about ritual murder in St. Lucia. However, when combined with an incident known as the "Monchy Murder" that occurred the following year, one would expect widespread speculation that ritual murder was becoming a problem on the island. In 1904, three men were convicted of strangling and mutilating a twelve-year-old boy "for purposes of Obeah."[45] Allegedly, the boy was a servant in the house of one of the accused. The men were arrested after the police raided one of their homes and found a tin can containing the boy's severed hands and heart.

They later uncovered the rest of the body buried in the backyard.[46] All three men were convicted and sentenced to death.[47] At sentencing, despite the fact that the prosecution had tried the case as a simple charge of murder, the Chief Justice of St. Lucia's Supreme Court determined that "there could be no doubt that . . . the boy had been murdered in order that parts of his body might be obtained for this abominable practice."[48]

Contrary to what one might expect of such a sensational story about ritual murder, there was very limited newspaper coverage of this trial in the United States. The first story was only two sentences long and was published under titles such as "Barbarous Superstition," and "Ghastly Crime."[49] The author explained, "Barbarous superstition which prevails among a portion of the population of the West Indian Islands is the basis of a ghastly and extraordinary crime that has come to light in the island of St. Lucia. The finding of the heart and hands of a white child in the possession of an Obeah man (a negro sorcerer), led to the discovery that the child had been murdered and the body mutilated in order that superstitious natives might, through the possession of parts of the body, be able to work spells."

Only one newspaper seems to have followed up on this story, providing greater detail. Two days after the original report, the *Times Picayune* published a two-paragraph article titled "Barbarism in St. Lucia: Further Details of the Murder of a White Child by Obeah Man." The author explained that a "seemingly intelligent negro butcher" had been arrested for "the murder of a white boy" and that this case revealed the "barbarous superstition and diabolism that suvives [sic] to a startling extent in the West Indies, the heritage of savage ancestry."[50] After this, there appears to have been no reports of this case in the United States. There were no publications at any time that linked it to "voodoo."

Compared to the U.S. coverage, the stories of this murder in other parts of the Anglophone world were often extensive and followed the case from inception to conclusion. The *Gleaner*, published in Kingston, Jamaica, provides the best example. The first article about the Monchy murder appeared in the *Gleaner* on October 14, 1904. The author reported that they had just received a cable-gram the day before describing a "ghastly and extraordinary crime."[51] After providing a brief description of the events—that the head and hand of a white child were found in an "Obeah practitioner's" possession—the author lamented that this case was becoming so widely known that they feared that "through it the West Indies may come to be regarded as lapsing once more into barbarism—a view which many persons are only to inclined to take already." The author went on to explain that although such practices were common among Africans when they first arrived in the colonies, they were unheard of in Jamaica over the preceding years and so rare in the British Caribbean that they surprised everyone when they occurred.

Despite the editor's initial concerns that widespread knowledge of this case might cultivate a negative view of the West Indies, the following day, the *Daily Gleaner* published an enormous story about it that comprised a third of page six of the paper.[52] The *Gleaner* reprinted the entire story from the *Voice* (a newspaper in St. Lucia), which detailed the process of the arrest and the statements of the accused and the sergeant. They also reprinted the *Voice*'s reflections on the story, where the author opined, "this murder is complicated with ignorance and savage superstition, and is only a startling indication of a widespread evil, making for a relapse to barbarism, to which we have been for years vainly striving to attract the serious attention of the authorities."

The *Gleaner* followed this story until the end of December, when all three men had been convicted, sentenced, and executed for the crime.[53] In later articles, they continued to report concerns printed in St. Lucian newspapers about the widespread belief in Obeah on the island and condemnations that patrons of the Obeah practitioners for divination and other minor rituals were encouraging the more "nefarious" or "heinous" practices.[54]

Legislators, officials, and the media in the British Caribbean would continue to reflect on this trial over the subsequent years. First, in the same year that this case took place, legislators in St. Lucia passed a new law prohibiting the practice of Obeah.[55] Second, in 1905, an unidentified author published a book about the case titled *The Monchy Murder: The Strangling and Mutilation of a Boy for Purposes of Obeah, at St. Lucia*. Ten years later, John Udal (lawyer, judge, and former Chief Justice of the Leeward Islands) wrote an article titled "Obeah in the West Indies," in which he recounted the facts of the case. Even as late as 1926, Frank Wesley Pitman published an article in the *Journal of Negro History* about slavery in the West Indies, wherein he argued the ritual sacrifice of children was common among Black people in St. Lucia.[56]

Clearly legislators and the media in St. Lucia, as well as other British colonies, saw broad implications of this murder. They expressed concern that the island was "relapsing" into barbarism and that the broader population might be complicit in the persistence of dangerous "superstitions" by patronizing Obeah devotees for other services. They passed laws to suppress "Obeah" to avoid future ritual murders and characterized these measures as necessary to prevent the spread of similar practices throughout the British Caribbean.

Despite the similarities in the purported acts of ritual murder in St. Lucia and Cuba (white children allegedly murdered for their body parts by Black sorcerers) and the trials occurring during the same year, the United States largely ignored the former and focused on the latter. The story about this ritual murder in St. Lucia was treated as a "one-off" in the U.S. media; they didn't republish any of the reflections on how this case was a problem of governance or the potential ripple effect throughout the Caribbean. This is particularly striking because reports about ritual murder in St. Lucia—printed in English and circulated throughout the Anglophone world in newspapers, books, and journal articles—would have been much more accessible than the Spanish-language reports about the Niña Zoila case.

Even more telling than the frequency of such stories about St. Lucia versus Cuba is the language used to describe the ritual murder. Unlike the Cuban cases, where "brujeria" and "nanigoismo" were translated as "voodoo," the few reports of the St. Lucia murders that appeared in U.S. presses maintained the local terminology of "Obeah men" and "Obeah practitioners." In doing so, they encouraged comparisons between "voodoo" in Haiti and Cuba without drawing similar analogies between St. Lucia and Haiti.

In these ways, one can begin to see how the labeling of ritual murder in Cuba as "voodoo" was an indication of imperial interest. St. Lucia remained a British colony; thus, purported ritual murder there was of little political value and generated little notice in North American presses. Cuba's Niña Zoila case, on the other hand, was followed extensively and was spoken of in terms of its broader significance. Journalists constantly reminded readers why the United States would keep a close eye on Cuba and perhaps reoccupy the nation at the first sign of breakdowns in governance.

The End of the Second Occupation (1908–1909)

During the next two years of the second U.S. occupation, reports about Cuban "voodoo" and human sacrifice basically disappeared until September 1908, when President Roosevelt announced that the United States would withdraw its troops from Cuba on January 28, 1909. This announcement sparked a surge of articles that reflected on the purported rampant "voodooism" on the island and its relationship to the end of the occupation. For instance, an identical article appeared in the *Baltimore Sun* on September 6, 1908, under the title "To Evacuate Cuba January 28," and in the *Galveston Daily News* on September 14, 1908, under the title "Troops Quit Cuba Jan 28."[57] The first line of the article reported that President Roosevelt had agreed to withdraw U.S. troops from Cuba on January 28, 1909. Without any attempted transition, the author then stated that local Cuban newspapers had documented an "extraordinary revival" in "voodoo" practices where people sacrifice children, as they were reported to do in Haiti, and that these practices were not confined to Black Cubans. The author said that many white people, if not actual participants in the human sacrifice, at least believed in "voodoo."

These reports multiplied as the time for the withdrawal of the troops drew nearer, and they increasingly reflected on how these purported practices flourished in both Cuba and Haiti. For instance, in October 1908, a sensational article about "voodoo" circulated in several U.S. newspapers with the title "Horrors of Voodooism Break Out Again: Babies Stolen in Cuba and Hayti for Human Sacrifices to Sacred Serpents."[58] The full-page article featured a giant image of a baby in the clutches of a boa constrictor being strangled, while Black people bowed to the snake in the background. The author alleged that children were frequently offered as sacrifices to snakes, whom Haitians and Cubans worshipped as gods. The writer emphasizes, "While civilization stands aghast at such deeds, done almost at the door of the American Republic, the hideous practices appear to be going on unchecked."

The article went on to describe three rumored cases of attempted or actual child sacrifice in Cuba. The author started with the case of Irene Rodriguez, who had been allegedly sentenced to death in June for sacrificing a three-year-old white child, Luesa Valdes. Rodriguez's two accomplices were sentenced to life imprisonment. Glossing over the fact that this case ended in convictions and harsh sentences for the perpetrators, the author concluded that "this case reveals the fact that the brujos, or voodoo worshipers, have in all the provinces leaders or high priests who command powerful influence over the people." To emphasize this point, the author cited two other alleged cases where "voodoo" practitioners attempted to snatch children for their rituals and concluded that the practice is "rampant." The author asserted that while "voodoo" practices were brought to Cuba by enslaved persons, they had been "fostered by constant communication with the natives of Hayti, only 60 miles away."

As the U.S. coverage of purported "voodoo" sacrifices in Cuba increased, journalists often linked the two nations and argued for similar policies in each. For instance, in December 1908, the last full month of the U.S. occupation of Cuba, an unidentified author wrote an article for the *Oregonian* that was simply titled "Hayti."[59] The author averred that "civilization" was gradually seeping out of the country and that Africans were reverting to their "savage" practices, including "voodoo worship." They claimed that the supposed degradation of the Black population in Hayti had caused warlike conflict between the mixed-race and Black people. Like many authors had before, they reported that "the inhabitants of Hayti have enjoyed an abundant opportunity to develop a stable government if they had possessed the ability, but the clear verdict of history is that they do not possess it." The author asserted that "the world may tolerate anarchy and slaughter in this unhappy island for a few years long, but it is only a question of time when some civilizing power will step in and compel the people to give up perpetual fighting for peaceful industry. *What nation that will be can perhaps be surmised from recent events in Cuba.*"[60]

Ironically, it was the United States who had fostered greater contact between Cuba and Haiti. Following independence from Spain, Cuba had banned nonwhite immigration. During the second U.S. occupation, Spanish immigration was permitted, but it substantially declined. Meanwhile, more seasonal labors from the British Caribbean and Haiti arrived in Cuba—9,000 from the British Caribbean and 1,400 from Haiti between 1906 and 1908. Around one-third of these laborers stayed in Cuba. Scholars argue that this was the first time that there was a significant flow of Haitian immigrants to Cuba after independence.[61]

A Race War in Cuba? (1908–1917)

There was approximately an eight-year gap between the second and third major U.S. interventions in Cuba (1909–1917). During that time, the U.S. media was filled with constant allegations that "voodoo" cannibalism and murder were rampant in Cuba. In many cases, these stories became an entry point to debate whether the United States' permanent acquisition of Cuba was necessary. Most of these debates centered around race relations in Cuba, and concerns about "voodoo" coincided with restrictions on Afro-Cuban political participation.

The earliest account that "voodoo" practices might be a source of racial tensions in Cuba was a series of stories appearing in July 1908, when three

Afro-Cuban "brujos" were reportedly arrested for the murder of a white female child, Luisa Valdes, in Alacranes, Matanzas. U.S. newspapers reported this controversy under titles such as "Race War Feared in Cuba" and "Voodoo Murder May Cause War."[62] The authors claimed that Black Cubans were assembling outside the jail, plotting to rescue the prisoners, while "rival bodies of armed whites" were trying to prevent the jail break and possibly lynch the prisoners.[63]

These harbingers of a "race war" in Cuba came just a month before the establishment of the Partido Independiente de Color ("PIC")—"the first black [political] party in the Western hemisphere."[64] The PIC opposed post-emancipation efforts to represent Cuba as a predominantly white country and stressed that Afro-Cubans had been an integral part of the liberation army during the war for independence from Spain. They sought to allow nonwhite immigration, ban racial discrimination, as well as improve access to jobs and socioeconomic conditions for Afro-Cubans.[65] The PIC published a newspaper that included reports of when Afro-Cubans experienced racism, such as being turned down for jobs or being denied service.

The PIC sparked major controversies in Cuba. In January 1910, the Cuban Senate passed a bill criminalizing the party.[66] The government seized the party's newspaper and "the leaders and hundreds of members of the party were arrested and persecuted for allegedly conspiring to transform Cuba into a black republic."[67] They were ultimately found not guilty; however, the government refused to lift its ban on Black political parties. Opponents accused the PIC of trying to turn Cuba into another Haiti and opined that the suppression of the party was necessary to prevent that.[68] In April 1910, the PIC wrote to the U.S. foreign minister in Havana and to the U.S. president asking them to help the PIC's cause.[69]

Shortly thereafter, in May 1910, Frederic Haskin wrote a three-part series titled "Trouble in Cuba," that was featured in numerous U.S. newspapers. In each essay, Haskin reflected on race relations in Cuba and on the question of further U.S. intervention. The first article in the series was subtitled "The Danger of Revolution."[70] In it, Haskin focused on the first two U.S. interventions in Cuba, describing the occupations as "protection and guidance from an older and stronger power" for this "infant nation." Haskin lamented that despite "the memory of America's chivalrous intervention," Cuba still "does not like the Yankees" because of "ingratitude" or "prejudice." However, he asserted that politically savvy Cubans, despite their dislike for the United States, knew that their annexation to the United States was "inevitable," because "nothing short of a miracle" could prevent Cuba from "complete political disaster" as it faced an impending "race war."

In the second article, titled "The Race Question," Haskin turned away from the previous U.S. interventions to focus on what he regarded as the central issue that threatened "the very life of the republic" of Cuba.[71] After reporting that members of the "negro party" of Cuba (the PIC) had been jailed for planning a revolution against the current government, Haskin claimed that two of the key problems in Cuba were that more than half the population had African heritage and that so many Black Cubans had participated in the revolution against the Spanish for "sheer love of fighting" as opposed to belief in a clear cause. Their high percentage of the population and their bellicose nature, Haskin claimed, made Cuba like a powder keg ready to explode if Black people were given an opportunity to fight.

Under the subtitle, "Holy War Feared," Haskin argued that the different types of slavery in the United States and Cuba led to enslaved persons having fewer "civilizing" interactions with their masters in the latter than in the former. As such, "voodoo" was more prevalent among Black Cubans, and they would follow any political leader who could gain the support of the "voodoo" priest. Haskin warned that a "voodoo" priest could preach for the extermination of white people and the establishment of an all-Black government, and a "holy war" would follow, with the Black population doing exactly as the "voodoo" priest ordered.

Haskin conceded that there were educated Black people in Cuba who would be capable of becoming leaders; however, if they were elected at the head of a "negro organization" or political party, they "would be unable to hold in check the passions and prejudices of their own followers. They would be overthrown by more intemperate and more radical and blacker negroes and the fair island of Cuba would be reduced to the low level of semisavage [sic] Hayti."[72] Some newspapers printed this essay with titles suggesting both an impending "holy war" and a war between the races.[73]

In Haskin's third essay, titled "The Problem of Annexation," he argued that Cubans did not want to be seized by the United States, and people from the United States did not want to annex Cuba.[74] Nevertheless, he contended that it was the duty of the United States to ensure that there was peace in Cuba. In part, he reasoned that this intervention was an obligation that the United States had undertaken following the Spanish-American war and the Platt Amendment. Moreover, Haskin pointed out that Cuba was a main supplier of food for the United States and the provider of one-third of the nation's sugar. Therefore, it was in the United States' self-interest to ensure that Cuba remained politically stable.

Over the next two years, the PIC continued to petition the United States to exercise their authority under the Platt Amendment and step in to protect the PIC's rights.[75] Then, on May 20, 1912, 10 years after the end of the first U.S. occupation, the Party staged an armed rebellion, trying to force the government to rescind the restriction on Black political parties.[76] The PIC army did not harm anyone in the uprising, and they primarily carried out attacks on foreign property.[77] Some scholars argue that the PIC's strategy was not really to attack the government, but rather to force the United States to intervene by threatening the security of foreign property.[78] The PIC's purported strategy succeeded, as foreign investors indeed asked the State Department for assistance.[79]

Despite the lack of aggression against people, the Cuban media "depicted the uprising as an unabashed campaign of black-on-white violence inspired by nothing more than racial hatred,"[80] and some argued that this was the beginning of another Haitian revolution. The government sent in the army and "zealous white volunteers" to put down the "rebellion."[81] Between 2,000 and 6,000 Afro-Cubans were killed, including party leaders and members, as well as numerous Black civilians.[82] By contrast, only 16 members of the military forces were killed, eight of whom died from friendly fire when white people assumed that Black soldiers were working with the PIC.[83] Nevertheless, the Gomez administration depicted the PIC uprising as a "race war" and argued that the government had saved the nation by murdering these Afro-Cubans.[84]

Exactly one year later, on May 20, 1913, President Gomez's term in office ended and Mario García Menocal assumed the presidency. Later that year, reports of "voodoo" murder resurfaced in a significant number for the first time since Haskin's 1910 predictions of a racialized "holy war" on the island. These reports denounced Gomez's handling of "voodoo" practices during his presidency and suggested that President Menocal was much more responsive to the problem. The favorable depictions of Menocal's handling of "voodoo" may have been, in part, that he was, as one scholar described, "[k]nown for his willingness to repress black strikers during his tenure as chief of Havana's city police during the first U.S. occupation" and he had "shown his commitment to pro-imperialist nationalist values by working as the manager for the largest U.S.-owned sugar plantation in Oriente."[85]

For example, an article appeared in several newspapers, including the *L.A. Times* and the *Washington Post*, between late December 1913 and April 1914, titled "Cuba Wars on Voodoo: President Menocal Striving to Stamp Out Orgies" or "Cuba Stops Voodooism."[86] The author argued that the Spanish had attempted to place a check on "voodoo" during the colonial period by deporting the people who engaged in such practices and inflicting "barbarous" punishments on the perpetrators. However, they had failed to stop the practice. Following independence, the author averred that "Voodooism received its first substantial checks during the American Intervention" because the U.S. forces "cared nothing for voodoo curses and evil consequences, but broke up their meetings and ceremonials with indifference."[87] The author claimed that following the U.S. occupation, under the Gomez administration, "voodoo" had regained strength because he had issued "a presidential decree [that] allowed public ceremonies, which had been stopped by the Spanish." By 1913, the author asserted, Black "voodoo" practitioners had developed an "extensive organization," which had "relations with strong political factions, who in return for legal protection control their votes." Through this political control, they claimed, many heinous crimes, like human sacrifice, had gone unpunished. However, the author argued, extreme public outrage had caused the administration to take action in a recent case where a Cuban child had allegedly been murdered by "voodoo" practitioners. Now, President Menocal was taking "dramatic measures" to try to stop such practices.

The Third Occupation of Cuba (1917–1922)

Over the next five years, reports about "voodoo" in Cuba were exceedingly rare. The few accounts that did surface were brief—merely one sentence or two—and provided only blurbs about an incident without reflection on the implications.[88] The final surges of publications about "voodoo" in Cuba occurred during the last major U.S. military intervention.

In 1916, President Menocal used fraud to get re-elected.[89] Once again, the Liberal Party asked the United States to intervene under the Platt Amendment and to help Cuba hold free elections.[90] They protested during the harvest and damaged property.[91] In Santiago, they had some success and forced Republicans out of government positions which they took over themselves. Menocal tried to quash the opposition by arresting civilians.[92] On March 30, 1917, U.S. marines and Cuban government forces arrived to help suppress the rebellion.[93]

The first two years of the third occupation brought waves of press about "voodoo" practices in Cuba back to U.S. newspapers. In 1918, an article titled "Awful Rites of Voodoo" circulated in several newspapers. The correspondent reported that a seven-year-old girl had become "the victim of the blood sacrifices of Voodoo witch-doctors," in Havana.[94] The author lamented that "Voodooism, the mystic, blood witchcraft-religion of Haiti, believed stamped out in Cuba, has reappeared on the island in its most repellant form." They claimed that the people who "participated in the sacrificial rites" had been arrested but criticized that "no attempt is being made to round up other voodooists, a Havana judge having held that voodooism is a religion and the Cuban laws forbids government interference with religious worship."

Stories about "voodoo" in Cuba escalated the following year, in 1919, when a series of strikes began sweeping across the island.[95] Strikes halted industries such as sugar and maritime shipping, which cost U.S. investors hundreds of millions of dollars.[96] When the local governments struggled to suppress the strikes, the United States sent thousands of marines to "Havana, Cienfuegos, and Gibara, and their presence intimidated workers and forced them to return to their jobs."[97] As with the previous occupation, U.S. reporters often questioned Cuban authorities' ability to suppress voodoo sacrifices and suggested that white Cubans secretly participated in ceremonies.[98]

While the mere renewed presence of U.S. forces in Cuba seems to have fueled the resurfacing of similar narratives about "voodoo" practices there, events within the United States also appear to have left their mark on how the U.S. media interpreted Cuban responses to these cases. In 1915, the Ku Klux Klan was reborn following the release of the film *The Birth of a Nation*, which depicted the Klan as heroes or saviors. Racial tensions reached a pinnacle during the so-called Red Summer of 1919, when race riots broke out across the country. These riots frequently began with the arrest of a Black male on allegations of a crime against a white person—typically the rape of a white woman. Alleging concerns that the legal system would not bring the Black men to justice, white mobs gathered around jails and courthouses throughout the country seeking to lynch the accused men rather than allow the case to go to trial. Riots frequently ensued as these mobs either simply subsequently targeted larger Black communities or faced opposition from Black protestors who sought to prevent vigilante attacks on the accused.

These U.S. struggles with lynching and mob violence against Black civilians seeped into reports of white Cubans' responses to accused "voodoo" murderers.[99] In 1919, U.S. journalists asserted that a white girl in one Cuban town disappeared when she was running an errand. When she was found with an Afro-Cuban male, members of the community put a rope around the man's neck and tied him to the back of a horse and flogged the horse to a gallop. The correspondent averred that this action was "justified" because Cuban law did not include the death penalty. Not surprisingly, the U.S. journalists did not reprint a statement in the prominent Cuban newspaper, *La Prensa*, in which a white worker claimed that the purported "brujo" was actually an immigrant laborer who was lynched because he was a "scab" worker[100]—ironically, likely breaking those same strikes that U.S. marines had come in to suppress.

Around the same time as this lynching, a second girl disappeared. The child's body was discovered in a cemetery, missing her brains, heart, tongue, and blood. Upon hearing of this incident, a "mob of several thousand" stormed a prison where eight Black men were being held on the accusation that they had killed the white girl and used her organs for "voodoo." While soldiers fired into the crowd to try to push them back, guards took five of the accused from their cells and executed them in another part of the prison. The media reported that they were killed while trying to escape.[101]

The first reports on these incidents in the United States surfaced in June, before the majority of the race riots of the "Red Summer" had taken place. They centered on the second case where the public had stormed the prison. The most widely circulated version stated, "Five alleged negro voodoo worshippers held in San Servino prison at Matanzas, on a charge of complicity in the murder of a little girl, were shot and killed last night by soldiers when they attempted to escape while being removed from the prison to a place of greater safety after a mob had attempted to storm the castle for the purpose of lynching the prisoners. Two members of the mob were killed and eleven injured when the soldiers fired on the would be lynchers a couple of hours earlier."[102] It is notable that the article focused on the attempted lynching and the subsequent murder of the "voodoo" practitioners. This was a distinct shift from earlier reports of "voodoo" in Cuba, which had typically concentrated on the descriptions of the young, white victim and the serpents or demons to which the children would purportedly be sacrificed. Rather than titles about children dying in the clutches of "voodoo doctors," these 1919 reports featured headlines such as "Guards Shoot Negro Voodoo Worshippers," and "Voodoo Worshippers Slain."

In August of that year, after the volatile month of July when race riots surged throughout several major U.S. cities, a similar story about Cuban "voodoo" appeared in newspapers throughout the country. This time, the titles depicted the Cubans who carried out mob violence as the heroes of the story, with phrases like "Lynchers Fighting Voodoo Cannibals,"[103] "Cubans Invoke Lynch Law to Curb Voodoos,"[104] and "Revival of Voodoo Practices in Cuba Causes Lynchings."[105] The author alleged that six "of the Voodoo" were killed "by the application of lynch law for the first time in this country's history" or the "first instance of mob violence known in [the] Island."[106] In at least one newspaper, this story about the lynching of Cuban "voodoo" practitioners was published right next to an article about participants in the Chicago race riots (one of the most deadly race riots in the U.S. in the summer of 1919) being jailed for murder and assault.[107]

In November of that year, yet another version of this story reflected on both incidents of mob violence in greater detail. Once again, the author stressed that in June of that year "for the first time since the cessation of Spanish rule cases of lynching have occurred."[108] This time, the body of the article focused on attempting to rationalize this act of mob violence, explaining, "These outrages growing in number greatly excited public opinion," and that "many of the newspapers justified this because of the leniency of the law to voodoo culprits."[109] The author described both cases in detail and claimed that similar charges had surfaced, and that "other negroes have been arrested on charges of a similar character, and raids have been made wherever the practice of voodoo rites has been known."[110] As if concurring with the Cuban newspapers that had purportedly defended the lynching because of "leniency" in these cases, the author stressed that although "several negroes have been convicted and have received heavy sentences; there is no death sentence in Cuba."[111] Ironically, at least as recently as 1916, there had been numerous articles suggesting that accused "voodoo" practitioners had been executed, with titles such as "Sorcerers to Die for Voodoo Murder."[112]

Once again, if we compare the reports on this case in the U.S. news to those in other international presses, there are interesting contrasts. For instance, an article about the same incidents appeared in the *Jamaican Gleaner* in July 1919.[113] The author likewise explained that a mob had descended on the jail and that the prisoners had been killed after they had "mysteriously" found a method to escape in the chaos. However, the reporter for the *Gleaner* did not refer to this as lynching, but rather as the "Mexican method" or "Ley de fuga." They explained that the mob would likely have caused significant damage at the jail if the prisoners had not been killed, so they were released and then shot down as they were escaping. They described the motive of the mob as "public indignation," but did not suggest that there was a lack of accountability for the "voodoo" practitioners or that it was because there was no death penalty in Cuba. The differences between these reports, especially the U.S. fixation on justifying the murder of Black "voodoo" practitioners, was likely connected to the prevalence of such violence against Black Americans and opposition to recent efforts to pass anti-lynching laws in the United States (discussed further in Chapter 3).

This connection between U.S. lynching and the response to the alleged "voodoo" practitioners was not lost on contemporary Cubans. Scholars confirm that white Cubans did not typically employ mob violence against Black Cubans who were accused of crimes.[114] At least one supporter of lynching wrote an editorial in a Havana newspaper, praising the mob and comparing Cuba to the U.S. South where people already "know[] how to lynch."[115] Several intellectuals, in particular members of an association of Black Cubans in Havana known as Club Atenas, denounced both the alleged crimes and the lynching of the accused as barbaric actions that were too uncivilized to be permitted in Cuba. One politician, Juan Felipe Risquet, described lynching as "the symbol of human injustice" and the "savage human beast which harms everything in its way."[116] Risquet averred that the vigilantes "imitated North American lynchers."[117]

Post-Occupation: Haitian "Voodoo" Practitioners in Cuba (1920s)

Stories about Cuban "voodoo" in the U.S. media reached their peak during the occupations. However, a smaller wave of reports of "voodoo" practice in Cuba began shortly after the end of the final U.S. intervention in 1922. Reporters almost universally attributed these practices to Haitians living in Cuba. For instance, a white girl was found with her heart cut out, and authorities assumed that she had been killed for ritual purposes. Reporters noted that one of the six suspects who had been taken into custody was Haitian and stressed that he was presumably the leader.[118] That same year, another white child was reported to have been kidnapped from the same plantation. The correspondent attributed this kidnapping to the failure to convict the murderers of the first child. The author claimed, "Nobody doubts that the child has been sacrificed on some rude jungle altar," and indicated that three Haitians and two Cubans were arrested for the act.[119] The following year, in 1923, another article reported that police found body parts thought to be those belonging to a white child in the home of a Black Cuban male. Everyone in the house was arrested and their "paraphernalia" for their "voodoo rites" was confiscated. The author explained, "The house is situated in the Villa Alegre district where there are a number of Haitians, many of whom are alleged to be devotees of voodooism."[120]

The U.S. press was not the only foreign press printing such allegations. On October 8, 1919, the *Times* of London, England, reprinted one of the U.S. articles about the recent purported "voodoo" murders and the subsequent "lynchings" of the accused individuals under the title "The Cult of Human Sacrifices." In response, the *Times* received several letters to the editor attributing such practices to Haitian influences. C. W. Lowther wrote the first of these, explaining that he had been in Cuba 12 years earlier and there had been no evidence that "voodoo" was practiced there at the time. Lowther observed that "voodoo" had been well-documented on the neighboring island of Haiti and speculated that since the United States had occupied the nation, the "voodoo" priests from Haiti had "taken refuge in Cuba" and therefore "voodoo" had increased in Cuba "in its more hideous form."[121] A few days later, George Musgrave made similar comments in another letter to the editor. He asserted, "As Mr. Lowther suggests, most of these murders in other localities have been traced to superstitious fanatics who have escaped from Haiti. Such occurrences in Cuba are as anomalous as degenerate murders in England."[122]

Some modern scholars have argued that these stereotypes arose due to Haitian immigration into Cuba in the early to mid-twentieth century and conflicts that arose in the context thereof. Historical records indicate that "between 1917 and 1931 some 300,000 Haitians, Jamaicans, and other workers from the Caribbean region entered the island to work on sugar plantations."[123] Historian Barry Carr, in his work on Black immigrant workers in Cuba, claims that Haitian workers were both mocked and feared. He contends that tales about their "voodoo" practices circulated through the sugar plantations, underscoring the supposed barbarism of the Haitian people. Carr quoted a 1922 article from a Cuban newspaper *El Heraldo de Cuba* which said, "In the province of Oriente, Haitians are devotees of witchcraft ("brujeria"), contaminating black Cubans in an atavistic leap backwards in time. They practice the superstitious 'Vodu' cult which is full of black magic . . . and [are] led by a priest known as 'papa Bocu.'"[124] Historian Marc McLeod, in his examination of Haitian and West Indian immigrant workers in Cuba between 1912 and 1939, makes similar claims. McLeod argues that Afro-Cuban religions were viewed as witchcraft by white Cubans. Thus, when Haitians brought their religions to Cuba, they were regarded negatively due to "a common heritage in Catholicism and West African religions." McLeod argues that "Vodou" was thus referred to as "brujeria" and portrayed as cannibalism.[125]

However, one must also consider the influence that U.S. imperialist agendas played in the reporting of the Haitian involvement. While the United States had just concluded its third and final intervention in Cuba, it would continue to occupy Haiti for more than a decade after the last U.S. marines left Cuba. Reports that Haitian immigrants were behind "voodoo" murders in Cuba would have reinforced the claims that U.S. forces and reporters made about similar practices in Haiti itself. Therefore, these reports simultaneously justified its continued occupation of Haiti and its relinquishing of Cuba by suggesting that Haitians were the real actors perpetuating "voodoo" in Cuba and that stamping out the problem at its source (Haiti) would eliminate future incidents in Cuba.

By the late 1920s and early 1930s, U.S. reports on "voodoo" in Cuba decreased, and the few that surfaced continued to stress that these occasional cases of "voodoo" in Cuba were linked to immigrant workers. In January 1929, one reporter averred that the Cuban government had successfully suppressed "voodoo" and that "it was largely in connection with the government's campaign against Obeahism and Nanigoism that measures were adopted curtailing the immigration of illiterate workers from Haiti and Jamaica."[126] The same author also opined that in the Oriente, the region of Cuba closest to Haiti, "voodoo" priests have the most power and human sacrifices were possibly still taking place.[127]

Not only did reporters continue to blame immigrants for the occasional resurfacing of "voodoo" throughout the late 1920s, but they also claimed that the Cuban government dealt harshly with the accused whenever these cases surfaced. For instance, in April 1927, police arrested several Afro-Cubans who were suspected of trying to abduct a seven-year-old girl and use her in a sacrifice. In this article, and many that would come later, they reported that the police invaded the purported "voodoo doctor's" house and arrested everyone there.[128] The subtitle of the article emphasized that the attempts to kidnap the girl had failed. In 1929, an article about another case circulated in the U.S. media. The author reported that "Cuba has dealt severely with Voodooism, and it is believed its more ghastly forms have been eliminated," and referenced "the persistent efforts of the Cuban police authorities and the severe penalties measured out by the judges."[129] The following year, an additional report indicated that "Voodooism in any form is sternly frowned upon, but occasionally crops up in spite of the vigilance of authorities. Whenever one of the secret meeting places is discovered it is immediately broken up, and the paraphernalia used in their incantations" is destroyed.[130]

Conclusion

One will recall that before the United States began taking an interest in the annexation of Cuba during the second war of independence from Spain, the only known reference to "voodoo" in the U.S. media was an article that compared "nanigos" in Cuba to "voodoo" practices in Haiti. However, during the occupation, this terminology was rarely used. When the U.S. interest in the annexation of Cuba declined, the media returned to using local terminology—that is, "nanigoism," "brujos" ("witches"), and "brujeria" ("witchcraft")—interchangeably with the word "voodoo" to describe acts of purported ritual violence. This use of Spanish phrases makes "voodoo" appear to be more of a translation for a practice that does not exist in English vocabulary than a definition of what was happening in Cuba. They also, as the previous section demonstrated, occasionally employed other terminology, such as "Obeah," "witches," and "witch doctors," to describe what once would have only been glossed as "voodoo" and "voodoo doctors."[131] The use of terminology deployed in Africa and the British Caribbean drew parallels with beliefs and practices common in other parts of the world where the United States did not have and was not attempting to obtain dominion. The clarity of this transition is powerful—when the annexation of Cuba became an unlikely outcome, not only did the U.S. media suggest that the Cuban government had a handle on "voodoo," but they also implied that what was happening there was not so much "voodoo" at all, but some local problem for which there was no English translation and a common vice among Black people throughout the world.

Of course, the end of U.S. imperialism in Cuba did not signify the end of racialized preoccupations about "voodoo" and the rights or liberties of people of African descent. In 1922, the same year that the final U.S. "occupation" of Cuba ended, reports began surfacing of "voodoo"-related "love cults" in the Mid-Atlantic region of the United States. Like the allegations about early twentieth-century Cuba, white people were reportedly the victims of these Black "voodoo" rituals. To understand these cases, the next chapter explores how the United States itself dealt with controversies about race relations (particularly interracial mixing of Black men and white women) and returns to some of the issues raised in this chapter, such as lynching and the race riots of the 1910s and 1920s.

3
Love Cults and "White Slaves" in the 1920s

Chapter 1 explored how the term "voodoo" emerged following the U.S. capture of New Orleans and was used to broadly refer to African American "superstitions," which were supposedly evidence that Black people were unprepared for emancipation or political participation. Chapters 1 and 2 examined how, as the rights of African Americans were slowly eroded in the late nineteenth century, attention turned to Black "voodoo" practices abroad. In particular, in the 1900s and 1910s, "voodoo" became more than just vague "superstitions," as U.S. news articles and English-language travelogues frequently made scandalous claims about cannibalism, human sacrifice, and other brutalities among adherents in Cuba and Haiti. However, once U.S. imperialism in the Caribbean waned, sensational cases about "voodoo" within the United States caught public attention and caused the meaning of the term to evolve once more.

Just as the last U.S. occupation of Cuba was ending, from 1922 to 1929, a series of cases arose in several mid-Atlantic states (Pennsylvania, New Jersey, and West Virginia) and Oklahoma where Black male "voodoo doctors" were accused of kidnapping, enslaving, and murdering women. In most of these cases, the alleged victims were white. In those where the victims were nonwhite, reports connected the "voodoo doctors" back to white patronage—either through an abundance of white clients or from donations/financial backing from white people. Just as depictions of Caribbean "voodoo" reflected U.S. imperial designs on certain nations, domestic claims about "voodoo" revealed twentieth-century anxieties about African Americans and race relations. These cases reflect the complex combination of concerns that arose following African Americans' migrations from the South to the North and the West during World War I (1914 to 1919) and the race conflicts that occurred during the "Red Summer" of 1919 and the early 1920s.

Voodoo. Danielle N. Boaz, Oxford University Press. © Oxford University Press 2023.
DOI: 10.1093/oso/9780197689400.003.0003

White Slavery and "Love Cults" (1913–1922)

In the late nineteenth century, the phrase "white slavery" became a shorthand way in which Europeans referred to trafficking in women and girls, particularly for the purposes of sexual exploitation. This purported problem became a matter of public discourse in or before 1881, when England's House of Lords established a special committee to examine the trafficking of girls in and out of the country. Four years later, in 1885, tens of thousands of people gathered in Hyde Park in London to protest "white slavery" and demand legislation to address the issue.[1] Ultimately, the laws that were passed in England and the international conventions on "White Slave Traffic" that followed would lead to the development of the first widely accepted definitions of human trafficking.[2]

Trafficking in women was referred to as "white slavery" for several reasons. First, although problems about trafficking and forced prostitution were being discussed and investigated in various parts of the world, the stereotypical victims that led to these new public discourses and laws were white women, and the perpetrators were depicted as foreign men.[3] Second, the phrase was meant to invoke comparisons to transatlantic slavery, which was fully abolished in the Americas in the 1880s. Referring to trafficking in women as "white slavery" both established it as a separate problem from Atlantic chattel slavery and brought it under the umbrella of the broader efforts to eradicate slavery around the world.[4]

These discourses represent a shift in views about sex work and promiscuity. In the late nineteenth century, physicians blamed prostitutes for spreading venereal disease and called for public health measures to "protect" middle and upper classes. However, in the early twentieth century, James Morone avers, "Suddenly, the remorseless white slaver stalked onto the scene. Foreign devils snatched innocent daughters off the family farm, dragged them to the dangerous city, and chained them in brothels till they perished."[5] These concerns about white slavery swept through numerous countries for different reasons. In the United States, scholars have attributed it to "rapid urbanization, the rise of women in the workforce, and the changing racial composition of American cities,"[6] as well as industrialization after the Civil War, "complemented by a massive influx of immigrants from southern and eastern Europe after 1880."[7] Although various contemporary police forces and crime reports undermined the notion that white slavery was common,[8] in the first two decades of the twentieth century, dozens of books, pamphlets, plays, movies, and other forms of media featured stories about white slavery and "sexual danger."[9]

During this time, many countries drafted legislation and created infrastructures to address "white slavery." In the United States, in the years leading up to World War I, over 30 cities launched vice investigations, and 44 states passed laws to stop forced prostitution. At the federal level, in 1910, the United States passed a law known as the Mann Act. This legislation prohibited any person from knowingly transporting "any woman or girl" across state lines "for the purpose of prostitution or debauchery, or for any other immoral purpose, or with the intent . . . to induce, entice or compel such a woman or girl to become a prostitute or give herself up to debauchery or engage in any other immoral practice."[10] Although speaking less than 50 years after the end of the Civil War and the enslavement of Black people, in the debates over the Mann Act, Representative Coy of Indiana described white slave trading as "[a] thousand times worse and more degrading in its consequences on humanity than any species of human slavery that ever existed in this country."[11]

In the first eight years after the passage of the Mann Act, law enforcement officers arrested more than 2,000 people for violations of this law.[12] The FBI (then known as the Bureau of Investigation) created a "special commissioner for the Suppression of the White Slave Traffic" and opened offices in major cities.[13] The FBI investigated cases of "immorality," which was often a coded word for sexual relationships that were considered improper at the time.[14] They frequently arrested Black men for having sexual relationships with white women. Perhaps the most significant of these was a Black boxer named Jack Johnson.

On December 26, 1908, Johnson became the first Black fighter to contend for the world heavyweight championship title. His opponent was Canadian champion Tommy Burns. Before this fight, many people believed that Black fighters lacked the courage, intelligence, and stamina to outperform white boxers.[15] After fourteen rounds, Johnson defeated Burns, beating him so badly that the police had to intervene.[16]

After Johnson's victory, white boxers and their fans throughout the world argued that Johnson had not officially won the heavyweight title. Burns had not defeated former heavyweight title holder James Jeffries to become the heavyweight champion; instead, when Jeffries retired, the title had passed to Burns.[17] Therefore, Jeffries was coaxed out of retirement to challenge Johnson. Supporters referred to Jeffries as "the Great White Hope."

On July 4, 1910, Johnson fought Jeffries in Reno, Nevada. Despite significant hype about Jeffries's return to the ring, Johnson defeated him in round fifteen and became the undisputed heavyweight champion. Starting the evening of the fight and continuing for several weeks, white Americans carried out extreme violence against Black Americans as an act of "collective grief."[18] White mobs murdered Black people in Arkansas, Virginia, Louisiana, and New York.[19] Phillip Hutchison argues "Jeffries's resounding defeat threw white America into a Johnson-related funk that lasted nearly five years."[20]

Shortly thereafter, Johnson aggravated these negative public perceptions by marrying a white woman named Etta Duryea. Not long into their union, in September 1912, Duryea shot and killed herself. Some reporters blamed Johnson, claiming that his alleged physical abuse and infidelity drove Duryea to commit suicide.[21] Criticism against Johnson increased when merely two weeks "after the coroner official ruled Duryea's death a suicide, the champion appeared in public with Lucille Cameron, a fawning nineteen-year-old blonde, on his arm."[22] Cameron's mother hired an attorney and told the media that Johnson had kidnapped Cameron.[23] Johnson denied these allegations, telling reporters that Cameron was "crazy about" him and that "he could 'get any white woman he wanted.' "[24]

Despite his public assertions about Cameron's willing participation in their tryst, authorities arrested Johnson for violating the Mann Act. Some people in Chicago (where Johnson was arrested) called for Johnson to be lynched; however, the district attorney asked them to let the legal process play out, while averring that the sentence should "set an example to Johnson's race."[25] Unfortunately for the prosecution, Cameron testified before the grand jury that she had been living in Chicago for months prior to her first encounter with Johnson.[26] This destroyed the prosecution's case against Johnson because he did not transport her across state lines—a requirement of this federal anti-trafficking law. Cameron further undermined the case when she married Johnson in early December 1912.

The media drew links, both direct and indirect, between this scandalous case and "voodoo" in Black communities. Less than two months after Cameron and Johnson married, on January 27, 1913, police in Evansville, Indiana, raided the "temple" owned by William Johnson with orders to arrest everyone inside.[27] Reporters described Johnson as a "Reverend" and a "voodoo" man. They alleged that "a young girl lay for three days in a hypnotic trance in the 'temple' " during the week prior to the raid, and the police arrived to enforce "orders for the negro to leave town and the band to disperse."[28]

When the raid began, 10 white women allegedly rushed out of the temple and jumped the fence around the property to evade the authorities.[29] At least two white women remained inside as the police searched the premises. Police sergeant William Fuches encountered one of them when he entered an area that reporters described as the "throne room." Fuches claimed that he saw Johnson instructing the young white woman to take off her corset and "anointing" her with olive oil on the face and shoulders.[30] However, when she noticed Fuches, the woman "hastily grabbed up the wearing apparel she had discarded and jumped through a window."[31] Authorities were unable to identify or locate this woman after she fled.[32]

Another white woman named "Sister" Jackson was found in the home during the raid. Reporters described her as Johnson's "accomplice," although it was unclear how or in what acts she aided him. Jackson was a 29-year-old married woman; journalists asserted that her "husband had gone insane over her connection with the negro doctor."[33] In fact, reporters averred that the majority of the white "saints" who frequented Johnson's temple were "young married women who have left their homes and husbands."[34] This allegation would become a theme during the next 10–15 years; authorities and journalists often stressed that it was young *married* white women who were kidnapped, abused, or duped by Black "voodoo doctors."

Reports of the breakup of this meeting were laden with descriptions of behavior so irrational and bizarre that one would assume that Johnson was running a cult. For instance, on the day of the raid, reporters claimed "the feeling tonight in the neighborhood of the 'temple' is so intense that the police are guarding it for fear of arson or dynamite."[35] It is unclear whether they feared that the devotees would attack the site out of anger over the raid or if concerned neighbors would engage in vigilante violence against a place where they believed their wives and daughters had been held. Reports also stressed the overwhelming support of Johnson's white "saints," claiming that forty of these women testified for the "negro voodoo doctor."[36] Despite this robust defense, the judge sentenced Johnson to sixty days imprisonment "for maintaining a disorderly house."[37] When they heard the verdict, the white women allegedly shouted at the judge, "the Lord will strike you dead!"[38]

Interestingly, although the predominant theme of "white slave trafficking" was forced prostitution, reports of William Johnson's temple contain no overt statements about sexual abuse or prostitution. However, several aspects of this case may have sent subtle clues to readers at the time that this "voodoo doctor" was holding these women in sexual bondage. First, the allusions to white women's purported involvement in "voodoo" has always had some form of sexual undertones. One will recall that the earliest references to "voodoo" in New Orleans were reports of white women engaging in naked orgies with women of color (Chapter 1). Second, repeated references to nudity and "anointing" the bodies of the white "priestesses" or "saints" certainly indicated that acts that would have been regarded as lewd were taking place in the "temple." Reporters' descriptions of the women's fervent defense of the "voodoo doctor" would have implied that their support was the result of psychological abuse.

The public would have seen numerous parallels between the arrests of William Johnson and Jack Johnson, which occurred in neighboring states and just a few months apart. The most obvious is the report that Black men were engaged in "lewd" behavior with white women; this is something which Jack proudly admitted, and which was implied by reports that a young white woman was removing her corset in William's presence when the police entered. Moreover, the white "saints" who defended William likely resurrected bitterness over Lucille Cameron's defense of Jack in her testimony and subsequent marriage. One does not have to guess whether journalists and their readers understood this case in the context of Jack Johnson's recent arrest and failed prosecution. At least one of the articles written about the Evansville incident was titled "William Johnson Disciple of Jack."[39]

Pittsburgh, PA (1922)

Around 10 years later, another case emerged that was centered on a Black man using "voodoo" to subjugate a white woman. In late March 1922, police entered the home of an African American man named Henry Washington in Pittsburgh, Pennsylvania, and allegedly found an emaciated and filthy 45-year-old white woman named Charlotte Wyles laying on top of a mass of rags in the attic.[40] Wyles had been missing for several years (reports varied between 7 and 11 years). She vanished a short time after her husband had disappeared and left her alone with their two children.[41] Police located Wyles based on a mysterious tip provided by her sister-in-law, Margaret Serberline, who never disclosed the source of her information.[42]

Authorities arrested Washington and charged him with "immorality, cruelty and neglect."[43] He appeared in morals court before Magistrate Tensard DeWolfe. Unfortunately, reporters do not appear to have followed his case after the initial arrest and it is unclear what ultimately happened in this prosecution. However, news reports from the first few days after Washington's arrest suggest that perceptions of domestic "voodoo" during the 1920s remained rooted in concerns about "white slavery."

Similar to the raid on William Johnson's "temple," reports about Wyles's "rescue" and Washington's arrest contain no explicit language about the sexual nature of Wyles's purported bondage. However, Washington was charged with "immorality" and appeared in "morals court." Discussions about "immorality" were often coded ways of referring to supposed sexual misconduct such as extramarital, interracial, or homosexual intercourse, as well as prostitution. Furthermore, with or without the overt sexual component, the case of Henry Washington's alleged abuse of Charlotte Wyles embodies many of the white slavery tropes from the 1910s.

First, at the height of the "white slave trafficking" scare, slavery tropes were about "villainous rogues and hapless maidens."[44] In the case of Charlotte Wyles, reporters implied that Washington had dominated Wyles through physical and mental abuse. They stressed the filthy conditions of the home and claimed that Wyles was emaciated when taken into custody. They described Washington as a "negro exponent of Voodooism"[45] who had used his "alleged control over 'evil spirits'" to bring "Wyles into subjection."[46] Several articles emphasized, "The police surgeon has doubts whether Mrs. Wyles will ever recover her sanity."[47] Yet, while suggesting the need for state intervention to protect Wyles (a vulnerable white woman), reporters stressed Washington's alleged powers "held no terror" for the magistrate who heard his case.

Like the Johnson case in 1913, descriptions of Wyles's response to being "rescued" also reflected the paradoxes of white "slaves" refusing to be freed from "captivity." Some reports indicated that Wyles had fought tirelessly for her freedom, but her efforts had been in vain. These journalists claimed that Wyles had attempted escape multiple times, but Washington and his wife had locked her inside the upper level of the home and closely guarded Wyles whenever she was permitted to leave.[48]

Other news articles described how Wyles "fought police and she had to be carried into an ambulance" when they found her.[49] Most of the reporters who referenced Wyles's hesitance to leave Washington suggested that she had been driven into submission over years of captivity. They explained that Wyles had initially wanted her freedom but had eventually "resigned herself to her fate and the doctrine of Voodooism had taken root. She did not want to leave."[50] Most stressed that Wyles's response was connected to "cult" indoctrination, indicating that Washington "made her believe she would be seized by his voodoo witches if she escaped."[51] Even after her "rescue," it appears that Wyles never explained her own circumstances; she refused to talk during Washington's trial.[52]

Through this language of "voodooism," journalists and authorities were able suggest that Wyles, a "white slave," had been so horribly abused and indoctrinated that she did not desire her own freedom. Similarly, as the FBI began investigating other cases of purported white slavery in the United States, they discovered that some of the women were willingly involved in prostitution and were not "victims." Moreover, the women were not stolen from their families; they were running away from them.[53]

Reports of Wyles's condition also reinforced common narratives about "white slavery" in other ways. Descriptions of Wyles's "rescue" emphasized that the house was dirty and that chickens, cats, and more than a dozen dogs were permitted to freely roam the premises.[54] By contrast, reports indicate that Washington was well-dressed, appearing before the court with "spurious diamonds dangling from his ears."[55] Several articles described Washington as dressed in a "white vest and swallow-tailed coat" which he "neatly folded under his bunk" in jail.[56] Other depictions of purported traffickers of "white slaves" frequently stressed their public displays of wealth and contrasted this against the poor conditions in which the "enslaved" women were held.

Nevertheless, the Washington/Wyles case was an interesting paradox in the narratives of "slavery" and prostitution. Scholars argue that the "white slavery" panic ended by 1917 and was replaced by policies that no longer treated sex workers as hapless victims, but rather regarded them as threats to public morality and a potential downfall of the white race. Instead of "rescuing" sex workers from their foreign/racially other "captors," new task forces and laws focused on policing, incarcerating, and even sterilizing these women. However, amidst this shift, reporters still depicted Wyles as a victim and deployed the previous decade's tropes about the use of coercion and force.

Legal Lynching and the Protection of White Women (1922–1924)

In Chapter 2, I discussed how accounts of "voodoo" in Cuba incorporated discussions about lynching in the second half of 1919. Journalists reported that mobs attacked persons who were accused of committing murder and lynched them. This was framed as a way to ensure that the Cuban people could get justice for alleged "voodoo" atrocities that supposedly would not otherwise be prosecuted. As briefly mentioned in that chapter, this was connected to events going on within the United States.

The introduction of a federal anti-lynching bill in 1918 and a surge in race riots in 1919 brought claims about Black men physically attacking white women to the forefront of national conversations in the late 1910s and early 1920s. In addition to shaping narratives about "voodoo" in Cuba, these events seem to have shifted the focus of the dangers of "voodoo" in the United States. Instead of anxieties about "white slaves" captured by "voodoo cults," allegations about Black "voodoo doctors" murdering white girls and women became part of nationwide debates about lynching, interracial violence, and the protection of white women.

It is well established that vigilante violence known as "lynching" became an immense problem in the South following the U.S. Civil War and the period known as Reconstruction (1865–1877). Scholars estimate that between 1882 and 1930, at least 2,462 African Americans were lynched by Southern mobs.[57] Lynching was described as a punishment and a preventive measure against the assault of white women. However, lynchings were often carried out for other perceived slights against white people and were rarely connected to real incidents of Black men sexually assaulting white women.[58]

In 1918, activists made significant strides in calling national attention to the problem of lynching and introducing measures to combat it. The National Association for the Advancement of Colored People (NAACP) organized a major conference on lynching, during which eleven state governors and other influential people signed a declaration calling for a federal investigation of lynching.[59] Both President Woodrow Wilson and the American Bar Association openly denounced lynching.[60] Perhaps most significantly, the Dyer Anti-Lynching Bill was introduced to Congress. It sought to make lynching a federal offense and to make those who participated in lynch mobs subject to murder charges.[61] Members of law enforcement who negligently allowed a lynching to occur could themselves be imprisoned for up to five years and fined up to $5,000. Counties where a lynching occurred could also be sued for up to $10,000.[62] The bill passed the house in January 1922 but "under the threat of a Southern filibuster, was buried in the Senate."[63]

Shortly after the Anti-lynching Bill passed the House, media reports across the nation suggested that a series of Black "voodoo" doctors were attacking and murdering white women and girls in Pennsylvania and West Virginia. One of these alleged cases took place in Martinsburg, West Virginia. On March 14, 1922, a Black man named Monroe S. Peyton was convicted of "criminally attacking" a 10-year-old white girl named Hazel Johnson. No other information was provided about his purported crime. Instead, reporters focused on the proceedings themselves, proudly announcing that the jury deliberated less than fifteen minutes before returning a guilty verdict and that the judge sentenced him to death by hanging.[64] Media reports claimed that Peyton was the first person in the county to ever be sentenced to death.[65]

Peyton was held in jail for over a month following his brief trial while he awaited execution. Approximately one week before he was to be hanged, Peyton escaped. However, the authorities discovered him in the home of another Black person a few days later.[66] Shortly thereafter, days before the sentence was carried out, unknown persons sent a request to the state pardon attorney, seeking to get Peyton's sentence reduced to life imprisonment.[67] However, reporters explained, "The sheriff immediately sent a transcript of the evidence of the case to the state's chief executive."[68] His execution was carried out on May 4, 1922. Peyton maintained his innocence until the day of his death.[69]

A second, more notorious case took place the following year involving Elsie Barthel, a white nurse, and Lorenzo Savage, a Black butler, who were both working in the home of a white medical doctor in Pittsburgh, Pennsylvania.[70] In the fall of 1923, authorities discovered Barthel's body at an abandoned mansion. Someone had murdered the 28-year-old by smashing her head with a heavy object. Several playing cards were found in an envelope near Barthel's body.[71]

Police initially suspected that a taxicab driver named Walter Hauley (also spelled Haule or Hanley), Barthel's alleged "sweetheart," had murdered her.[72] Barthel was killed on a Sunday morning; by that evening, the police had brought Hauley in for questioning.[73] The police found two of Barthel's handkerchiefs in Hauley's possession[74] and Hauley told the police "several conflicting stories about his movements" that night, including that he had picked up Savage from the abandoned mansion where Barthel was killed.[75] Captain Louis Leff expressed that "he was not satisfied with the stories Hauley told."[76]

However, the police began to turn their suspicions toward Lorenzo Savage after Barthel's mother reported that Barthel had made an appointment to have Savage tell her fortune.[77] Detectives went to Savage's home, searched it, and found that playing cards were missing from his deck.[78] The police questioned Savage at home and then brought him to the police station for further interrogation.[79] In the middle of the night, Captain Leff took Savage to the abandoned mansion where Barthel killed.[80] It was there, "after hours of grilling," that Savage allegedly "made a startling confession."[81]

According to police, Savage reported that Barthel had asked him to make her a charm because she was unmarried and had become pregnant by Hauley.[82] Savage had given her several playing cards, which he told her had been imbued with a spell to help her with this problem.[83] On the night of the Barthel's death, she was supposed to meet Savage at the abandoned mansion to return the cards and pay Savage $395 for the ritual.[84] Barthel brought the money but refused to pay him. Savage purportedly confessed that he had become angry and hit Barthel in the head with a brick, then dropped a large stone (weighing at least 50 pounds) on Barthel's head.[85] Savage allegedly took the money from Barthel's body but accidentally dropped the playing cards.[86] Following this purported confession, Savage was convicted of first-degree murder.[87] On March 31, 1924, he was electrocuted, and his body was buried in the prison cemetery.[88]

Read together, Peyton's and Savage's cases illustrate some common trends in reports of "voodoo" during this time that would have undermined efforts to oppose lynching and reinforced stereotypes about Black male violence against white women and girls. First, they emphasized the innocence and vulnerability of the alleged victims of "voodoo doctors." For instance, in the case of Monroe Peyton, every report stressed that Hazel Johnson, the child who he purportedly assaulted, was merely 10 years old. Several also emphasized that she was white.[89] Although the details of Peyton's purported attack on Johnson were not described, one must recall that this case occurred amid widespread reports of "voodoo" practitioners in Cuba killing white children and sacrificing them to their gods. The use of the language of "voodoo" to describe Peyton's attack likely encouraged the public to make certain assumptions about the motive.

The case of Savage received much more attention, as did the tales of Barthel's purportedly unique virtues. Like Hazel Johnson, reports noted that Barthel was young. Nearly every article about her murder described Barthel as a nurse. This, perhaps, would have been a stark juxtaposition to descriptions of Savage as a "voodoo doctor," engaged in what many would have seen as quack "medicine." In addition to emphasizing that she was a nurse, most reporters also described Barthel as "pretty."[90] Furthermore, reporters depicted Barthel as an innocent client, rather than part of Savage's "dark arts." Several journalists claimed that Barthel's parents and employer had come forward "to defend her character against suggestions that she was involved in a voodoo cult of any sort."[91]

Reporters also generally hid elements of the case that would have questioned Barthel's virtue. The *Baltimore Afro-American*, a Black newspaper, appears to have been one of the only newspapers to report a scandalous aspect of Savage's purported confession— that Barthel was unwed and pregnant, and that she was consulting Savage to abort the child. Instead, most journalists simply averred that Barthel was buying a "love charm,"[92] or vaguely reported that she had "approached him [Savage] when she had difficulties with her sweetheart"[93] or paid him for "curing her love ills."[94] One particularly sympathetic reporter described Savage's alleged victim as "pretty Elsie Barthel, a white trained nurse, who sacrificed her life in quest of a mystic love charm."[95]

In this way, the Savage-Barthel case is reminiscent of many of the trials of Black men for assaulting white women in the early to mid-twentieth century. In particular, cases of sexual assault were sometimes the women's attempts to hide their own promiscuity. One of the best examples is the famous trial of the Scottsboro boys that would take place less than 10 years later in 1931. In that case, nine African American teenagers, aged 13 to 19, were accused of raping two white women on a train. After a first trial (in which all nine defendants were convicted despite overwhelming evidence of their innocence), one of the alleged victims admitted that they had fabricated the entire case to prevent being arrested for prostitution. Reports of Savage's trial likewise hid Barthel's acts that would have transgressed the boundaries of what society permitted at the time—sex outside the confines of marriage—and portrayed her as Savage's victim.

Unlike the case of the Scottsboro boys, an actual crime took place in the case of Barthel. The manner in which she died—being crushed by a heavy stone—makes it clear that Barthel did not take her own life. However, was Savage merely another example of a Black scapegoat or "bogeyman" who was often blamed for crimes against white women? Police initially suspected Barthel's lover, who admitted to being at the scene of the crime and who had reason to quarrel with Barthel over the scandalous pregnancy. Did Hauley cover up his crimes by blaming the Black man who offered to help Barthel abort his child?

Indeed, both Peyton's and Savage's trials appear to have been rife with inconsistencies or opportunities for misconduct. For instance, Peyton's case was reportedly the first death penalty case in the history of the county. However, the jury deliberated for a mere fifteen minutes before convicting him, and the judge immediately sentenced him to death.[96] The early twentieth century is full of similar cases where juries deliberated for only seconds or minutes before issuing a death sentence to a Black defendant who was accused of harming a white woman.

In Savage's case, the authorities simply dismissed their prime suspect and zeroed in on Savage, then obtained his confession in a very suspicious manner. One will recall that police questioned Savage for hours at his home and then at the police station. However, it was only after they took Savage out to an abandoned mansion in the middle of the night that he finally supposedly admitted to this crime. It is impossible to know what was said or done to Savage during that interrogation. Did the officers beat him? Did they threaten him with stories of brutal lynchings of Black men in other parts of the country who had been accused of crimes against white women? Was Savage compelled to confess and face a swift execution instead of future torture at the hands of the police or a mob?

Multiple sources report that both men professed their innocence until the end of their lives.[97] However, these same reports often depicted the men as callous and unfeeling. Reporters averred that the "voodoo doctors" showed no remorse during the proceedings. They claimed that Payton "received the sentence unemotionally."[98] One article about his execution was titled "Went to Death Calmly."[99] Another noted that although he had previously claimed his innocence, Peyton "was mute on the gallows" and refused the opportunity to make a final statement.[100] In contradiction of his claims of innocence, one reporter claimed that when Savage was executed, he "declared that he will never be punished and that the dread Voodoo will devastate all who seek to enforce the law against him."[101] He allegedly told the arresting officers that they couldn't harm him and threatened to "blast" them with his "power," cause their children to die, their houses to fall down and their "souls [to] shrivel up."[102]

These cases demonstrate a pattern among Northern states at the time. Similar to the accused ritual murderers in Cuba in 1919, in the U.S. South, Black men who were accused of harming white women were typically lynched, including many being ripped from their jail cells by white mobs as they were awaiting trial. These lynchings took place regardless of the evidence of the accused's innocence, including in scenarios where it would have been virtually impossible for the accused to have committed the crime. Research has shown that guilt was irrelevant; the accused's real "crime" was frequently something uncharged, such as insulting a white person or refusing to work on a plantation. Scholars have argued that in the Northern states, the death penalty took the place of extralegal violence, essentially serving as a lawful form of lynching. These criminal proceedings against men like Savage and Peyton could have served as an overtly legal method of killing these two men, whose true "crimes," if they committed any, might never be known.

Another curious aspect of Savage's case is journalists' constant reflections on the broader implications of the crime, in the industrial city of Pittsburgh. Like other Northern cities, Pittsburgh was deeply impacted by the Great Migration. The Black population of the city increased more than 200% between 1900 and 1940, dwarfing the 42% increase in the non-Black residents.[103] Narratives of "voodoo" among the Black community served as a way of discrediting this growing population. For instance, reporters claimed that the investigation revealed "an astoundingly widespread following of the Voodoo doctor."[104] Another claimed that Savage had "for a long time terrorized a large part of Pittsburgh's colored population. Posing as 'high priest' of Voodoo he has performed feats which amazed and awed the colored folk to such an extent that thousands firmly believe his claims to supernatural power."[105] They asserted that Savage's "former subjects are rejoicing over the lifting of the yoke."[106] Less than 10 years later, Detroit—another major city rapidly changed by migration in the 1910s and suffering from racial conflict in the interwar period—would see similar claims of widespread belief in "voodoo" and "superstition" following an alleged act of human sacrifice among Black Muslims (Chapter 4).

Several reports also emphasized Savage's Caribbean heritage as the root of his purported depravity. For instance, one reporter wrote that Savage allegedly came from Jamaica, "where Voodooism flourishes among the superstitious natives."[107] They claimed that Savage was "beating on his steel bars a fantastic rhythm, reminiscent of the booming 'drum talk' of the cane brakes of Jamaica."[108] Even African American newspapers embraced this widely held stereotype about a wild Caribbean, overrun by voodoo-practicing barbarians. The *Baltimore Afro-American*, perhaps trying to distance Savage's alleged crimes from the U.S.-based Black residents of Pittsburgh, appears to have been the only newspaper to report the following:

One room of his establishment had been fitted up to resemble a Voodoo temple in the jungle. Tropical plants and grasses, several stuffed snakes and one live snake as well as human skulls and other bones were part of the properties of this occult workshop. A huge West Indian drum the tympan of which he claimed was made from human skin, hung over the altar of rough stones, which occupied one end of the room, screened by imitation vines. Just what rites were performed in this temple those who participated in them are loath to say. It is known that small animals were sacrificed on the altar, however, and there are unconfirmed rumors whispered that at least one human sacrifice was made there.[109]

All-Black Towns and "Voodoo" Predators (1925–1929)

A third trend in media reports about "voodoo" in the United States in the 1920s is the denunciation of all-Black towns and districts as hotbeds of "superstitious" practices that threatened neighboring white communities. In the late nineteenth and early twentieth centuries, Black Americans built hundreds of self-governing districts and towns throughout the United States.[110] These areas, which were settled primarily or exclusively by African Americans, represented opportunities for Black people to own property and businesses, and to escape everyday racial violence. The early 1920s saw the violent destruction of several of these areas, most notably the Greenwood district in Tulsa, Oklahoma, in 1921 and the town of Rosewood, Florida, in 1923.

In the late 1890s and 1900s, several Black entrepreneurs began buying land in Tulsa, Oklahoma, with the intention of building up a Black-owned community near the segregated white town. By the 1910s, this area, the Greenwood district, had become a thriving community of almost ten thousand people with a wealthy business district that many would describe as the Black Wall Street. White residents of Tulsa resented Greenwood's prosperity and felt threatened by its wealth and growth. Researchers have emphasized that this resentment became the foundation for the incredibly violent response to an accusation that a Black man, Dick Rowland, had attempted to sexually assault a white woman during an elevator ride in the Drexel Building on May 30, 1921.

Authorities took Rowland to the jail above the Tulsa County Courthouse. As news of the alleged crime spread, white Tulsans gathered around the building, demanding that Rowland be turned over to them so that he could be lynched. Armed Black men from Greenwood went to the courthouse steps to help defend Rowland and the jail from the white mob. A white man approached one of the Black men, questioned the man's right to have a weapon, and tried to take it away from him. During the confrontation, the Black man's gun went off. Both sides opened fire and the greatly outnumbered African Americans retreated to the Greenwood district.[111] White Tulsans attacked the entire Greenwood district, burning houses and businesses, and shooting at residents as they fled. Before the massacre ended, Greenwood was irrevocably damaged. Between 100 and 300 people were dead, 1,256 homes were destroyed, and most businesses and places of worship had been demolished.[112]

In the days following the riot, the Tulsa City Commission imposed a new fire code to attempt to prevent businesses from rebuilding in the Greenwood district. According to the Oklahoma Commission to Study the Tulsa Race Riot of 1921, "Despite the Herculean efforts of the American Red Cross, thousands of black Tulsans were forced to spend the winter of 1921–22 living in tents. Others simply left."[113]

The town of Rosewood, Florida, met a similar demise two years later. Rosewood had been settled by both Black and white people in the nineteenth century. However, by the early twentieth century, due to segregation laws, the area had developed into two small towns of a few hundred people—Black Rosewood and white Sumner. In 1923, a Black man was accused of sexually assaulting a white woman in Sumner. After a standoff at the home of Sarah Carrier, who worked as a laundress for the woman who had allegedly been assaulted, a white mob descended on Rosewood, murdering several residents, and burning the entire town.

While revenge for the sexual assault of white women was the overt justification for white mobs to destroy Black towns, many researchers argue that (as in the case of lynching) these claims were a pretext to act on other concerns. These Black towns, particularly in the case of Greenwood, fueled white anxieties of Black self-governance and resentments of Black profitability away from white rule. One can easily see the parallels between the desires to destroy independent Black towns and those to destroy the independent Black nation of Haiti, which was being occupied by U.S. forces during this time (1915–1934).

The following cases from two all-Black towns—Lawnside, New Jersey, and Greenwood district, Oklahoma—illustrate yet another juncture of these communities and the nation of Haiti. Residents of several Black towns were accused of participating in heinous practices associated with "voodoo" in the mid- to late 1920s. Accusations about sexual assault and innuendos about murder were woven together with reports of the financial success of Black "voodoo doctors." Following just two to five years after the destruction of Rosewood and four to seven years after the destruction of Greenwood, these cases must be seen as a reflection on "voodoo," sexual assault, and Black self-governance.

Lawnside, New Jersey (1925–1929)

Lawnside, New Jersey, is a town of great significance in African American history. In the eighteenth century, formerly enslaved persons began settling in Camden County, New Jersey, near Quaker abolitionists. They believed that residing together and close to the Quakers would protect them from kidnapping and re-enslavement.[114] Over time, this area became a stop on the Underground Railroad.

Historically, Lawnside was merely one part of an area known as Center Township. However, in response to a growing independence movement, the governor dissolved the township and created the Borough of Lawnside.[115] The following month, local residents voted to establish their own government in a special election, and became the "first independent self-governing African-American community north of the Mason-Dixon Line."[116] From 1925 to 1929, Lawnside and a neighboring area of Camden would become the site of three highly publicized cases about "voodoo doctors" who were allegedly using white people's money to finance their "heinous" practices and were tricking white women into taking part in scandalous rituals.

The first of these cases began in 1925, when 71-year-old Ebbinger H. H. Hyghcock was arrested in Lawnside for practicing medicine without a license and obtaining money under false pretenses.[117] A Black woman named Lottie Ingram complained to police that she had paid Hyghcock $25 to help her with a problem with her heart. However, he had taken her to the passages underneath his house and her condition had worsened after her "experiences" there.[118]

Authorities were preparing to release Hyghcock when his seven-year-old daughter told someone that her father had shot a "light colored" woman and put her body in a cemetery.[119] Hyghcock dismissed the story as his daughter's imagination; however, police decided to search the property. They found a series of tunnels or passages under the house containing chicken carcasses, dried meat, painted dolls, and other things.[120] They also found a list of names of people "to go" and others "to be ruined."[121] One of the passageways held the bodies of two infants.[122] For reasons that were never stated in news reports, authorities assumed that the infants were African American. Hyghcock averred that they were medical specimens that he had received from local physicians as a gift.[123]

After they did not find the body of an adult woman, the police questioned Hyghcock's daughter again. She reported that she saw someone remove the body from the house one night but could not recall when.[124] Although it appears that no adult bodies were ever recovered and police do not seem to have suspected that the infants were murdered, dozens of newspapers throughout the country printed the story under titles that suggested that Hyghcock had committed homicide.[125] A few days later, around April 13, police and firemen went to Hyghcock's home with axes and shovels to destroy the tunnels and chambers.[126]

At the time, little seems to have been published about this case after the first five days following the seven-year-old's murder claims. However, over subsequent years, a few reporters blamed the local white community for Hyghcock's affluence. In one story from 1929, the author described Hyghcock as "a prosperous citizen of the town" and explained that although he "was colored, very many of his clients were white. They paid handsomely to have spells cast on their enemies."[127] The author asserted that five hundred letters from prospective clients had been found on the property, "many of them from white people." One of them was from "[a] white woman who had applied to the doctor for a spell to put on another woman who had stolen her husband's love." This woman "described her experiences when she ventured into the dark underground labyrinth where he performed his alleged miracles."

The year following Hyghcock's arrest, in August 1926, authorities claimed to have broken up a "love cult" in Lawnside.[128] They reported that Abby Yancy, supposed high priestess of a "voodoo cult," held African American girls captive in her home, chained to the floor and tortured, and threatened them with a razor if they cried during their beatings. When the girls turned 14 years old, they were sent to Elder Robinson, who would sexually assault the girls, promising them that they would ascend to heaven if they obeyed him and bore him children.

While Yancy, Robinson, and the girls whom they allegedly enslaved were all African American, one reporter, Jane Grey, once again connected "voodoo" in Lawnside to white patrons. Grey averred that "white folks' money financed the vicious scheme" at the Lawnside home. Grey also reported that some of the children in Robinson's "cult" had been sent to white neighborhoods begging for alms, claiming to be from an orphanage for Black children. They earned the most money in Jewish neighborhoods, Grey claimed, because they pretended to be Black Jews and even spoke a little "Jewish language."

A couple of months later, in October 1926, the arrest of "Rev." George Gaines closed out this spree of voodoo-related arrests in and near Lawnside. Gaines had a shop with a sign in front advertising himself as a "Spiritualist Healer."[129] Reports do not specify whether this shop was located in Lawnside or the neighboring white area of Camden. One day, a 22-year-old white woman from Camden, Carmella di Francisco, wandered into Gaines's shop. After Di Francisco entered, Gaines said prayers in the four corners of the room and then told Di Francisco that she had been cursed by her mother-in-law. He prescribed "anointment" as treatment and informed her that it would cost $200. He instructed Di Francisco to strip naked to the waist and rubbed a salve into her skin. Initially impressed by Gaines, Di Francisco encouraged her sister-in-law to see Gaines. Her sister-in-law was also cursed, Gaines averred. He charged her $100 for a similar anointment.

The two women later decided that they had been duped. They tricked Gaines into coming to Di Francisco's home, where he was arrested for obtaining money under false pretenses, defamation of character, and practicing medicine without a license. When they arrested him, police found lists of Gaines's "patients." Reporters claimed that many of these clients were "beautiful, rich, and socially distinguished women."[130] The discovery of this list led to what one reporter described as "a smashing expose"—that "white people's money" had "financed many of the voodoo ventures in New Jersey."[131] Because of this case, the journalist claimed, "the authorities delved deeper into the epidemic of 'black magic' and the capitalization of voodoo practices at the expense of superstitious and gullible persons."[132] The author cited both the Gaines case as well as that of Elder Robinson, which had "links in a chain of Caucasian cash-backing."[133]

Greenwood, Oklahoma (1928)

Around the same time that George Gaines was arrested for allegedly "terrorizing" white women in New Jersey, a similar case arose in Tulsa, Oklahoma. Lillian Walker, a 25-year-old violinist, went to the home of 55-year-old Dr. William Woods, a Black chiropractor[134] who was also a renowned crystal gazer. Walker reportedly ventured to Greenwood, the "heart of the negro section" of town,[135] for a séance or to have her fortune told.[136] After her session with Woods, Walker went to the hospital for treatment of "cuts and wounds."[137] She initially told authorities that Woods had tried to rob her. She later claimed that Woods held her captive and that she had bruised her head and knee when she jumped out a window to avoid his "advances."[138] Reporters explained the discrepancy by declaring that Walker was "hysterical when first asked to relate her story."[139]

Initial reports did not indicate that any criminal charges were brought against Woods; rather, he was held in jail "for investigation."[140] However, some weeks later, the *Miami News Record* reported that a charge of attempted assault had been brought against Walker for his purported advances against the "pretty professional violinist."[141] I have found no record of the outcome of the trial, but an African American man named S. L. Harris testified in Walker's case, claiming to having been there at the time of the alleged assault. Harris testified that Woods had offered to pay him and his wife $2,500 and give them a car if they would fraudulently testify that Walker was drunk when they arrived and was demonstrating a dance for Woods.[142]

After Woods's arrest, reporters averred that local police had "turned their attention to determining the scope of voodooism in the city."[143] They described Woods as the "Lord High Seer" of a "voodoo ring" that was patronized by wealthy, white customers.[144] Woods allegedly held "nightly seances" at his home on North Greenwood avenue, "in the heart of the negro district."[145] Journalists claimed that Woods had confessed to "making a small fortune out of his voodooism."[146]

While authorities were purportedly exploring the extent of "voodoo" practices in Greenwood, Walker pursued a civil case against Woods. She sued him for $102,500 in damages for "injuries" that she suffered when Woods supposedly held her captive. Around four months later, the jury reached a verdict. After deliberating for three hours, they decided to award her $750—a tiny fraction of the amount that Walker sought, but a hefty fine for the time.[147]

One must wonder about the public perceptions of this case in 1927–1928, just a few years after the race riot that had demolished most of the Greenwood district in 1921. While studies have documented a profound official and media silence on the matter in the decades following the massacre, the traumatic events of 1921 would not have faded from the memories of the Greenwood residents who stayed in the area. It seems certain that allegations that a Black man had tried to sexually assault a white woman would have generated much concern about another wave of attacks on Greenwood district. Repeated references to Woods's wealth and the prosperity of "voodoo" practitioners may have also caused both white and Black Tulsans to reflect on the Black community's ability (or lack thereof) to rebuild their once thriving economy. For these reasons, this case would have hit several nerves in this fragile community.

Conclusion

In many ways, these cases show the evolution of public understandings of "voodoo" in the early twentieth century. One will recall that when the term became widely used following the U.S. Civil War, it described the "superstitions" that Black Americans would "revert" to once freed from slavery and which purportedly prevented them from having the capacity to vote or hold public office. The cases in this chapter further demonstrate the complex relationship between public interpretations of "voodoo" and the institution of slavery. By the early twentieth century, "voodoo" was not only a "barbaric" practice that would flourish in the absence of the strong white governance of Black people, it also was a religion that supposedly incorporated the very institution of slavery—holding believers captive through mental and spiritual torment. In Chapter 6, I will discuss how these connections continue until the present day in cases about human trafficking.

These cases also illustrate the deep connections between reports of "voodoo," lynching, and the death penalty. In Chapter 2, I discussed how the use of "voodoo" to support U.S. interventions in Cuba declined as reports emerged that white Cubans were lynching Black "voodoo doctors." I argued that when Cubans used this form of vigilante violence, it appears to have resonated with white Americans and demonstrated that Cubans were willing to take seriously their "obligations" to maintain Western standards of "civilization" in their country. The cases in this chapter represent the other side of this equation—the use of state-sanctioned lynching (the death penalty) to terrorize Black communities in the United States as they migrated north during and following World War I.

Furthermore, as Chapters 1 and 2 discussed, the reports of "voodoo" in Haiti and Cuba during the late nineteenth and early twentieth centuries described practices that were violent and, in the case of the latter, targeted white victims. The cases in this chapter suggest that public understandings of voodoo in the United States took on some of the characteristics of reports in these other countries. The preoccupation with "voodoo" in all-Black towns in the United States parallels concerns about independent all-Black or predominantly nonwhite nations like Cuba and Haiti. The media referred to these cases of "voodoo" as evidence of the kinds of "barbarism" that Blacks would "revert" to if not carefully governed by white people and the threat that the degradation of Black communities could pose to neighboring white ones. The next chapter will elaborate further on this issue, discussing allegations that Black people in Detroit, like those in the Caribbean, had engaged in human sacrifices.

4

Human Sacrifice and African American Muslims in the 1930s

In 1932, in Detroit, Michigan, an African American Muslim named Robert Harris killed his tenant on an altar in his home, as a purported human sacrifice to Allah. In the weeks that followed, as Harris was prosecuted for murder and ultimately was sent to an insane asylum, newspapers across the country declared that Detroit was home to a "voodoo cult," and that Black Muslims in the city offered human sacrifices to their "gods." The actions of this unstable man led to an entirely new interpretation of domestic "voodoo" and had serious repercussions for the Nation of Islam that continue to the present day.

At this time, the late 1920s and early 1930s, most stories about "voodoo" sacrifices were occurring in Haiti and Cuba—places where the United States sent its forces to occupy and "civilize." While there were numerous reports of "voodoo doctors" committing murders in the United States during this period, these were instances where someone was killed in a dispute over charms (i.e., the Lorenzo Savage/Elsie Barthel case discussed in Chapter 3), or they were cases where "voodooism" played no part in the alleged crime, but the authorities suspected that the accused sold charms or engaged in other "superstitions." However, Robert Harris's sacrificial killing in 1932 would be the first time that Black people in the United States were suspected of belonging to a religious organization centered on ritual murder. Similar to reports of child sacrifice and cannibalism in Haiti, allegations that the Nation's early leaders supported human sacrifice still cloud the histories written of this organization to the present day.

The Harris murder occurred during the final years of the U.S. occupation of Haiti (1915–1934), during the height of North American fascination with "voodooism." As stamping out "voodooism" and ritual sacrifice had been one of the justifications for U.S. imperialism in the Caribbean, Detroit police would have been under tremendous pressure to swiftly disband their own "voodoo cult" or risk undermining the notion that the United States could exert a "civilizing" influence through its occupation of more racially diverse countries. As I will discuss in this chapter, this murder had a profound impact on the early organization and leadership of the Nation of Islam beyond the mere damage to their public image/reputation.

"Voodoo" Murders in the Late 1920s

The events in Detroit in 1932 followed a series of brutal murders that were characterized as "hex" or "voodoo" killings in the late 1920s. In December 1928, Cleveland police officers shot an African American man named Doss Wade as he was running from a house that they were surveilling. While in the hospital for his injuries, Wade confessed that two days prior he had murdered Nehemiah Gibbs after robbing him of $35. Wade claimed that he had struck Gibbs with a piece of iron, dragged his body to the basement of a house, and then chopped off his head with an ax.[1] The police indeed discovered a headless body in the basement of the house from which Wade had emerged, and also located a severed head in an old cupboard; however, police found Wade's purported victim, Nehemiah Gibbs, alive.[2] When questioned further about the identity of his victim, Wade identified him as Gibbs's brother, but he was also found unharmed.[3]

No resolution to this mysterious murder appears to have ever been reported. It seems that the police were unable to determine who the victim was, whether Wade had killed him, and what might have been the motive for the murder. However, reporters continued to emphasize the possibility of a ritual purpose, stating that "[d]etectives would assign no other reason for the decapitation other than some Voodoo rite."[4] Even while reporting that "police are somewhat doubtful of the [voodoo] 'doctor's' confession" because Gibbs was found alive, they continued to use sensational titles such as "Headless Body of Man and Story of 'Voodoo' Mystify."[5] Aside from referring to Wade as a "voodoo doctor," or "voodoo healer," most news articles gave little other indication of why "voodoo" was suspected to have been involved.[6] However, some reporters added that Wade was arrested a year prior to this incident for practicing medicine without a license, presumably to further the suggestion that some kind of "cult" killing had taken place.[7]

Approximately two months after Doss Wade purportedly confessed to decapitating a man in Cleveland, Ohio, an alleged "voodoo doctor" known as Bishop Adams was indicted for the murder and robbery of a white grocer named William Glober in Austin, Texas. Glober's body was discovered in his store with bruising on his head and his throat slit from ear to ear.[8] Adams confessed to killing Glober in the process of robbing the store, and blood was found on Adams's shoes, as well as on a handkerchief and a razor in Adams's home.[9] The jury found Adams guilty after only about three hours of deliberation.[10] He was sentenced to death. In November 1929, the Appellate Court affirmed the sentence given to Adams.[11] He was executed on March 13, 1930, at a state prison in Texas.[12]

Similar to the case of Doss Wade, there was never any indication of why Adams was characterized as a "voodoo doctor." Several reports asserted that Adams had a reputation in the Black community as a "voodoo doctor."[13] Another alleged that Adams "believ[ed] his 'voodoo' would save him from the [electric] chair," and that he had requested "implements to make his 'witchcraft.'"[14] Despite the lack of any ritual element to the crime, journalists reported about his trial, appeal, and execution repeatedly using "voodoo" in the title.[15]

Perhaps the most notorious "voodoo" or "hex" murder of the late 1920s was that of Italian immigrant Benny Evangelist (born Benedetto Evangelista), his wife Santina, and their four children on July 3, 1929, in Detroit, Michigan. The brutality of this murder garnered immediate attention. Evangelista was beheaded and his wife's head was nearly severed. Their children were very young, ranging from age 18 months to 7 years. However, it was Evangelista's profession that triggered significant speculation about the cause of the family's demise.

Evangelista was a "mystical healer" who performed readings and rituals for his clientele, as well as prescribed herbal medicines.[16] The *Detroit Free Press* described the killing, stating, "Behind the tragedy was a grotesque background of religious insanity paralleling in its weirdness and barbarism any voodoo fetish of the West Indies." The author explained that "Ben's followers, many of them intelligent and wealthy members of the community, believed in 'Voodooism,' or devil worship. Evangelista was thought to commune with the stars and the wind. Revenge or jealousy or even fear of the evil eye were regarded by police as motives behind the killings—which have not been solved."[17]

Between the reports of "negro voodoo doctors" committing brutal murders and allegations of human sacrifice in Cuba and Haiti, the U.S. public had competing narratives about the nature of "voodooism" at this time. The domestic murders were typically gruesome—involving decapitation, bludgeoning, and so on—but they were neither ritualized nor a component of a larger religious sect. Therefore, when African American Muslims were accused of forming a "voodoo cult," this was perhaps the first instance in which a large group of Black people in the United States had ever been linked to ritual murder based on the teachings of a religious organization. In a time period when the imagined practice of human sacrifice as a "voodoo" ritual in Haiti and Cuba played a central role in justifying the need for the United States to provide a "civilizing influence" through occupation, reports of similar domestic practices would have suggested to the public that African Americans had been granted too many liberties and rights since emancipation and were experiencing a regression similar to that which was supposedly occurring in the Caribbean.

The Moorish Science Temple (1929)

Shortly after the Evangelista murders, the first allegations of voodoo cult practices among Black Muslims emerged against the Moorish Science Temple of America, an organization founded by Noble Drew Ali in 1913. Ali pronounced that the Temple was a Muslim organization and wrote a religious text that he referred to as the Holy Koran of the Moorish Science Temple; however, Susan Nance explains that the Moorish Science Temple was better described as "a black Spiritualist-style religion steeped in the philosophies of mystical Freemasonry" than as an Islamic group.[18] The Temple originated in Newark, New Jersey, but spread to other major cities in the Northeast and Midwest, especially Chicago.[19] Ali theorized that African Americans were actually Asiatic peoples or "Moors."[20] Ali sought to unite virtually all non-European populations, claiming that the Japanese, Chinese, Egyptians, African Americans, Indians, Brazilians, Argentinians, Mexicans, and others were all Asiatic peoples who belonged to the one true religion—Islam.[21] He also taught his followers that the United States' racial hierarchy would soon be reversed, when whites were destroyed and "Asiatics" ruled.[22]

Ali died, rather mysteriously, in the summer of 1929. In September of that year, police officers learned that several different factions who had been fighting for leadership of the Temple planned to hold a "conclave." The police organized a raid to locate Kirkman Bey, who had allegedly been kidnapped by rival Temple leaders.[23] When the police arrived at the meeting site, the Temple members shot at the patrolmen, killing one and injuring two. The police returned fire, killing two Temple members.[24] Dozens of African

Americans were taken to police headquarters for questioning after the shootout. Journalists reported that this "gun battle stripped secrecy from the Moorish Science Temple," which they described as a "cult in which Mohammedan titles, voodooism, Confucianism, Buddhism and 'jungle magic' were strangely intermixed."[25]

The Allah Temple of Islam/Nation of Islam (1932–Present)

Although reporters passingly referred to the Moorish Science temple in 1929 as a cult where "voodoo" and "jungle magic" were practiced, allegations that Black Muslims were members of a "voodoo cult" did not begin in earnest until November 1932. At that time, as noted earlier, an African American Muslim named Robert Harris murdered his black tenant, James Smith, as a purported human sacrifice to Allah. According to Harris's confession, Smith voluntarily climbed onto a makeshift altar in a back room of Harris's home, after Harris promised him that his sacrifice would make him the "savior of the world."[26] Harris set a clock and waited until it was precisely noon (the hour the murder must take place pursuant to his "supernatural instructions") then stabbed Smith in the heart and struck him over the head with an automobile axle.[27] He forced his wife and two children, ages 9 and 12, to serve as witnesses to the "rite."[28]

Harris was a member of the Allah Temple of Islam, an organization of African American Muslims which had been founded by an immigrant trader named Wallace Fard (also known as W. D. Fard, Wallace Farad, and Fard Muhammad) in Detroit in 1930.[29] Like the Moorish Science Temple before it, the Allah Temple of Islam (later renamed the Nation of Islam) taught their followers that Allah would bring about the cataclysmic destruction of white "devils" and empowered African Americans through lessons about the great historical achievements of Black people.[30] Both Islamic Temples had swiftly gained a following in Northern U.S. cities like Chicago and Detroit, where numerous African Americans had moved during World War I, to fill labor shortages as well as to escape lynching and other pervasive forms of racial discrimination in the South.[31] The murder of James Smith, with the subsequent arrest and trial of Robert Harris, was one of the earliest stories that gained widespread media attention for Allah Temple of Islam, which numbered approximately 8,000 members in the early 1930s, as reports of this "human sacrifice" reached newspapers in every corner of the nation.[32]

The media immediately drew subtle connections between African American Muslims and "voodoo" practitioners in Cuba and Haiti by emphasizing that although Harris had only confessed to murdering a Black man, authorities believed that he had previously targeted white victims. First, as reports of this "voodoo" murder began to circulate, the police initially suspected that Harris was responsible for the Evangelista murders in 1929. For example, on November 21, the *Circleville Herald* reported that "[p]olice immediately started a roundup of all members of the Order of Islam, in the hope that light be shed on other murders," particularly that of Benny Evangelista.[33] On the same date, the *Sarasota Herald Tribune* claimed, "Police, recalling the slaying of Benny Evangelista, leader of a fantastic religious cult, his wife and four children here in 1929, said they would take Harris' palm prints to determine whether he was the wielder of the ax that killed the Evangelistas. Detectives have expressed the belief the Evangelistas were killed by the head of some rival cult."[34] However, Harris was swiftly exonerated for this crime because his fingerprints did not match those found at the Evangelista home.[35]

Reports that did not link Harris to the Evangelista murder emphasized his alleged plans to execute other white people in Detroit. For example, the *Nevada State Journal* reported that Harris had initially intended to sacrifice Gladys Smith (no relationship to Harris's actual victim), a "21-year-old white welfare worker."[36] The journalist claimed, however, that "Miss Smith seemed unperturbed at her narrow escape as Detroit's first white voodoo victim. 'He threatened me, but I paid no attention,' she said 'We welfare workers are accustomed to such threats.' "[37] Another report indicated that Harris "is said by detectives to have admitted plans to kill Judges Edward J. Jeffries and Arthur E. Gordon. They said Harris also admitted planning to kill a woman welfare worker whose name he could not remember."[38] Additionally, this same source claimed that Harris had announced that he was "going to kill lots of Christians."[39]

Newspaper descriptions also made Harris appear to have a cult-like following analogous to the purported support shown to "voodoo" priests in Haiti and Cuba. Although Fard was unquestionably the leader of the Allah Temple of Islam in 1932, the media described Robert Harris as the "high priest" of this "voodoo cult" and asserted that hundreds of members gathered in support of Harris throughout the proceedings.[40] Other Temple members, including Harris's own family, adamantly denied these claims. Robert Harris's wife asserted that he had a history of mental illness and violent outbursts, and had threatened several times to decapitate her and their children.[41] Under the misleading title "Leader of Cult Called Insane," the *Detroit News* reported that Harris's brother Edward, who was also a Muslim, explained that Harris had no standing in the Temple and the members were well aware of his mental health issues.[42] Edward attributed his brother's erratic behavior to financial concerns, not to their religious beliefs.[43] The homicide investigator assigned to Harris's case seemed to support the significance of these economic problems in Harris's mental breakdown, as he reported that Harris's plots to kill the social worker began when she had recently terminated welfare benefits to Harris's family.[44]

Despite the growing evidence that Robert Harris committed murder because of mental illness and financial stress, the police continued to harass Temple members, seeking to establish a connection to their religious teachings. Homicide detectives questioned Wallace Fard, founder of the Temple; Ugan Ali, the Temple secretary; and Edward Harris about the tenets of their faith, searching for a relationship to "human sacrifice."[45] Edward reaffirmed that his brother was suffering from a mental breakdown, and that "nobody paid much attention to him."[46] Ali expressed a similar opinion, stating that Harris had "no standing" in the Temple and "[m]any people avoided him because of the wild things he sometimes said."[47] Fard responded that he did not know Robert Harris and that nothing in their teachings encouraged human sacrifice.[48]

The police continued to detain Fard, Ali, and several other Temple members despite their unequivocal denunciations of Harris's actions. Hundreds of Black Muslims marched on the police station in protest of these seemingly unwarranted confinements. Unfortunately, misleading newspaper accounts about these demonstrations fueled speculation that the Temple had encouraged Harris's "human sacrifice." The *Morning Herald*, a newspaper in Hagerstown, Maryland, published one such distorted report, claiming "five hundred members of the negro Voodoo-Moslem cult recently revealed in Detroit marched to the Central police station today to demand the release of their leaders, held for questioning as a result of the investigation growing out of the 'sacrificial' slaying of James H. Smith last Sunday."[49] They failed to mention that Harris was suffering from mental illness and that the Temple leaders had condemned his actions.

While some reporters omitted key facts in the Harris case to suggest the culpability of the entire Temple, others instead persisted in attributing the murder to their religious teachings even while recounting events that contradicted the Temple's involvement. For example, under the title "Cult Slayer Pleads Guilty," the *Detroit Press* described Harris's extremely erratic behavior at his arraignment but still suggested that his crime might be linked to Islamic teachings.[50] The author claimed that Judge Scallen ordered Harris to remove his hat in the courtroom, but Harris refused, replying, "I'm king here." This resulted in a dispute between Scallen and Harris about who was "king," and a court officer was forced to remove the hat from Harris's head. During this exchange, the judge asked Harris whether he admitted to killing James Smith. Harris replied in the affirmative; then, after struggling with the court officer to attempt to replace the hat on his head, he explained that Smith had to die because "[i]t was crucifixion time."[51] Immediately after his confession, Harris informed the judge, "Well, I've got to go now," and attempted to leave the courtroom. However, officers restrained him and returned him to his cell. While the *Detroit Press* reported that due to this bizarre behavior it was likely that the judge would appoint a sanity commission to evaluate Harris, they continued to refer to him as the "cult leader," and claimed that as a result of this murder the deputy chief of detectives had ordered a special investigation into the "activities of the Order of Islam [referring to the Temple]."[52]

Similar contradictory articles emerged over the following days, as Harris was transferred to the mental health ward of the local hospital after he became agitated and began destroying things in his cell. Judge Scallen appointed a three-member sanity commission to evaluate Harris, and they adjudged him legally insane and sent him to the state asylum in Ionia, Michigan.[53] Even as the media described Harris's bizarre behavior and the sanity commission's findings, they continued to characterize him as the leader of a "voodoo cult" and his actions as representative of all Black Muslims, employing misleading titles such as "Negro Cult Leader Admits Killing Man in Voodoo Worship," and "Cult Chief Admits He Killed Victim" to report these events.[54]

The attribution of the actions of one mentally unstable person to the members of the Allah Temple of Islam and its leaders is consistent with the sensationalized depictions of "voodoo" in Cuba and Haiti in the late nineteenth and early twentieth centuries. Travelers and reporters conflated isolated allegations of ritual murder on these islands with the beliefs and desires of the entire Black population, and emphasized that the rulers of these countries supported "voodoo" and ritual murder or were too afraid to suppress it. One will recall that in Spenser St. John's book, *Hayti or the Black Republic* (1884), he asserted that voodoo, human sacrifice, and cannibalism permeated all classes of Haitian society, and claimed "[a] black Government dares not greatly interfere, as its power is founded on the goodwill of the masses, ignorant and deeply tainted with fetish-worship."[55] In the 1910s and 1920s, as discussed in Chapter 2, journalists made analogous claims that white government officials in Cuba and other influential people were collaborators or co-worshippers of "voodoo" and refused to punish their Black counterparts, even for heinous crimes like human sacrifice.[56]

As historian Richard Brent Turner has pointed out, following Marcus Garvey's conviction for mail fraud and deportation to Jamaica in 1927 and the death of Noble Drew Ali in 1929, the Allah Temple of Islam (and its later incarnation as the Nation of Islam) "may have been the most important Pan-Africanist organization in Americas in the 1930s."[57] Particularly because of Fard's teachings about the racial superiority of Black people, as well as his encouragement of Black self-sufficiency and self-segregation, linking this leader of such a significant source of African American empowerment to human sacrifice would have been a particularly effective manner of discrediting him and all of his followers in the 1930s.

Due to the widespread public understandings of "voodoo" and human sacrifice as components of uncivilized Black societies and the close link between reports of these practices and U.S. imperialism, these repeated claims that the Temple was involved in Harris's crime had a substantial impact on the organization. First, the founder of the Temple, Wallace Fard, was detained by police until May 1933; he was instructed to leave Detroit immediately upon release.[58] Although official reasons for Fard's detention and banishment from the city are unknown, later FBI files indicate that Fard was "arrested on charge of investigation at the Fraymore Hotel as Chief of the Voodoos."[59] The media claimed that he was suspected of encouraging Harris's purported human sacrifice.[60]

After leaving Detroit, Fard spent a short time at the organization's second temple in Chicago, which had been established by his chief minister, Elijah Muhammad, in 1932. However, Fard disappeared in 1934, leaving Muhammad to take over Temple operations.[61] Muhammad changed the Temple's name to the Nation of Islam, purportedly to escape their negative reputation from Harris's so-called human sacrifice. The Chicago temple also became the Nation's main headquarters. Therefore, these characterizations of Black Muslims as a "voodoo cult," directly or indirectly, led to the first major changes in the organization's name, location, and leadership.

The University of Islam (1934)

When Elijah Muhammad became the leader of the Nation of Islam, one of his first initiatives was to create the University of Islam—a school for children in grades four through twelve. Muhammad's goal was to replace the public-school curriculum of white America with courses that reflected the history of the human race as the Nation understood it.[62] At the "University," Black students learned math, science, and other subjects from a less Eurocentric lens.[63] However, the Detroit Board of Education almost immediately attempted to close the University and force the children back into public schools. Police officers arrested Elijah Muhammad and other University teachers for contributing to the delinquency of minors.[64] The Board of Education also prosecuted parents for violating the state's education laws.

Ironically, considering that state-run segregated schools across the country were notoriously inadequate—understaffed, with outdated and insufficient materials, and unqualified teachers—the media cited the quality of education as the reason that the school was closed.[65] They claimed that school inspectors found that "none of the teachers apparently was the holder of a teaching license; the courses of instruction listed many subjects proper for school work, but the inspectors 'doubted the ability of teachers to instruct in these matters'; many so-called text books contained misinformation."[66] In addition to these complaints about subpar materials on standard subjects, reporters claimed that "over 400 pupils in [the] 'university of islam' [were] learning voodoo mysticism."[67] FBI files would later make similar claims that an inspection revealed that the teachers, facilities, and educational materials were too inadequate to "provide even the most rudimentary education for the colored children who were attending" and the information taught was "of a fantastic nature quite outside the realities of life."[68] The FBI files continued, "Those inside the movement know that the real purpose is to indoctrinate the students with Elijah's teaching while keeping them ignorant of American history and government and out of contact with the 'white devil' children."[69]

Approximately five hundred Nation members and supporters gathered to protest the arrest of the University teachers and the closing of the school.[70] The media referred to the demonstrations, which made front-page news across the United States, as a "mob" of "Negro 'Voodoo' Worshippers"[71] who had gathered to protest the closing of "a Negro cult."[72] In the course of these protests, about twenty people were injured, including several police officers.[73] Fifty police officers dispersed the crowd with the use of nightclubs, and they arrested thirty-five people.[74] Local newspapers reported that other members of the group were released to avoid further "race riots." However, they alleged that Elijah Muhammad was sentenced to pay a fine or serve a short jail sentence for "contributing to the delinquency of a minor child and voodooism."[75] At least one journalist claimed that "police feared the teaching of the cult might precipitate another series of voodoo atrocities such as was climaxed with a weird murder here two years ago."[76]

Perhaps the most bizarre and demeaning response to police attempts to close the University of Islam was an editorial in the *Helena Independent Records* approximately five days after the protests. The author appeared to question the validity of African Americans' struggles to find work and food during the Great Depression, describing their "evil" "rites and customs" as "proof against unemployment, poverty and hunger."[77] The author argued, "A ritual murder committed a while ago by one of its members, who confessed that he slew a lodge brother on an altar at his house, and the outbreak against the police, indicates [sic] that these colored people not only do not live by bread alone [a biblical reference to Matthew 4:4, meaning that physical nourishment is not sufficient to survive], but require emotional elements in their lives both weird and tragic."[78] The author declared that if such actions "were not tinged with evil," the rest of society might just "let the negroes blissfully revel in them, since the uplift by education of intelligence so often produces crooks who prey upon society."

Vernon McQueen and the Japanese Conspiracy (1937–1940s)

The period between 1937 and 1942 was a significant and tumultuous time for the Nation of Islam. First, the Nation was rocked by allegations of yet another purported instance of human sacrifice in Detroit. Several years later, in 1942, many Nation leaders and members, including Elijah Muhummad himself, were arrested for sedition and encouraging others to avoid the draft. The Nation's reputation as a "voodoo-practicing" cult that engages in human sacrifice continued during this period; however, the media and police began to question whether the Japanese were the masterminds behind these occult practices.

Despite Fard's departure and the restructuring and renaming of the Temple, narratives of Muslim "voodoo practices" in Detroit resurfaced in

1937 when a man named Vernon McQueen was charged for preparing to boil his wife and daughter alive at a "gathering of worshippers of Allah."[79] McQueen's arrest made front-page headlines across the country, as reporters alleged that the police were forced to hide McQueen's wife and child out of fear of reprisals from the other members of the "cult."[80] The media linked McQueen to Harris's murder of Smith in 1932 and the arrest of Wallace Fard shortly thereafter.[81] They characterized these events as evidence of "a new uprising of Detroit's Negro voodoo cult," which police thought had been eradicated when Fard had been ordered to leave the city.[82] Reporters further contended that McQueen's arrest provoked detectives to investigate the rest of the "Voodoo cult," which had spread to Chicago, New York, and Canada.[83]

The following year, in 1938, Erdmann Beynon published the first scholarly article ever written about the Nation of Islam in *The American Journal of Sociology*. Beynon titled this work "The Voodoo Cult among the Negro Migrants of Detroit,"[84] which he explained reflected the name that the police used to describe the Nation of Islam. He clarified that he did not intend "to trace relationship between this cult and Voodooism in Haiti or other West Indian islands"; rather, the name was "solely because of cases of human sacrifice."[85] This article would become central to the Nation of Islam's reputation because virtually every scholar writing about Wallace Fard, Elijah Muhammad, and Malcolm X since the 1930s has relied on Beynon for their work.[86]

Without citing a single source, Beynon recounted the details of the Harris and McQueen cases and the alleged response of other Black Muslims. He contended that Robert Harris was "a prominent member" of the Nation of Islam and McQueen was the brother of one of the assistant ministers.[87] Beynon claimed that these sacrifices caused substantial internal dissension in the organization, leading one group known as "Rebels against the Will of Allah" to break off from the others "to avoid human sacrifice, the necessity of which as an expiation of sin forms one of the most hotly debated subjects among cult members."[88] While Beynon conceded that Wallace Fard's official position on human sacrifice was not known, he suggested that the practice was a natural extension of Fard's teaching that his followers could gain access to Mecca if they killed four "white devils," and that members of the Nation were expected to give themselves over to Allah and the movement unto the point of death, if necessary.[89]

Beynon raised another key issue that was hotly debated in the press and investigated by the FBI at the time. He claimed that leaders of other "cults," especially a Japanese officer named Major Takahashi, sought to infiltrate the Nation and convince their members to join other fringe movements. Over the subsequent years, especially leading up to and during World War II, some U.S. journalists would make similar allegations, even speculating that the Japanese were the true masterminds behind the Nation of Islam's human sacrifices.

Ernest Allen explains that the Japanese defeat of the Russians in the Russo-Japanese war of 1904–1905 had significant implications for the entire world. The Japanese became a symbol of hope to colonized peoples of Africa and Asia; to Europeans it sparked a fear of uprisings against colonial or occupying authorities.[90] African Americans found increasing ties to Japan after their "principal delegate to the 1919 Peace Conference, submitted an amendment (ultimately rejected) to the League of Nations Covenant supporting the principal of racial equality."[91] During this same time period, Marcus Garvey, the founder of the Universal Negro Improvement Association (UNIA), envisioned Japan as an ally against whites and argued that Asians should have autonomous control over Asia just as Africans should of Africa.[92] A retired Japanese general thereafter penned a novel depicting a war in which the Japanese invaded the United States and Garvey led an army of 10 million African Americans in support of them.[93]

In 1932, a Japanese man by the name of Satokata Takahashi (born Naka Nakane) appeared in the Midwestern United States at a meeting of the UNIA in Chicago. He moved to Detroit in 1932, around the time that Robert Harris committed his famous "sacrifice." Takahashi represented himself to be an agent of the Japanese government sent to the United States to unify people of color and help them organize their own government.[94] In 1933, he became the leader an organization known as "The Development of Our Own" and used it "to join with all other colored people—yellow, brown, and black—against all white people."[95] After Fard and Muhammad left Detroit, many of their followers joined Takahashi.[96] Takahashi was deported in April 1934 for failing to possess a valid visa and being a foreigner ineligible for citizenship. He reappeared in Canada later that year, and collaborated with his African American wife, Pearl Sherrod (whom he had wed two months prior to his deportation) to continue to run The Development of Our Own until 1939, when Takahashi was arrested for re-entering the United States.[97]

At first, the speculations about Japanese involvement in Black Muslims' purported human sacrifices were sparse and equivocal. At the time of the McQueen incident, several newspapers reported that investigation of this case revealed "that a Japanese deported after a cult murder in 1932, was directing the organization's weird ceremonies from a Canadian hideout."[98] An article in the *Mexia Weekly Herald* continued, "Detective Lieutenant Walter Williams said his investigation revealed the Japanese was known to cultist [sic] as the 'Little God of the East' [a nickname given to Takahashi because of his 5 ft. 5 in. stature] who had charge of the 'Big Book' containing commands of Allah."[99]

Then in September 1942, Elijah Muhammad and other Nation members were arrested for evading the draft and "maintaining relations with the Japanese government."[100] These arrests "were part of a federal sweep of African-American pro-Japanese organizations that resulted in the arrest of more than eighty black people in 1942 and 1943,"[101] and led to much greater public speculation that the Japanese had directed Black Muslims to practice human sacrifice. On September 21, 1942, the *Freeport Journal Standard* reported that the FBI had arrested eighty-one members of three different Afrocentric organizations: the Peace Movement of Ethiopia, the Temple of Islam, and the Brotherhood of Liberty for the Black People of America. They were charged with encouraging others to refuse to register for selective service, and with teaching "that negroes owe allegiance to Japan."[102] Emphasizing the widespread influence of these organizations, the author reported that they claimed to have four million members across forty-six states between them, and that all believe that "they belong to the same race as the Japanese and therefore owe allegiance to Japan."[103]

Around this same time, the *Chicago Herald American* apparently printed a convoluted recount of these arrests that collapsed the events of the previous 10 years as if they had occurred at once. I have not been able to find the *Chicago Herald* story but have located a partial reprint in the *Waterloo Daily Courier* on September 23, 1942.[104] The story began by describing the Nation as "[f]anatical members of a Jap-inspired 'fifth column' [resistance movement]" who had "once planned to seize and offer high Detroit city officials on their altar of sacrifice." The author argued that the purpose of the Nation was to "drive the white devils into the sea" in order to accomplish "a fantastic scheme to unite the world's dark-skinned races with the Japs and on the arming of 30,000,000 soldiers to carry out the plan." The author explained that members of the Nation had been charged with sedition and draft evasion, but they also described the case of Robert Harris, which had taken place more than a decade earlier, as if Harris was the current leader of the Detroit branch of the Nation and this purported sacrifice had recently been uncovered by federal investigators looking for evidence of sedition. The author averred, "The troubled mind of King Robert Harris (of the Allah temple of Islam) had been inflamed against the white race by his Japanese teachers. It was filled with the blood lusts of the ancient Moslem prophets."

The reporter titled the article "Murphy on Negro Cult's Sacrifice List," emphasizing that one of the initial targets of Harris's purported sacrifice to Allah had been an associate justice of the Supreme Court, Frank Murphy, who was the mayor of Detroit at the time of the incident. They claimed that Harris had also considered killing two aldermen, a judge, and a welfare worker, but had abandoned his plans because their bodyguards made them difficult to kidnap or kill. Turning James Smith from a supposedly willing sacrifice into a hapless patriot, the reporter argued that "[a]fter two weeks of futile hunting for a victim, Harris reached home one night discouraged. His blood-shot eyes rested on the sleeping figure of a roomer who had spurned the pro-Japanese organization" and killed him at high noon "after a weird voodoo ceremony." The author argued that Smith's purported acquiescence to the sacrifice had actually been obtained by striking him over the head with a crank handle.

Despite all these allegations, in July 1943, the Detroit Field Division of the FBI concluded that the "investigation of the Allah Temple of Islam failed to reveal any evidence of pro-Japanese influence."[105]

The Civil Rights Movement (1960s–1970s)

Ultimately, the FBI later admitted that the charges of Fard's connection with human sacrifice "may or may not have been trumped up."[106] However, over the next forty years, newspaper reports and scholarly publications on the Nation of Islam, Elijah Muhammad, and Malcolm X periodically repeated these allegations that Fard was connected to "voodooism" and human sacrifice, particularly during the height of the organization's prominence in the early 1960s. These stories undermined the Nation of Islam in two distinct and somewhat competing ways. First, they emphasized that the so-called human sacrifices of the 1930s were a component of the Nation's strong anti-white agenda, which required hatred and violence against white Americans. Second, they depicted Wallace Fard as a white man who had duped African Americans into following him, tapping into their "primitive" instincts, and convincing them into committing the debased practice of human sacrifice.

C. Eric Lincoln's book *The Black Muslims in America*, which appears to have been the first monograph published about the Nation of Islam, unquestioningly adopted sensationalized depictions of the Harris murder from the 1930s. Lincoln argued that amidst the Great Depression and the increasing difficulties African Americans faced attempting to secure housing and employment in the North, welfare workers and police officers "became the symbolic targets of a virulent hatred of the white man growing in the breasts of Fard's Black Nation."[107] Citing a lengthy quote from Beynon's 1938 article, Lincoln contended that Harris's threats to kill to welfare workers "for human sacrifice as infidels" was "one extreme example" of this hatred and targeting.[108]

While Lincoln depicted Harris's crime as representative of broader sentiments of a disgruntled and disillusioned African American community, most reporters and scholars writing in the 1960s and 1970s characterized Fard as a criminal and a charlatan who was solely responsible for the formation of this "voodoo cult." For instance, in February 1961, dozens of newspapers circulated a virtually identical story written by George Sokolsky about the Nation of Islam. Sokolsky drafted this article in response to a protest that the Nation, under the leadership of Malcolm X, led in front of the United Nations Security Council meetings in New York City following the death of Patrice Lumumba. Sokolsky emphasized the swift growth of the Nation of Islam, which had at least thirty temples in the United States at this time and claimed 250,000 members. Sokolsky described the Nation as a "Negro Cult" and asserted that their founder was a criminal who taught his followers to hate whites and commit acts of violence:

> The organizer, W.D. Fard, who has disappeared and who the votaries of this sect believe is Allah, that is God, was a peddler in Detroit after serving a three year period in San Quentin penitentiary for violating the narcotics law. He went by many names and preached violence.
>
> At first Fard preached the Bible but very soon abandoned and ridiculed the testament and preached racial hatred instead. On Nov. 21, 1932, Detroit was shocked by a frightful story of human sacrifice. Robert Harris induced his roomer, John J. Smith, to present himself as a human sacrifice so that he might become "the savior of the world." At the appointed time and place, Harris plunged a knife into Smith's heart. Harris was arrested and adjudged insane. Fard disappeared in May 1933.[109]

Ed Montgomery made similar claims about Fard in his now-famous article, titled "Black Muslim Founder Exposed as a White," published in the *Herald Examiner* in 1963.[110] Montgomery declared that Fard, who Nation of Islam members believe was from Mecca, was actually named Wallace Dodd, and was born to a British father and a Polynesian mother. He depicted Fard as "an enterprising, racketeering fake" who posed as an Arab and intentionally targeted African Americans to steal their money. Within this multi-page article, Montgomery included a large section titled "Detroit Ousted Him for Human Sacrifice." Montgomery claimed that this "human sacrifice" demonstrated "the potential dangerousness and the primitive instincts of some of his followers."[111] He asserted that Fard was arrested in connection with the sacrificial murder and then ordered to leave Detroit, but not before he admitted that his teachings were a racket.[112]

Throughout the 1960s and in the early 1970s, both the media and scholars continued to resurrect these allegations that the founders of the Nation of Islam practiced human sacrifice. For example, in 1965, Lee Brown, a member of the San Jose Police Department, published an article titled "Black Muslims and the Police" in *The Journal of Criminal Law*.[113] The primary purpose of the article was to describe a series of violent conflicts between African American Muslims and the police in California; however, Brown inserted a sensationalized version of Robert Harris's murder into his narrative as background information. He recounted these events without mentioning that Harris was declared insane and that Temple leaders denied ordering or supporting his actions. Brown also contended that there were additional unconfirmed reports of human sacrifice associated with the Nation of Islam.[114] However, despite his negative depictions of the organization's origins, Brown ultimately concluded that the Nation posed no threat to police or society and had made substantial strides in reducing drug and alcohol abuse as well as criminal recidivism rates among African Americans.[115]

Merv Block was less equivocal in his depictions of the Nation of Islam in a newspaper article that he wrote in March 1972 that was circulated in several papers.[116] In addition to focusing on the departure of several prominent members (such as the late Malcolm X) and on claims that the millions of dollars raised for the poor were being siphoned off for Muhammad's personal use, Block emphasized the criminal history of many of the Nation's leaders, including their controversial founder, Wallace Fard. Block accepted as true the recent contentions that Fard was a white man of New Zealand ancestry who had served time in San Quentin prison. Of Fard's early activities with the Nation of Islam in the 1930s, Block asserted, "The cult came to notice in 1932 after one member sacrificed another. In 1933, Detroit police arrested Fard as chief of the 'Voodoo Cult,' and authorities told him to leave. He soon dropped from sight."

It is worth noting the irony of these allegations, which may have been somewhat lost on the media by the 1960s and 1970s. At the time that Harris offered Smith as a purported sacrifice to Allah, the United States had sent forces to Cuba multiple times and had occupied Haiti for nearly two decades, at least partially under the pretext of bringing "civilization" to these countries and suppressing ritual murder and cannibalism. As discussed previously, the U.S. media and English-language travelogues emphasized that Black people would not dare to intervene in such practices and that only the introduction of more white or mixed-race people would put an end to them. When news of Harris's actions broke, the media reflected on the popularity of this "Negro Voodoo Cult," and African Americans' support of the practice of human sacrifice. Yet, if Wallace Fard were indeed a white man posing as an Arab, and if he encouraged Harris and/or McQueen in their actions, then Fard would have had the opposite of the civilizing influence that many claimed white leaders would bring to the Caribbean.

Present Day

Searches of major newspaper databases have produced no recent references to the Nation of Islam as a "voodoo cult"; however, claims that their founder encouraged human sacrifice still haunt this legendary organization in scholarly literature. In the 1990s and 2000s, researchers frequently asserted that the murder of James Smith was an extension of Fard's alleged instructions that his followers should murder four white "devils" to gain access to heaven.[117] One of the most sensationalized interpretations of Fard's influence on Robert Harris appears in Karl Evanzz's biography of Elijah Muhammad published in 1999, which says:

> According to Fard, not only white devils were to be targets for ritual slayings, but also African Americans who placed their loyalty to the American government before their loyalty to the temple and God. Fard referred to these blacks as "imps," meaning they were "impersonating" white people in their thinking and behavior. Most of Fard's followers preferred to forego the rewards he promised for carrying out ritualistic murder, but there were a

handful for whom the salvation he assured them meant everything. Robert Harris, whom Fard had renamed Robert Karriem, was one of them. His desire to please Fard led him into an unspeakable act that had the city of Detroit in shock during Thanksgiving week of 1932.[118]

Without weighing in on the long-standing debate about whether Fard encouraged his followers to kill "white devils," the purported link between such an instruction and the murder of James Smith or the attempted murder of Vernon McQueen's wife and children is extremely problematic. Smith and the McQueen family were all African Americans who, at least according to media reports, were Temple members. As neither whites nor African American non-believers, it is unclear how their deaths would further Fard's purported teachings about murdering "white devils" or "imps." This is particularly true in the case of James Smith who, according to Robert Harris's confession, was so devout that he offered himself as a sacrifice to Allah.

Furthermore, there is a substantial distinction between murdering "white devils" or "imps" and engaging in human sacrifice. The above-cited scholars suggest that Fard urged the murder of "white devils" as a type of holy war against the oppressors and their collaborators, and that he claimed that such killings would earn the slayer access to Mecca. Human sacrifice, on the other hand, suggests the believer must utilize a ritualized method of killing to make a propitiatory offering to appease a god or gods. This would have been particularly true of public perceptions of voodoo-related human sacrifices in the 1930s. However, despite the contemporaneous descriptions of the Nation of Islam as a "voodoo cult" and the bizarre ritualized crimes of Harris (sacrificing Smith on an altar) and McQueen (attempting to boil his family alive), no reporter or scholar appears to have uncovered any evidence that Fard gave specific instructions about a ceremonial method of killing, nor that he ever suggested that the blood or life force of the victim would serve any spiritual purpose beyond proving the follower's loyalty. One must therefore question whether even recent scholarship continues to deploy racialized stereotypes about "voodooism" and human sacrifice that were common in the 1930s.

Conclusion

This chapter has explored how narratives about "voodoo" practitioners in Haiti and Cuba in the early twentieth century informed the public interpretations of the founders of the Nation of Islam who, in the early 1930s, were likewise characterized as leaders of a "voodoo cult." Despite substantial evidence to the contrary, the media immediately characterized the actions of one insane individual as indicative of the beliefs and teachings of an entire African American religious community. These allegations of human sacrifice drew the swift attention of the authorities in the 1930s and have permanently tainted public and scholarly perceptions of the Nation of Islam. In the years following Robert Harris's famous trial, the founder of the Nation was banished from Detroit and the police attempted to close the organization's private schools. Unable to endure police surveillance in Detroit, Elijah Muhammad attempted to rebuild the Nation by changing its headquarters to the Chicago temple and changing the organization's name. Yet, allegations of human sacrifice re-emerged from the extreme forms of domestic violence taking place in the McQueen household back in Detroit. At this time, the media began to wonder if Black Muslims posed an even greater threat than previously supposed—if they had allied themselves with, or were perhaps even being directed by, Japanese instigators.

From the first scholarly literature on the Nation of Islam, including Erdmann Beynon's "The Voodoo Cult among Negro Migrants in Detroit" and C. Eric Lincoln's *The Black Muslims in America*, U.S. universities have continually reproduced these racialized allegations without grasping the full meaning at the time they were uttered. As the previous chapters have illustrated, from the inception of the term, the concept of "voodoo" has denoted a group of persons of African descent who are incapable of voting, holding public office, and governing themselves. This particular "Negro Voodoo Cult," as the Nation was often called, reflected many of the things that the American public found threatening about Haiti and Cuba. They rejected white supremacy, sought their own political and educational autonomy, and engaged in physical struggles against oppression. This, not human sacrifice, was the true meaning of a "voodoo cult" in the 1930s.

5
"Sacrifices at Sea" and Haitian Refugees in the 1980s

In August 2017, Canadian law enforcement officers discovered a 54-page immigration file in a wooded area near the border between Canada and the United States.[1] The documents were from a Haitian man who had sought to immigrate to the United States but recently had fled to Canada after hearing rumors that the United States was placing greater restrictions on immigration from Haiti. The file indicated that when the man initially arrived in the United States, he had said that he wanted to "look for a better life." Later, he changed his story and claimed that if he returned to Haiti, he feared that he would be killed because of his Christian faith. In an interview with a U.S. asylum officer from December 2016, the man alleged that he had faced physical abuse from his half-siblings, who were "voodoo" practitioners. The man told of an alleged incident in which his half-brother had beaten him with a stick and had broken his finger because he was sharing the Christian gospel. Later, he claimed that his half-siblings had hired a gang to attack him because he wanted to bury their father according to Christian rites. This case is just one example of how, for nearly 50 years, claims about the threat of "voodoo" practices have played a role in immigration cases and debates in the United States.

The United States made significant changes to its immigration policies in the early 1980s. These policies significantly and negatively impacted Haitian refugees who were attempting to reach the United States in small, rickety boats and who were then detained in horrible conditions in detention centers while waiting for asylum hearings. Simultaneously, a series of fateful voyages took place where Haitian smugglers allegedly sacrificed passengers as part of "voodoo" rituals to ensure safe passage to the United States. Because of these supposed sacrifices, discussions of "voodoo" featured prominently in debates about immigration policies in the 1980s and their impact on Haitian asylum seekers.

Nearly half a century after the end of the U.S. occupation, these refugee cases drew public attention back to alleged barbarous rituals of Haitian "voodoo." In particular, they resurrected claims that Black religious communities practiced human sacrifice, stereotypes which had largely faded out by the late 1930s. However, instead of supporting U.S. imperialism in the Caribbean, reports of these "voodoo sacrifices" seem to have been meant to garner sympathy for Haitian refugees by illustrating the atrocities to which they would be subjected if not granted asylum in the United States.

Race and Immigration before the 1980s

The United States, like most countries in the Americas, has a long history of discriminating against nonwhite people in its immigration policies. Specifically, in 1915, the Senate passed a bill that would exclude "all members of the African or black race" from immigrating. However, the NAACP fought the bill, and it was defeated in the House.[2] Nevertheless, new race-related immigration policies were imposed just a few years later. In 1921, Congress implemented a "national-origin quota system, which assigned to each country a number of immigrants based upon the number of persons of that nationality residing in the United States on a given date."[3] By favoring immigration from predominantly white countries, this national-origin quota system essentially became another form of restricting immigration based on race.

The quota system remained in effect until 1952. Then, from 1952 to 1965, revised immigration policies no longer explicitly limited the entry of certain racial groups; however, they gave preferential treatment to immigrants from Western Europe. Finally, in 1965, the United States eliminated all immigration preferences based on race or national origin.

Political upheaval in Haiti corresponded with and led to changes in U.S. immigration policies after the end of these national origin regulations. From 1957 to 1986, Haiti was ruled by two consecutive dictators—Francois "Papa Doc" Duvalier and his son, Jean Claude "Baby Doc" Duvalier. Both leaders harassed and eliminated potential opponents, employing a vast network of secret police known as the Tonton Macoutes. Under their rule, formal political and judicial systems lost their power and meaning—Haitians could be deprived of their land, imprisoned, or killed at the whim of the Tonton Macoutes and other government officials.

The Haitian population of the United States increased exponentially during the Duvalier dictatorships. During the regime of "Papa Doc," middle- and upper-class Haitians migrated to the United States by overstaying tourist visas, "a practice that was largely tolerated" by the U.S. government.[4] However, during the economic and political turmoil of Jean-Claude "Baby Doc" Duvalier (1971–1986), tourist visas were difficult for Haitians to obtain, and refugees had to resort to other measures.[5]

In 1972, a boat of 65 Haitians left for the United States. They stopped in Cuba and the Bahamas, before finally landing in Pompano Beach, Florida. They had very little food or water and were in a boat that could barely stay afloat. After this voyage, Haitians increasingly fled to the United States across the ocean in small vessels,[6] earning them the moniker of "boat people."[7] Studies estimate that in the 1970s, around 40,000–50,000 Haitians filed asylum claims in the United States.[8] Many of them were so-called boat people.

Far from receiving the asylum seekers with open arms, the United States only approved around 25 of these claims and began deporting the others.[9] From 1970 to 1978, "the INS (Immigration and Naturalization Service) knowingly allowed the accumulation of as many as 7,000 Haitian deportation claims."[10] Shortly thereafter, the INS created an acceleration program to process asylum cases that reduced refugees' chances of having their claims approved. One of the creators of this program, Mario Noto, explained that its purpose was to protect the United States from what he described as the "Haitian threat."[11]

Within a matter of months, the immigration court in Miami that handled Haitian deportation hearings suddenly went from scheduling between one and 10 deportation cases per day to a minimum of 55 cases per day.[12] By 1980, this number had increased to perhaps 80 cases.[13] Immigration attorneys were placed in similar positions—frequently having to juggle three cases in a single hour that were often scheduled in different locations.[14] Although the INS was aware of these issues, they made no effort to resolve scheduling conflicts.[15] The hearing times for asylum cases were also reduced from 90 to 30 minutes, giving asylum seekers and their attorneys little time to argue the case.[16] More than 4,000 Haitian asylum seekers were processed through this accelerated program, and none of them were granted asylum.[17]

Alongside these specific changes to the processing of Haitian asylum cases, a new Refugee Act went into effect. The stated purpose of the law was to "provide a permanent and systematic procedure for the admission to this country of refugees."[18] This law defined a refugee as someone who "is unable or unwilling to return to" their country "because of persecution or a well-founded fear of persecution on account of race, religion, nationality, membership in a particularly social group, or political opinion."[19] This was the first time that U.S. law actually defined the meaning of "refugees."[20] However, the protections of this law only applied to people already inside the United States, not people on the way to the United States or at the border.[21] As the next section will discuss, this laid the foundation for new policies over the next few years that would focus on stopping asylum seekers, especially Haitians, before they could reach the United States and before any legal protections would be offered to them under this new law.

By the early 1980s, there were approximately 800,000 Haitians and Haitian-Americans (children of immigrants) in the United States, approximately half of whom were undocumented.[22] Because of the recent large influx of Haitians, in the early 1980s, much media attention was given to "boat people."[23] In 1984, in one of the first studies of Haitian immigrants in the United States, Michel Laguerre observed "little reporting in the press about Haitian Americans fails to make sensationalist statements about their voodoo practices."[24]

Sacrifices at Sea: Haitian Immigration in the Early 1980s

Between June 1980 and October 1981, there were at least three cases of purported voodoo-related violence among Haitians on vessels en route to the United States. There was a close relationship between the attention that the media gave to these supposed "voodoo" cases and major shifts in refugee policies. When lawmakers introduced new policies encouraging the interception and return of Haitian migrants on the open seas, or when concerns arose about the conditions of Haitian migrants in detention centers, journalists featured more stories about violence against the migrants on their journey to the United States and were more likely to characterize this violence as "voodoo." The first of these cases was the Dieu Qui Donne.

Dieu Qui Donne (June 1980)

On June 28, 1980, approximately 240 refugees boarded a ship known as the *Dieu Qui Donne* ("God who gives") in Gonave, Haiti, to sail toward the

United States.[25] The voyage was delayed by a lack of winds, and witnesses reported that the crew became suspicious that one of the passengers, Menasse Seme, had an evil spirit attached to him that was impeding the ship's progress. The crew searched Menasse to see if he possessed a "voodoo talisman" that was destroying the boat. They found nothing but a bible and his brother's Miami address in his bag, but they threw his satchel overboard anyway. One night, about two days before the boat reached Miami, the crew also tossed Menasse overboard. His brothers, Gulbert Seme and Jean-Pierre Seme, who had left Haiti many years prior, contacted the FBI, the U.S. State Department, and the Miami Dade County State Attorney's Office, seeking their assistance in bringing their brother's murderers to justice. However, all these offices refused to help the brothers, asserting that Haiti was the only country with jurisdiction to prosecute the murder of a Haitian national on the open sea. The director of the Haitian Coalition, a refugee assistant organization in Miami, reported that this case was the first time that they had heard of Haitians throwing each other overboard.

The following year, in 1981, allegations of Haitian refugees' "voodoo" sacrifices would make headline news across the nation. However, in the summer of 1980, these salacious claims about the *Dieu Que Donne* appear to have only been reported in a few newspapers.[26] One can perhaps understand the lack of reporting with the recent success of several efforts to defend the rights of Haitian refugees. First, in June 1979, the International Human Rights Law Group filed a complaint against the United States with the Inter-American Commission on Human Rights, asserting that the United States was discriminating against Haitians and depriving them of their right to life and liberty, among other things.[27] In April 1980, after the Commission began hearing testimony about the complaint, they sent a cablegram to the Secretary of State, asking him to halt deportations until it could review the case.[28] This case would have still been pending before the Commission when the *Dieu Que Donne* came ashore; however, this initial cablegram would have suggested that the Commission might be sympathetic to the plight of the refugees.

Second, on July 2, 1980, just a few days before this alleged sacrifice would have taken place, the U.S. District Court for the Southern District of Florida issued a decision which found that the accelerated asylum claim processing program was discriminatory against Haitians.[29] The court stressed that these policies showed intentional discrimination based on race and national origin, targeting Haitians who were "the first substantial flight of *black* refugees from a repressive regime to" the United States.[30] They found that the INS intentionally and systematically expelled Haitians.[31] The court also emphasized that there was substantial evidence that refugees who had been deported and returned to Haiti were at risk for significant mistreatment—surveillance, arbitrary imprisonment, torture, and death.[32] The decision barred the government from deporting any additional Haitians or holding any deportation hearings until they submitted a plan for a fair and nondiscriminatory evaluation of each asylum claim on a case-by-case basis.[33]

While this case and the initial response of the Inter-American Commission seemed favorable to Haitians, over the following year, Haitian asylum seekers experienced a series of traumas and legal setbacks that catapulted their plight to front-page news. Instead of focusing on the discriminatory INS policies about asylum hearings and deportation, these policies and incidents centered on the voyage from Haiti to the United States. These policies and cases seem to have encouraged the media to fixate on "voodoo sacrifices" in a way that they did not when the *Dieu Que Donne* first came ashore. One of the first incidents that drew attention to the dangers facing Haitian refugees took place on the island of Cayo Lobos in the Bahamas.

Cayo Lobos (September 1980)

In September 1980, just one month after reports surfaced about the murder of Menasse Seme, more than 100 Haitians were en route to Miami when their ship encountered a storm, and they were stranded on the Bahamian island of Cayo Lobos.[34] U.S. forces discovered them in early October and started to drop off supplies while the United States and the Bahamas fought about what would happen to the refugees. At first, the Bahamian police tried to round them up, and the refugees used whatever they could find, including knives, bottles, and sticks, to fight off the police. The refugees expressed fear that if they went back to Haiti, they would be jailed or killed. The police returned on November 12, "armed with nightsticks and tear gas," and they beat and kicked the refugees and forced them onto a Bahamian ship and took them back to Haiti.[35] An NBC television crew flew in a helicopter over the island and filmed much of the violence.[36]

When the refugees arrived in Haiti, a doctor from the Red Cross told reporters that approximately 25 of the returnees suffered from "cracked ribs, bruises, other signs of beatings and malnutrition."[37] Nine of them had to be carried off the boat on stretchers.[38] Their injuries primarily occurred when the Bahamian police forced them onto the boat. The refugees also reported that they had not been fed enough during the trip between the Bahamas and Haiti. There were no allegations that "voodoo" played any role in the voyage that stranded these Haitians in the Bahamas, nor in the beatings and starvation that they suffered while on the island; however, reporters would frequently mention this traumatic incident over the following years when they discussed allegations of human sacrifice on other voyages.

The *Jesula* (July 1981)

The second voyage that would be rumored to include "voodoo sacrifices" took place in July 1981. A 33-foot wooden sailboat named the *Jesula* left Haiti carrying about 215 refugees to the United States. The U.S. Coast Guard seized the ship and arrested its passengers near Key West, Florida, on July 25, 1981. By this time, the ship carried only 165 people.[39] Federal prosecutors charged two men whom they believed to be the captains or leaders of the voyage, Kersazan Tacius and Belony Saintil, with violating 8 U.S.C. § 1324(a)(1), which prohibits any person from bringing any "aliens" (persons not "lawfully entitled to enter or reside within the United States") into the country.[40]

Nine of the passengers testified for the prosecution, claiming that Tacius and Saintil not only were in charge of their illegal voyage, but also were responsible for the death of the 50 passengers who did not make it to the United States. Most of these individuals starved to death; the passengers attributed these deaths to Tacius and Saintil because they were the captains of the ship and oversaw the distribution of food and water.[41] The witnesses also accused Saintil and Tacius of beating the passengers with their hands, a rock, and a machete, killing some of them. Additionally, they alleged that the two men made sexual advances toward some of the women and threatened to throw overboard those who would refuse.[42]

This tragic voyage seems to have received little attention at the time that it came to shore in July. A search of newspaper databases revealed not a single article about this incident in the first two to three months after the voyage took place. However, changes to refugee law and the arrival of another ship with more sensational stories about passenger deaths at sea would bring media attention to what happened on the *Jesula*.

In July 1981, a cabinet task force, led by the U.S. attorney general, recommended that the United States develop policies to intercept and seize unregistered ships near its shores.[43] A couple of months later, "on September 23, 1981, Secretary of State James Baker entered into an agreement with Jean-Claude Duvalier (Baby Doc) to prevent the illegal migration of undocumented Haitians to the United States by sea."[44] This agreement allowed the U.S. Coast Guard to "stop and board Haitian vessels" and to return the boat to Haiti if they violated any law of Haiti or the United States. However, they weren't supposed to send back anyone who would qualify as a refugee in the United States.[45]

Later, on September 29, 1981, President Ronald Reagan issued Proclamation 4865, calling "illegal migration by sea of large numbers of undocumented aliens" a "serious national problem detrimental to the interests of the United States."[46] He prohibited "the entry of undocumented aliens from the high seas" and authorized the "interdiction of certain vessels carrying such aliens."[47] Reagan indicated that this proclamation was a follow-up to discussions with "the Governments of affected foreign countries" (presumably referencing his conversation with Duvalier). That same day, Reagan issued Executive Order number 12324, which specified the protocols for interdiction (boarding vessels that appeared to be "engaged in the irregular transportation of persons" and examining the documents of the people on board) and gave the Coast Guard the authority to carry out the procedures.[48] Thus, late September marked the first period when the U.S. Coast Guard had the official approval to intercept boats of Haitians on the open ocean and to prevent them from reaching the United States.[49]

The other major change during this period was the increasing visibility of the horrible state of Krome Detention Center, where Haitian refugees were being held prior to their asylum hearings. On October 23, 1980, the Dade County Department of Health found conditions at the Center to be so poor that they ordered it to be closed. However, the federal government refused and continued to use the detention center.[50] In July 1981, the same period that the *Jesula* came ashore, the governor of Florida sued the federal government, demanding that they either comply with the health requirements or close Krome Detention Center. The lawsuit asserted that the government was putting 1,600 people in a facility that was only built to hold around 500 people.[51]

Following the governor's lawsuit, Haitians detained at the Krome Detention Center staged a protest on September 3, 1981. They threatened to destroy the detention center if they were not freed. Nearly one hundred of the detainees managed to tear down a fence and escape. However, authorities came in with tear gas, ended the protest, and recaptured the escapees.[52] After the protests, the INS spent over $900,000 to remodel the Center and reduced the number of people held there from 1,500 to 600.[53] However, this was not the end of abuses at Krome Detention Center, and stories about "voodoo sacrifices" would often appear alongside news about neglect and cruelty at the facility.

Reports about the *Jesula* (October 1981)

The first time that the *Jesula* appeared in the news was on or around October 16, 1981—almost three months after it arrived in Key West.[54] At this time, journalists reported that most of the passengers had arrived suffering from starvation, dehydration, and sun exposure, and that the passengers "who tried to interfere or object to the way the voyage was being conducted were hacked to death with machetes by the captains." However, they mentioned nothing about voodoo.[55]

This sudden interest appears to have been driven primarily by the fact that the U.S. attorney's office began investigating the captains of the *Jesula* for "atrocities suffered" by the passengers.[56] However, the news about the *Jesula* also coincided with two important developments in U.S. immigration. First, the Coast Guard had just begun patrolling the Windward Passage between Haiti and Cuba trying to intercept refugees. Second, deportation hearings had just resumed at the Krome Detention Center after a month hiatus following a judge determining that such hearings could not be held without an attorney present.[57]

On October 22, 1981, Saintil and Tacius were charged with six counts of "conspiracy to bring 200 unauthorized aliens into the United States."[58] Although "voodoo" was not initially mentioned in the Saintil and Tacius voyage, the media quickly began to emphasize this aspect of the tale as stories from passengers were made public. For example, well-known journalist and political columnist William Safire referenced these voyages in an article exploring why crime rates were so high in Florida in 1981. Safire claimed that "[t]wo Haitian boat captains, illegally running immigrants into the United States, have been accused of carving up perhaps 16 of their starving passengers with machetes and throwing bodies overboard." He never referred to Saintil, Tacius, or their boat by name; instead, Safire referred to the vessel as a "voodoo death boat."

Safire averred that you don't have to be on a "death ship" to "be touched by crime." He claimed that one in 10 people in Miami had been the victim of crime in the past year. Safire briefly suggested that a "local narcotics war," or "the emptying of Fidel Castro's jails upon the population of Florida" might be the cause of the crime increase.[59] However, he argued "another reason given is the influx of Haitians, fleeing from hunger and overcrowding at home." Safire opined that it was insufficient for the federal government to police the oceans to try to stop Haitian immigration; he believed that they should "tie aid to Haiti to its cooperation with a voluntary blockade of its coast, thereby curtailing the need for odious detention centers here and stopping terror aboard the [voodoo] 'death ships.'" In at least one newspaper, this article appeared under the title "Terrorists Try to Destroy U.S."[60]

Another catastrophic incident increased the focus on the *Jesula* as an example of the terrifying experiences of Haitian refugees in their efforts to reach U.S. soil. In late October 1981, a 30-foot sailboat carrying 67 Haitian refugees capsized off the coast of Hillsboro Beach in Florida.[61] Thirty-three of the refugees—including two pregnant women—drowned as they tried to reach land and their bodies washed up on the beach. Stories about this tragedy often included comments about the *Jesula*.

On October 27, 1981, the *Colorado Springs Gazette* discussed the *Jesula* and the *Dieu Qui Donne* cases under the title "Seeking New Life, Many Find Death."[62] The author, George Stelon, claimed that the *Jesula* voyage involved a "voodoo-practicing captain" who killed 96 people and was indicted for smuggling. Stelon recounted that in the *Dieu Qui Donne* case, the crewmen had tossed Menasse Seme overboard because they "feared he was carrying an evil spirit." Stelon also detailed other tragedies such as the Cayo Lobos incident and two incidents from 1979 and 1980 in which the bodies of Haitian women and children washed up on the shores of Dania Beach and Palm Beach.

Stelon's article appeared next to a graphic and gruesome story titled "Beach Strewn with Refugees' Corpses," which explained that the bodies of 33 drowned Haitians had washed up on Hillsboro Beach. Below these articles was a third by Robert Shaw titled "Haitian Refugees Pose Unanswered Question." Shaw argued that the newly imposed interdiction policy had little chance of stopping hundreds or even thousands of Haitians from dying each year trying to enter the United States.

Articles like this continued well into the following year. For instance, in April 1982, the *Panama City News Herald* published a story titled "Flight for New Life to Florida Has Meant Death for Many Haitians."[63] The author began by emphasizing that "more than 50,000 Haitian refugees packed into hand-hewn wooden sailboats or hidden in the holds of smuggling ships have landed on South Florida shores in recent years." However, the author stressed, for many of these refugees, the voyage had been deadly. The author listed several incidents commonly invoked as examples of the plight of the "boat people," including the *Dieu Qui Donne* (the author notes that Seme was thrown overboard because "they feared the Haitian [was] carrying an evil spirit"), the Cayo Lobos incident, the *Jesula* and its "voodoo practicing crew" who "killed as many as 96 passengers," and the 33 Haitians who drowned off the coast of Hillsboro Beach. This article was published next to a larger piece about a recent tragedy in which another 21 Haitians had drowned off the coast of Hillsboro Beach. The paper titled this article "Police Become Experts on Haitian Drownings," and featured quotes from a police sergeant and other locals who lamented that Haitian bodies washing up on the beach had become such a common sight that people continued to "frolic in the waves" and walk along the sand, unfazed by and uninterested in the deceased refugees.

Reme and Pierrot (October 1981)

Within a few weeks after the protests over Krome Detention Center and the implementation of the interdiction policy, another voyage with alleged "voodoo sacrifices" made its way toward the United States. On October 1, 1981, Fritznel Reme, Fritz Pierrot, and approximately 90 other people boarded a 30-to-40-foot wooden sailboat in Haiti, beginning a three-week journey that ended with the vessel landing at Miami Beach, Florida.[64] The passengers, who did not have visas, passports, or other documentation to gain lawful entry into the United States, were detained.

Unlike the *Jesula*, there was little delay in federal officials proceeding against Reme and Pierrot. Within weeks of the arrival of the ship, both men were indicted for attempting to smuggle refugees into the United States. Journalists quickly picked up the story, publishing interviews with the refugees who were testifying against them. Most of these stories featured titles such as "Human-Sacrifice Voodoo Deaths of Haitians Probed," "Escape Boat Voodoo Deaths Report Probed," and "Refugee Voodoo Killings Target of U.S. Probe."[65] Available witness statements leave little doubt as to why the case was characterized in this way.

During the grand jury proceedings and the trial, the passengers asserted that Pierrot forced them to sing "voodoo songs" and had them searched for "valuables and black magic."[66] The witnesses also claimed that Reme, Pierrot, and some of the other defendants had killed two of the original passengers in a "voodoo ceremony" during their voyage. The Court summarized the story offered by one witness, Clement, as follows:

> Clement described a voodoo ceremony that led to the disappearance of the two missing passengers, Luc Alliance and Luc Vixamar. Prior to the voodoo rituals the boat's progress had been hindered by lack of wind. Pierrot had ascribed this to the presence of someone on the boat who had "black magic." He threatened to throw overboard anyone with black magic. Ultimately, searches of the passengers turned up black magic on Alliance and Vixamar. After a conference between Pierrot and four of the defendants who were acquitted, the two men were ordered undressed and bathed in special water. Then, pleading for their lives, they were made to sit crosslegged facing each other. All passengers other than Pierrot, Reme, several of the other defendants, and Vixamar and Alliance were sent below deck and remained there for the night. When everyone awoke the next morning, Alliance and Vixamar were gone.[67]

Although Clement is the only witness cited in available court documents, other statements appeared in the newspaper reports about this case during the investigation and trial. Nosilieu Guerrier testified that he had pretended to be in a "voodoo trance" and proclaimed that the men who were thrown overboard were guilty of placing a hex on the boat which caused the wind to stop blowing.[68] Another passenger testified that the men were searched and discovered to have cat feces, powders, and other items that (supposedly) suggested that they were "voodoo practitioners."[69]

Eli Joseph and Wilson Alexandre provided the most detailed interviews to reporters about what happened on their voyage. Joseph was an engineer who fled Haiti with his wife and three cousins because of political persecution.[70] Alexandre was a tailor who said that he left Haiti with his wife "to escape persecution by the secret police."[71] Joseph allegedly reported that there was a man called the "executioner" on the voyage, whose name was not disclosed in the media but presumably referred to Pierrot or Reme, who beat the passengers from Port-au-Prince with "ropes, sticks, spoons and iron bars."[72] Then, Joseph reported, three days into the voyage, "two women had the *mysteres* (went into trances) and were possessed by the *loa* (voodoo gods). The loa asked for a sacrifice. So the houngan (voodoo priest) chose two victims and his bourreau (executioner) threw them overboard."[73] Joseph claimed that after the "sacrifices," "bad luck" plagued the voyage.[74] They ran out of water on the fifth day of the trip and everyone nearly died because they tried to drink sea water to stay alive. On the seventh day, they came across a boat from Nassau and the passengers shared some bread and water with them. They encountered two islands on days seven and eight; on the first, they stopped and found fresh water, but on the second, an evangelical priest gave them food and water and a map to Miami. They ran out of water again four days later, then the boat began to break apart. Joseph reported that the ship was taking on water when they finally reached Miami Beach.[75]

Both men claimed that they took up their knives and attempted to "stop a voodoo priest and his 'executioner' from sacrificing more" people after Alliance and Vixamar were thrown overboard.[76] For example, when the captain asserted that the "voodoo spirits" had led them to find water on the first island, Joseph allegedly countered, "If it were left to the spirits, we would have already died out there on the sea."[77] Additionally, Joseph maintained that when he noticed the ship beginning to break apart, he took out a bible and began to pray that they would reach the United States. He explained, "Then we saw two boats. And then we saw light in the sky, like a reflection. God was with us. We started to see Miami."[78]

Voodoo in the Courts (1982–1988)

While every chapter of this book has mentioned at least a few court cases, the only available records of these proceedings have been surviving newspaper accounts that describe them. Court records, especially in cases that are more than 50 years old and were not appealed, have rarely been preserved and archived for future research. Therefore, the prosecution of the captains of these voyages provides unique insights into whether and how public discourses about "voodoo" were reflected in court documents. In the cases against Saintil and Tacius and against Reme and Pierrot, one can see that rumors of "voodoo sacrifices" were not only an important part of public debates about Haitian immigration, but that these allegations also featured prominently in the trials and had very serious repercussions for the accused individuals.

The Indictments (July 1982)

Over the next few months, the prosecution process proceeded slowly against Saintil and Tacius (from the *Jesula*) and against Reme and Pierrot. However, in July, these cases suddenly moved in different directions and launched them back into the media. First, on July 6, 1982, a federal judge dismissed the charges against Saintil and Tacius because there had been too many delays in their trial and the judge determined that their right to a speedy trial had been violated.[79] At this time, the U.S. Attorney, Atlee Wampler, reportedly stated that he "had long heard rumors of atrocities aboard smuggler-run ships from Haiti, and had decided to go ahead with this case."[80] The reporter who interviewed Wampler succinctly explained, "Survivors of the Jesula, which ran aground in the Marquesas Islands off Key West on July 25, 1981, told chilling tales of voodoo sacrifices, forced starvings and intentional drownings."[81]

Three days later, "on July 9, 1982, a grand jury returned a 15-count indictment against Pierrot, Reme, and eight others" for bringing or attempting to bring "illegal aliens" into the United States. When the prosecutors filed the indictment against Pierrot and Reme, some journalists reflected on the dismissal in Saintil and Tacius case and claimed "federal prosecutors are appealing a judge's ruling in another Haiti-to-Miami alien smuggling case in which refugees say human sacrifices also were offered during the voyage."[82] Other newspapers reported the indictment in a story about the general conditions that Haitian immigrants were living in. For instance, one story about the Krome Detention Center often appeared next to reports about the indictment of Reme and Pierrot.[83] On June 18, 1982, Judge Eugene Spellman ordered the release of the 1,800 Haitians who were being imprisoned at camps in Texas, Puerto Rico, New York, West Virginia, Louisiana, and Kentucky, and 451 who were held at the Krome Detention Center.[84] The story marked the first time that journalists had been allowed into the Krome camp since the order, and the reporters described the refugees' frustration that three weeks after the judge's order, they had not been released.[85] The refugees claimed that several people had tried to commit suicide and indicated that the judge was concerned about the psychological and emotional impact of the continued incarceration in the refugee camp, which was overrun with mosquitos, segregated by gender, and encased in barbed wire fences.[86] This story appeared on the same page as the story about Reme and Pierrot's indictment in the *Kokomo Tribune* and right above the story in the *Galveston Daily News*.

Convictions and Appeals (December 1982–February 1985)

The prosecution's case against Reme and Pierrot was based entirely on the testimony of five of the other passengers. Most of the case consisted of proving that Reme and Pierrot were in charge of the voyage and had control over the ship. The witnesses' testimony established that Pierrot was the captain of the ship, but that he and Reme both served in leadership capacities on the voyage.[87] Both men gave orders to the passengers, and both were observed steering the ship. Reme also allegedly helped navigate and gave instructions to the other passengers about what to say if they were seized by the authorities.[88]

In December 1982, Pierrot and Reme were found guilty. Pierrot was convicted on all 15 charges of smuggling or attempting to smuggle "illegal aliens" into the United States. However, the judge issued drastically different sentences—Pierrot was sentenced to 30 years of imprisonment and Reme was sentenced to five years of imprisonment. Both were sentenced to five years on each of the 15 counts of the indictment, but the difference in sentences emerged from the judge's decision to force Pierrot to serve six of the sentences consecutively (one after another), while all of Reme's sentences were to be served concurrently (at the same time).[89] When the judge imposed the sentence, they explained that the reason for the disparity was because the evidence indicated that Pierrot was the one who actually murdered the two men "at night after the voodoo ceremony."[90] Since Pierrot could not be charged with murder for a crime committed outside of U.S. territory, the judge gave Pierrot a more severe sentence on the trafficking charges.

Pierrot appealed his conviction, arguing that the trial court should not have allowed the prosecution to introduce evidence about the alleged "voodoo rituals" that led to the disappearance or death of Vixama and Alliance.[91] Pierrot claimed that this story about voodoo biased the jury against him because of negative public perceptions and stereotypes about "voodoo." Reme contested his conviction, claiming that he was just a regular passenger and had no idea that he was part of a smuggling operation.[92]

On August 9, 1984, Reme and Pierrot's cases reached the U.S. Court of Appeals for the Eleventh Circuit, which upheld their convictions.[93] The judges determined that the evidence of the "voodoo" rituals was properly admitted to show that Pierrot and Reme were in positions of leadership on the voyage and not just regular passengers. However, because of procedural issues with the testimony about Pierrot being the one who had committed the murder, the court invalidated his sentence and sent the case back to the district court for a new sentencing hearing.[94]

Although the Eleventh Circuit found that the evidence of the "voodoo ritual" was only used to show that the defendants had control of the ship (that it was not used to bias the jury against them), the evidence suggests otherwise. The U.S. Border Patrol agent who built the case against Pierrot and Reme reported that the national average sentence in such cases was a two-year sentence, and in south Florida it was a mere 10 months. Prior to this case, the most severe sentence had been exactly half that of Pierrot—15 years.[95] According to newspaper reports, upon sentencing Pierrot to 30 years in prison, "the stiffest penalty ever handed down in the United States" for smuggling "aliens," U.S. District Judge James King said that the "alleged sacrificial killings" resulted in a "sentence [that] is more severe than it otherwise would have been."[96]

In August 1982, while the Pierrot and Reme case was being heard by the trial court, the government filed an appeal challenging the dismissal of the indictments of Saintil and Tacius. In May 1983, the Eleventh Circuit Court of Appeals determined that Saintil and Tacius's rights to a speedy trial had not been violated after all.[97] Therefore, they invalidated the decision to dismiss the indictments and allowed Saintil and Tacius to be prosecuted.

Saintil and Tacius were put on trial later that year and each was sentenced to 30 years of imprisonment—the maximum sentenced allowed for the charges against them.[98] Saintil appealed his conviction, and on February 22, 1985, the case reached the Eleventh Circuit Court of Appeals. Like Reme and Pierrot, Saintil argued that the witnesses' testimony about the beatings and deaths should not have been allowed because they biased the jury against him without providing any useful evidence about the issues in the case. In a section titled "Admission of Testimony as to the Atrocities Committed on the Ship," the Eleventh Circuit ruled that *United States v. Reme* was analogous to this case. The Court held that these "atrocities" showed that the defendants were in control of the ship.

Aftermath of the Eleventh Circuit Appeals (December 1985)

In the months following the Eleventh Circuit's confirmation of these convictions, several reporters and politicians used these cases to reflect on emerging data about policies toward Haitian refugees. For instance, in December 1985, Perry Rivkind, district director of U.S. Immigration and Naturalization Service in Miami, reported that approximately 6,087 Haitians had been deported since October 1981, when the Haitian Interdiction Program began.[99] Rivkind also reported that at least 500 people had died in the crossing.[100] To contextualize these statistics, journalists reminded readers "on Dec. 1, 1982, a federal court jury convicted two Haitians of conspiracy and alien smuggling charges related to an ocean crossing marked by voodoo ceremonies and death" when they published articles about Rivkind's comments.[101]

During that same month, a reporter named Doralisa Pilarte detailed the plight of Haitian refugees in an article that circulated through several U.S. newspapers.[102] Pilarte began with the heartbreaking story of a 29-year-old Haitian woman whose temporary work permit had recently been revoked and she did not know how she would feed her 18-month-old son. After emphasizing that thousands of Haitians, whom she described as "paupers of the Americas," were fighting to stay in the United States, Pilarte discussed Rivkind who, while sitting in "his spacious office on the 11th floor of the INS building," argued that every nation had a right to defend its borders. Pilarte claimed that Haitian refugees had survived smugglers throwing children overboard from their "rickety, overcrowded boats." Furthermore, after emphasizing that the U.S. Coast Guard had sent over 6,000 people back to Haiti, Pilarte explained that the hazardous trip from Haiti to south Florida had killed at least 500 people, including those 90 who died in "an ocean crossing marked by voodoo ceremonies and death" (speaking of the Saintil and Tacius case). Pilarte also mentioned that the bodies of 33 Haitians washed up on Hillsboro Beach in October 1981, as well as a more recent incident from August 1985, when smugglers threw up to 100 refugees overboard in rough waters.[103]

The Final Appeals (1988)

Three years later, in 1988, these "voodoo" cases would have their final hearing in U.S. courts. For reasons that were not made clear in the available proceedings, a psychologist was hired to evaluate Pierrot's mental health and provide a report to the district court. Pierrot's defense team hired their own mental health professional—a psychiatrist—to perform a second evaluation. Both reached the same conclusion—that Pierrot was schizophrenic and needed treatment.[104] Accordingly, the district court issued a commitment order, sending Pierrot to a federal correctional institution–for psychiatric treatment. Pierrot appealed this order, arguing that cultural differences and problems with language and communication led to a flawed assessment. However, the Fourth Circuit Court of Appeal affirmed the district court's order.

This final hearing highlights the paradox of these allegations. Similar to how the cases of Robert Harris and Vernon McQueen flooded the 1930s with claims about the Nation of Islam practicing "voodoo sacrifices," the *Jesula* case and the Pierrot/Reme case caused the public to fixate on supposed "sacrifices at sea" among Haitian refugees. However, like Robert Harris, one of the main perpetrators of these "voodoo sacrifices" was determined to be suffering from severe mental illness. This reinforces the ease with which the alleged actions of one mentally unstable person could be conflated with an entire race or population.

Conclusion

In recent years, claims about "voodoo" have continued to play a role in discussions about Haitian immigration to the United States, but the tone of these conversations has changed. In the wake of the devastating 2010 earthquake in Haiti (discussed in the Introduction), Pat Robertson famously attributed the earthquake to Haitians making a "pact with the devil" that if he would assist them in earning their freedom from France, they would serve him. Robertson's heartless comments earned him substantial criticism from Christians and non-Christians alike; however, his remarks were similar to a broader series of discussions at the time about whether Haitian immigrants should be permitted to come to or remain in the United States following the earthquake and other natural disasters. Numerous organizations and individuals opposed any leniency, blaming "voodoo" practitioners and "devil-worshippers" for the disasters that have befallen Haiti, and expressing concern that allowing more Haitians into the country would bring more "voodoo" into the United States.

Three short days after the earthquake, Americans for Legal Immigration PAC published an article titled "South Florida Schools Prepare for Haitian Influx," discussing President Obama's policy to permit Haitian children orphaned by the earthquake to enroll in South Florida schools.[105] A person with the handle "swatchick" commented in opposition to this policy, "People in South Florida do not want anymore [sic] of them. Between not speaking English and voodoo it is a problem. The police departments actually get calls by people wanting a police report because someone else threatened them or have placed a voodoo curse on them. They used to call about how to deal with voodoo curses. Many teenagers are in gangs and/or out robbing people which mostly consist of their own."[106]

In September 2016, approximately one month before Hurricane Matthew would make landfall in Haiti as a Category 4 storm, the U.S. Department of Homeland Security announced that it would end preferential treatment to Haitians who had recently arrived in the United States but did not fall under temporary protected status.[107] Reporters claimed that this policy came in advance of an expected influx of 7,000 Haitians attempting to enter the United States by traveling through Mexico and crossing the border into Southern California. Bill Wisniewski, who claimed to be a writer at the U.S. Department of Veterans Affairs, opposed this new influx of Haitians, stating that San Diego was already suffering from a severe housing shortage that left refugees sleeping on the sidewalk. He added, "WE DON'T NEED NONE DAT [sic] HAITIAN VOODOO! NEITHER! NO-HOW!"[108]

Following Hurricane Matthew, U.S. newspapers published numerous articles about the effects of this powerful hurricane on Haiti, Cuba, and the Dominican Republic. The Charisma News identified the hurricane as "the worst humanitarian crisis to hit Haiti since a devastating 2010 earthquake," which was magnified by the fact that many people still resided in makeshift shelters.[109] Mark Romine Ministries made the first of four comments on the article, callously responding, "Haiti's national religion is effectively Voodoo. Maybe they should change religions." A user known as Paul M. asked Mark Romine Ministries about the difference between life in Haiti and the "other half of the island," to which Romine replied, "I think that it's much better in the Dominion [sic] Republic who are basically Catholic."[110]

Similarly, after Hurricane Matthew bypassed Florida and struck the Carolinas, Jackie Littleford of Winter Park, Florida, sent the following letter to the editor of the *Orlando Sentinel*, "Just a comment on Hurricane Matthew not being as destructive for us as we feared it might be: Thousands of believers in Central Florida, and our families and friends around the world, were praying that God would move the storm out to sea and protect us, which he did—first 20 miles out into the ocean and then another 5 miles out. (Thank you, Lord!) I'm very sorry for the people of Haiti (and my church has sent offerings to help them rebuild), but maybe their voodoo gods are powerless."[111] Like Pat Robertson, Littleford received some criticism of her editorial, with Tom Holt of Orlando sarcastically remarking that "the people of North and South Carolina must worship voodoo gods too since portions of their states were also devastated by Matthew, and several people died there," and suggesting that Littleford "become more educated about Haiti, where 90 percent of the population is Christian."[112] Similarly, Jeff Dolan pointed out that North Carolina suffered an estimated 1.5 billion dollars in damage, and suggested that "[m]aybe, just maybe, hurricanes move based on weather patterns with no 'assist' from any powerful deities."[113]

These examples show several changes to the commentary about the supposed relationship between "voodoo" and immigration. In recent years, it is rarer for journalists themselves to characterize "voodoo" as something that Haitians need to be saved from or to include stories about "voodoo" in sympathetic pieces about the status of Haitian immigrants. Instead, readers are offering their own comments and editorials about how "voodoo" is the cause of Haitian woes and that they shouldn't be granted asylum. However, the next chapter shows that claims about "voodoo" rituals are still used to garner sympathy for immigrants in other parts of the world in the way that they were for Haitians in the 1980s.

6
Sex Trafficking and Sacred Oaths in the 1990s to the Present

Over the past few decades, human trafficking networks have transported thousands of West African women and girls to Spain, Italy, the Netherlands, and other parts of Europe.[1] The organizers of some smuggling rings have administered ritual oaths to bind these women to their traffickers before they leave for Europe and to convince them that they will die a painful death if they abandon their service before repaying their debt. Once the women arrive in Europe, the madams who oversee their work as prostitutes reinforce these oaths with threats of spiritual retribution.

Scholars, police officers, and human rights experts have begun to refer to these rituals as "voodoo oaths," even though they have no connection to New Orleans Voodoo, Haitian Vodou, or West African Vodun. This chapter explores this most recent evolution of the term "voodoo" which, like its use in the first half of the twentieth century, suggests that African spiritual practices are used in the sexual exploitation of women and girls. Furthermore, like its application to Haitian refugees in the 1980s, these allegations of "voodoo" are deeply connected to investigations of the conditions of Black immigrants. Stories about these "voodoo oaths" seem designed to demonize the traffickers (as earlier accounts did with the Haitian boat captains) and portray these West African women as victims who have suffered a perilous journey to arrive in Europe.

Despite the familiar aspects of alleged "voodoo" practices among West African immigrants in Europe, this chapter represents a departure from the others in this book in at least one significant way. It is the only chapter where the practices categorized as "voodoo" are actual spiritual rites in Black communities. Therefore, in addition to examining the characterization of these rituals as "voodoo," this chapter also problematizes this terminology by exploring the possible origins of these rituals and the positive uses of similar sacred oaths in African societies.

The Sex Trafficking Cases

Human trafficking is defined as "the recruitment, transportation, transfer, harbouring or receipt of persons," through the "threat or use of force or other forms of coercion, of abduction, of fraud, of deception, of the abuse of power or of a position of vulnerability or of the giving or receiving of payments or benefits to achieve the consent of a person having control over another person, for the purpose of exploitation."[2] Except for Eastern Europeans, "the number of Nigerian victims of human trafficking for sexual exploitation is among the highest of any ethnicity in Western Europe."[3] For example, in 2002, two organizations reported to the Working Group on Contemporary Forms of Slavery that there were more than 30,000 Nigerian girls and women ranging between 15 and 25 years of age who were "currently victims of prostitution in Italy."[4] Specifically, around the turn of the twenty-first century, Nigerian women represented a large percentage of the sex workers in Palermo, the capital of Sicily, and nearly all those who worked in street prostitution.[5] Similarly, Nigerians represented slightly more than 10% of the more than fourteen thousand "potential trafficked victims" whose nationality was known in the United Kingdom between April 2009 and December 2016.[6]

For Nigerians, most of these journeys begin with the women and the traffickers forming a contract whereby the traffickers agree to arrange documentation and transportation to Europe in exchange for a fee and, in some cases, to assist the women with finding employment once they arrive in Europe.[7] In many circumstances, the women repay their debt by working as prostitutes under the traffickers' close and coercive supervision.[8] Madams who work with the traffickers oversee the women's work, taking a portion of their earnings for the woman's expenses and applying the rest toward her debt. Some women are unaware that they will be working as prostitutes before they leave for Europe; those who are aware are still often surprised by the difficult conditions they are subjected to when they arrive.[9]

The average debt that each woman incurs varies substantially from person to person and country to country; however, in every case, the sum appears to be substantial. For instance, Jeffrey Cole reports that around the turn of the twenty-first century in Palermo, Sicily, the original debt averaged between US$40,000 and US$50,000.[10] Around a decade later, in 2009, sources report a slightly higher sum, 50,000 euros (~US$56,800), for the average Nigerian woman's transportation to Spain.[11] However, one report from 2012 indicated that women trafficked from Nigeria to Italy had been forced to pay as much as US$91,000.[12] These hefty initial sums could be increased as the madams continually added to the debt, charging for lodging, food, "insubordination or late payment," or other expenses.[13]

In 2008, the Nigerian National Agency for Prohibition of Traffic in Persons declared that 90 percent of the women and children who had been trafficked from Nigeria to Europe had visited sacred shrines before their departure.[14] Trafficking victims report that when they went to these shrines, they took sacred oaths and performed spiritual rituals to bind them to their traffickers or madams, creating an added level of assurance that they would repay their debt and would not divulge the identities of the traffickers or the processes they used to transport them to Europe.[15] The details of these rituals vary widely. Several sources reported that the women were asked to consume the raw heart of a chicken and/or the raw body parts of a chicken or to drink chicken blood.[16] Some claimed that they were asked to climb in a coffin or to drink water that had been used to wash the body of a deceased person.[17] Others alleged that the women would be asked to bathe with a bloody cloth.[18] The priest would then make small incisions on the woman's body and rub medicines into them.[19] Some women also reported that there were animals sacrificed at the shrines to ensure their safety in travel.[20]

After the rituals, the priests of the shrine frequently keep nail clippings, hair (head, armpit, or pubic), and blood (sometimes menstrual) from the woman to reinforce the ritual if the woman fails to keep her contract.[21] They add other "signifiers embodying personal and spiritual power, beauty and sex appeal, protection and success" to packets containing the woman's "body-related material."[22] For instance, "pieces of twisted metal refer to the power of Ogun, soap and powder enhance beauty and sexual 'power,' the kola nut is an exchange of faithfulness between lovers, and so forth."[23] The priests warn the women that these substances would allow them to locate and kill the women if they escape.[24]

After the women arrive in Europe, the madams remind them of these oaths and packets to threaten them into compliance. Some of the madams also "re-enact the oaths" or do other rituals with the women in Europe.[25] According to police detectives and others who interviewed trafficking victims, the women believe that madness, illness, fertility problems, death, or other tragedies would result from breaking the oath.[26]

Literature Review

This question of "voodoo oaths" caught my attention through an abundance of online news articles on their use in human trafficking. For example, in 2009, the *Telegraph* reported the following on the arrest of several members of a trafficking group, "Police said the ring carried out 'voodoo rituals' and black magic to frighten the women and keep them always under control with the threat of 'destroying their souls' or 'making them crazy.'"[27] Similarly, a 2012 *Newsbank* article titled "Italian Police Break Up Prostitution Ring," indicated that traffickers "applied physical and psychological torture to their victims that included voodoo rituals."[28] That same year, the Interior Ministry in Spain told reporters that they had arrested seventeen smugglers who had forced Nigerian women into prostitution "using threats including claims they would cast Voodoo spells on them if they didn't comply."[29] Sixteen of the smugglers were from Nigeria and the other was from Uganda.[30] In 2015, Emma Anderson of the *Local* reported that trafficked women in Spain are subjected to "juju voodoo rituals" that "guarantee that the women complied with everything they demanded, under threat of death to them and their families."[31]

Since the late 1990s, international human rights experts have also expressed concern about the use of "voodoo" in their reports on human trafficking. For instance, in 1999, the Report of the Special Rapporteur on the sale of children, child prostitution, and child pornography, Ms. Ofelia Calcetas-Santos, on her mission to Belgium and the Netherlands, stated, "Many women and girls who arrive in Belgium from West Africa are victims of trafficking networks, which may use fear of voodoo to put pressure on them to cooperate."[32] Three years later, in 2002, the chairperson of the Working Group on Contemporary Forms of Slavery reported that two organizations who worked with Nigerian girls trafficked to Italy asserted that girls were "forced to become prostitutes and controlled through fear, by use of traditional rituals such as voodoo and threats of reprisals against their families back in their home countries."[33]

Later, these references would become much more common. In October 2013, Ana Dols Garcia published a research paper for the UN High Commissioner for Refugees titled "Voodoo, Witchcraft and Human Trafficking in Europe" in which Garcia purports to examine "the misuse of voodoo to enslave women for sexual purposes."[34] On April 1, 2014, Joy Ezeilo, the Special Rapporteur on trafficking in persons, wrote the following about her mission to Italy: "Victims are also psychologically and spiritually coerced through voodoo oaths which make it difficult for them to denounce or give away the madams, even when they are approached by social workers or the police."[35] Also in 2014, the Office to Monitor and Combat Trafficking in Persons at the U.S. Department of State claimed, "Nigerian traffickers rely on threats of voodoo curses to control Nigerian victims and force them into situations of prostitution or labor."[36]

Since at least the early 2000s, scholars have also been writing extensively about these oaths, emphasizing the role of "juju," "witchcraft," and "voodoo" in the trafficking of West African, especially Nigerian women. The first of these articles appears to have been "'Voodoo' on the Doorstep: Young Nigerian Prostitutes and Magic Policing in the Netherlands," by Rijk van Dijk, published in *Africa: Journal of the International African Institute* in 2001. As the title suggests, Van Dijk discussed the growing awareness of the widespread problem of underage Nigerian girls who were arriving unaccompanied in the Netherlands, applying for asylum, and then swiftly disappearing. When authorities later found them working in brothels, the girls described "certain religious rituals that had taken place before they left Nigeria and which they were forced to go through after arrival in the Netherlands."[37]

Van Dijk provides the most cited explanation of how "voodoo" became the way to describe these rituals, writing, "Almost immediately the term 'voodoo' was coined as a way of referring to the anxieties of supernatural origin the police recorded, the rituals that had supposedly taken place in relation to the girls' travel and the packets that one way or another seemed to keep them in bondage to their work as prostitutes."[38] Van Dijk explains that "voodoo" signified "a kind of 'inauthentic' ritual, not performed on the girls' behalf, not with their own but solely with the operators' commercial interests in mind, and not performed by ritual specialists who would want to safeguard their public status and prestige. 'Voodoo' became synonymous with spiritual entrapment and with being policed through occult means by their madams and pimps in every move they made."[39] Not certain about adopting this language, Van Dijk uses the term "voodoo" in quotes throughout the text.

In recent years, countless other articles have discussed the role of West African rituals in solidifying the relationship between human traffickers and their victims. For instance, in 2016, C. S. Baarda wrote an article titled "Human Trafficking for Sexual Exploitation from Nigeria into Western Europe: The Role of Voodoo Rituals in the Functioning of a Criminal Network," for the *European Journal of Criminology*. That same year, legal scholars Luz Nagle and Bolaji Owasanoye published an article titled "Fearing the Dark: The Use of Witchcraft to Control Human Trafficking Victims and Sustain Vulnerability" in the *Southwestern Law Review*, and May Ikeora published "The Role of African Traditional Religion and 'Juju' in Human Trafficking: Implications for Anti-trafficking," in the *Journal of International Women's Studies*. The following year, in 2017, Marcel van der Watt and Beatri Kruger published an article titled "Exploring 'Juju' and Human Trafficking: Towards a Demystified Perspective and Response" in the *South African Review of Sociology*.

Some of these scholars expand upon Van Dijk's explanations of the reasons for the use of the term "voodoo." For instance, Jeffrey Cole (talking about Palermo, Italy, at the turn of the twenty-first century) asserts that "social workers, scholars and police investigators" as well as "some women" use the term "voodoo."[40] However, "[t]he women themselves tend also to refer to the 'sacred oath,' as do some observers."[41] In an article about Nigerian women who had been trafficked to Italy, Simona Taliani argues that the term "voodoo" is used constantly in complaints that the women have filed with police. However, Taliani explains that "the girls use it with the intention of making clear to the Europeans what they are talking about. It is their way of talking with whites about certain 'things.' The most adventurous among them even say, 'Voodoo is a word that you use, not us.' "[42] Taliani argues that the term "voodoo" is a product of "the processes of comprehension, decoding and translation" that happens when the trafficked women are trying to explain their circumstances to the authorities in Europe. May Ikeora agrees, reasoning that descriptions of these oaths, in which people often use phrases like "black magic," are "tantamount to a projection of negative attributes and stereotypes onto magic" and "can be linked with the Western construction and imagination of blackness."[43] Ikeora begrudgingly uses the term "juju" in their paper "for the purpose of popular nomenclature and clarity of argument," but refers to "juju/voodoo" as "an unjustified reference to the discourse of human trafficking, being that 'traditional oath-taking' is truly the main method utilised."[44] Ikeora explains that "juju" (and presumably other terms like it) perpetuates the stereotype that there is nothing good or valuable in African indigenous/traditional religions.[45] "Ikeora argues, "we should begin to move away from the current nomenclature of ascribing all oath-taking in ATR [African Traditional Religions] as Juju/Voodoo, especially in the context of human trafficking."[46]

Unfortunately, other scholars are frequently applying language such as "voodoo" and "witchcraft" as if they are synonymous with one another and without problematizing the use of these terms. For instance, in 2008, Farrah Bokhari published an article about children trafficked into the United Kingdom, many of whom originated from West Africa, especially Nigeria.[47] Bokhari used the words "voodoo" and "witchcraft" interchangeably, averring that some children are "controlled through the use of culturally specific rituals such as voodoo (witchcraft), combined with threats to their person and their family."[48] Similarly, C. S. Baarda contends that "in the context of Nigerian human trafficking," the term "voodoo" is used to "refer to a variation on ancient West African religious traditions"[49] and that "Voodoo or juju is a form of witchcraft in Nigeria existing alongside Christian or Islamic belief."[50] Nagle and Owasanoye take this even further in their 2016 article, arguing that "witchcraft," "voodoo," "hoodoo," and "juju" are synonymous terms.[51]

Some of these scholarly publications perpetuate even more harmful prejudices and misinterpretations, incorrectly denouncing well-recognized spirits, entities, deities, and religions as "voodoo," "witchcraft," and satanic/evil practices. For instance, several sources indicate that some women may have performed oaths or other rituals to bind them to their traffickers in front of effigies or shrines for Eshu, an orisha (an entity or deity) honored in Nigerian Yoruba religion as well as in diasporic traditions such as Cuban Santería and Brazilian Candomblé. Marcel van der Watt and Beatri Kruger describe this orisha as "the evil god Eshu."[52]

Eshu (Exu in Brazil) is considered the divine messenger who facilitates communications between humans and the rest of the orishas. Prayers and rituals honoring him are typically performed at the opening of religious ceremonies; therefore, in regions where Eshu is venerated, it is plausible that he is indeed invoked before the sacred oaths used in human trafficking. However, Eshu is not an "evil god" and, assuming that he indeed plays a role in trafficking rituals, he is honored by millions of adepts of West African and African diaspora religions for religious purposes that have nothing to do with human trafficking or other criminal enterprises.[53]

Likely because of these prejudicial perceptions that African religions are composed entirely of evil practices, some of the more recent scholarship has called for the suppression of these rituals. For instance, legal scholars Nagle and Owasanoye argue that "witchcraft practices, especially if used to further a criminal enterprise, violate human rights standards and should fall outside the scope of freedom of religion under the law."[54] They contend that freedom of religion must be subservient to the obligation to protect the women against vulnerability and coercion.[55]

In all of the scholarly and human rights publications and in the media, the focus has been on the gravity of the problem of human trafficking from West Africa to Western Europe, the spectrum of abuses suffered by women and girls before and after their arrival in Europe, and proving that "voodoo" rituals play a role in the process. By emphasizing the issue of human trafficking, these reports and articles have ripped these oaths from their cultural context. By using sensationalized terminology such as "voodoo," "juju," and "witchcraft," they have also cultivated images of practices that resemble something from a horror film.

Most of the people who have written about these human trafficking rituals seem to have little knowledge of the history and importance of these shrines and oath-taking practices. Some have even questioned whether these "voodoo shrines" "originate[d] because of human trafficking."[56] On the contrary, as the following sections explore, these oaths have a long history in West African societies and have often been used for the benefit of the oath-taker and the broader community.

The Ayelala Shrine and the Origins of "Voodoo Oaths"

Based upon the superficial assessments that scholars and human rights officials have published about "voodoo oaths," it is impossible to identify their origins with certainty. However, the information provided about the origins and beliefs of the trafficked girls and women indicate that many of them swore oaths and underwent spiritual rituals in the Edo State of Nigeria. For instance, in 2014, the Special Rapporteur on Trafficking in Persons reported that "[v]ictims from the Edo State in Nigeria, particularly from Benin City, constitute a large proportion of the persons trafficked for sexual exploitation" in Italy.[57] Similarly, a report from the International Organization for Migration indicated that 18,125 of the 119,000 migrants who arrived in Italy in 2017 were Nigerian. More than 5,400 of the Nigerian migrants were women, approximately 80% of whom "were potential victims of trafficking, and that 94 percent were from Edo State."[58]

Scholarly publications point to same region as the source of many trafficking victims. In 2001, Rijk Van Dijk argued that in the case of women and girls arriving in the Netherlands, it was common that they came from the Edo region of Nigeria and had been living in Benin City prior to their departure for Europe. They reported visiting shrines there to make an agreement with their operators and allow them to assemble the package containing their human material.[59] In 2012, another article about the use of "fetishes" in the trafficking of Nigerian women in Italy cites several examples of women who had been raised in Benin City.[60] Similarly, C. S. Baarda explains that it is common for the victims of traffickers to "refer to an elaborate voodoo justice system set against the backdrop of ancient shrines situated in the Edo region of Nigeria."[61] Specifically, Baarda provides an example of a woman who was working as a prostitute in Italy who called home to her family in Nigeria and spoke to them about going before the Ayelala shrine, which Baarda refers to as a "voodoo temple in Benin City."[62]

Ayelala is one of the largest and best-known shrines in Edo State. It has a long and complex history. Legend says that the Ayelala shrine was established as the result of a war between the cities of Ilaje and Ijaw. The conflict began because an Ilaje man committed adultery with the wife of a high chief and then ran away to Ijaw, where he was granted asylum. Angered that the Ilaje adulterer had found sanctuary in Ijaw and could not be punished for his crimes against the high chief, Ilaje authorities executed an enslaved woman from Ijaw in his stead. The woman became known as Ayelala because she said this word while she was being executed. It means "the world is incomprehensible."[63]

Before Ayelala was executed, the Ilaje and Ijaw people reached "a covenant of reconciliation."[64] Ayelala is said to have vowed "to witness to and punish non-compliance to the terms of the covenant and all future covenants to be reached in her name."[65] After her death, some of the people who made the covenant did not abide by it and they died. Over time, "Ayelala became popular as a deity who dispenses justice and protects morality."[66]

As a deity, Ayelala is known to punish a wide range of crimes, such as lying, fighting, theft, and murder. If someone has been robbed, for example, they could go before the shrine and ask Ayelala to punish the thief. Ayelala would possess the robber and lead them to the shrine to confess.[67] A shrine to Ayelala can also be placed on someone's property (i.e., a farm) and thieves who attack the property would be struck with mumps until they confess and make retribution.[68] Most significantly for this chapter, "Ayelala can be invoked to sanction an oath made between two parties. Oath taking in the traditional sense is a condition where total loyalty or adherence[] to certain agreement and conditionality is prescribed and administered in the beneficiaries of the agreement, and the exercise is usually fetish. Anyone who has taken such oath will not escape the punishment or sanction of a particular supernatural force or deity if the oath is broken. Oath taking is usually done at the Ayelala's shrine."[69]

Itohan Mercy Idumwonyia and Solomon Ijeweimen Ikhidero argue that shrines like Ayelala are a central part of both traditional religion and the traditional justice system in Benin (Nigeria) because "[t]he power to discern and punish evildoers is one of the incontestable attributes of God in Benin traditional religion."[70] They explain:

> each of the traditional courts has an "Ogua-Edion" (ancestral shrine) where the people meet to dispense justice. The divine forces to this end are believed to be present as witnesses to proceedings of justice administration. The consciousness of the presence of these unseen forces induces the jury to try as much as possible to be fair in their cross-examination; otherwise the jury, like the offender, will be punished. Where the truth is in doubt, recourse is usually taken to oath and ordeals. The belief is that, after taking an oath, any of the parties that have given false information will earn divine wrath.[71]

In contrast to scholars of human trafficking who condemn sacred oath-taking practices, numerous Nigerian scholars have written in favor of reintroducing shrines like the Ayelala into the state's judicial processes. In 2009, religious and legal studies scholar Akhilomen Don observed that Nigerians have grown concerned about the judicial process, with problems of corruption, high costs, lengthy litigation, and so on. He argued that "the citizens of Nigeria seem to have lost confidence in the ability of the police to prevent and detect crime." Don claimed "unlike the police, the use of Ayelala has proven to be very efficient"[72] and that when people consult the shrine, the decision is swift (within one week) and is regarded as fair. He gives the example of two major markets that caught fire in Benin City in 2005. Looters used the opportunity to steal from shops that had been damaged by the fire as well as to break into those that had not. However, the day after the fire, a well-respected chief invited the high priest of the Ayelala shrine to Benin City. The priest "consequently issued a public warning that as many as have taken away goods which do not belong to them should return same immediately or face the wrath of Ayelala. The following morning, goods earlier carted away resurfaced in the market."[73]

Don argued that Edo State would benefit from greater recognition of the invocation of Ayelala as a formal part of the legal system. He denounced Nigeria's heavy reliance on colonial legal structures such as the police and courts and argued that the best idea would be to incorporate indigenous practices that align with the "beliefs and peculiar circumstances" of the people of Edo State. He recommended the reform of the police and judiciary, and suggested that one method of restructuring could be to request judges and law enforcement to "swear an oath administered by the priest of Ayelala," with the premise that "fear of the wrath of the goddess would deter them from such ignoble acts."[74]

Like Don, Idumwonyia and Ikhidero point out many limitations of the British legal system that was imposed during the colonial era. They contend that the British system is costly and slow, whereas the traditional justice systems are quick and cheap.[75] They further argue that the British legal system is limited because it only takes physical evidence into account. However, the people of Benin believe that deities and God can identify and punish criminals even when human beings do not know them.[76] Additionally, in the Western legal system, an accused "may jump bail, resist arrest or manipulate justice," but deities such as Ayelala will not let them escape.[77] For all these reasons, Idumwonyia and Ikhidero contend that traditional shrines are increasing in popularity once again in the postcolonial era.[78] Idumwonyia and Ikhidero also propose a merging of the English and tradition Benin justice systems, such as the invocation of spirits or deities in the English system. If witnesses or judges are asked to take traditional oaths to swear to be truthful or impartial, then this could reduce false testimony and corruption.[79]

In 2013, sociologist Matthias Olufemi Dada Ojo conducted a survey to determine whether the Ayelala could be incorporated into the Nigerian criminal justice system to combat corruption. The responses to the survey seem to support Idumwonyia and Ikhidero's observations about favorable public views of the shrine. For instance, 100 percent of respondents at least "somehow agreed" that Ayelala was really feared by people, and the vast majority agreed that they viewed the deity as very powerful.[80] Only 6% of people responded that they did not believe Ayelala to be efficient in punishing crime when invoked. The rest of respondents at least "somehow agreed" that Ayelala was efficient and efficacious at punishing crime.[81] By contrast, most people whom Ojo interviewed regarded the administration of justice by police or courts as very poor, poor, or fair. Ojo concludes that Ayelala should be incorporated into the Nigerian criminal justice system to reduce corruption and ensure justice. Like Don and Oronsaye, Ojo suggests that part of the problem with the criminal justice system in Nigeria is that it is a colonial system "which is totally alien to the cultures of the people of Nigeria."[82]

As for the problem of Edo State shrines and human trafficking, May Ikeora explains that some shrine priests are unaware that the oaths are being used this way and argues that there should be more efforts to raise awareness among shrine priests about this problem and to mobilize them to help identify and apprehend traffickers.[83] For those who are aware, the authorities could make targeted plans to arrest individuals who solicit and perform such specific oaths, while preserving the larger spiritual practices and shrines that likely serve other ritual functions in society at present and will continue to morph in the future. In fact, in 2013, Ikeora points out, "The Edo state Criminal Code (section 233(a)) in Nigeria was amended to include the criminalisation of the administration of any form of oath performed by a woman or girl to travel out of Nigeria for the purpose of prostitution."[84]

Furthermore, there is some evidence to suggest that these oaths and the shrines where they are performed can become powerful tools to combat human trafficking. Where priests were unaware of the purpose of the oath when it was administered, perhaps they would be willing to testify against the traffickers once they have been informed of the illicit purposes for which their shrine and deity were invoked. They could affirm the identity of the persons who came before them for the oath—proving the connection between the trafficker and the victim where other evidence might be unavailable. In cases where they are aware of the purpose of the oaths that they administered, the priests could be pressured into offering evidence by threatening them with prosecution as accomplices to human trafficking or with violations of laws such as that recently passed in Edo State. In such situations, the evidence offered by the priests could lend credibility to a victim's testimony or might even replace the victim's testimony if she is too afraid to confront the traffickers. Ikeora cites two examples where the priests who administered the oath were used in exactly this way. In both cases, the victims refused to testify, but the statements offered by the priests helped secure a conviction.[85]

Sacred Oaths in African Communities

Although the available evidence suggests that most, if not all, of the oaths administered to trafficked women took place at traditional shrines like those in the Edo region of Nigeria, sacred oaths have been used for centuries in many different communities of African descent in the Americas and West Africa. In these oaths, one can see some of the same beliefs and intended outcomes as the trafficking oaths—consumption of ritual substances, promises of fidelity and secrecy, and the belief that betraying the oath will result in physical pain or death. However, sacred oaths and other binding rituals have often been used to protect and uplift, including to help fight against enslavement and colonization.

Oaths and Rebellion in the Atlantic World

First and foremost, Africans enslaved in British colonies in the Americas employed sacred oaths as a part of preparations for insurrections from the early eighteenth century to the mid-nineteenth century. The widespread use of sacred oaths in anti-slavery and anti-colonial rebellions reminds us of the versatility of oaths in African societies over the centuries. From the eighteenth century to the twentieth, imbibed oaths were a mechanism to unite people of African descent and protect them from colonial authorities in their fight against oppression. Yet even these community-centered and liberatory oaths were proscribed because they were used in struggles that were deemed illegitimate at the time.

For example, enslaved persons took a sacred oath, allegedly sealed by drinking one another's blood, as they gathered to plan a rebellion in New York in January 1712.[86] They carried out the rebellion three months later, on April 7, 1712. The rebels armed themselves and set fire to a building, killing some of the whites who arrived to put out the fire. In the middle of the commotion, they tried to escape and flee to the north. However, the New York militia captured twenty-seven of the insurgents and executed most of them. Decades later, in 1741, another group of enslaved people in New York planned to start an uprising by burning the city and killing all the residents. One scholar argues that the insurgents swore "war oaths 'by thunder and lightning' "[87] and another asserts that they affirmed the oath by drinking a mixture made primarily of rum.[88] They also employed a ritual specialist to prepare poisons for them to take in case the rebellion failed.

In addition to these early accounts of sacred oaths in North America, countless others reportedly occurred in the Caribbean. One of the earliest examples of such oath-taking was in Antigua in 1736.[89] A group of enslaved persons planned to start a rebellion on October 11, while the colonists were hosting a ball to celebrate the anniversary of the coronation of Britain's King George II.[90] During their preparations, they took an oath of fidelity to one another and promised to carry out a plan to kill all the white people in the colony.[91] They affirmed these oaths by drinking a mixture composed of liquor, grave dirt, and chicken's blood.[92] Unfortunately for the rebels, the ball was delayed until the end of the month and the conspiracy was uncovered before the uprising actually began.[93]

Enslaved insurgents in nearby St. Croix took a similar oath in 1759. Two of the rebels cut their fingers and created a mixture of their blood, water, and grave dirt. The participants swore that they would not disclose the plans for the rebellion. To seal the oath, they drank the mixture.[94]

Only one year later, in 1760, the most famous sacred oath in the history of the British Caribbean reportedly occurred in Jamaica prior to a major uprising known as Tacky's rebellion. This revolt began in April 1760 and lasted for approximately a year and a half, until October 1761.[95] It is likely that more than one thousand insurgents participated in the rebellion. Before it was over, around sixty white people died and hundreds of rebels were killed in battle, had committed suicide, or were executed.[96]

In preparation for the rebellion, ritual specialists known as "Obeah practitioners" administered an oath, which was sealed by drinking a mixture of blood, rum, and grave dirt. Obeah practitioners also provided charms or rubbed a powder over the rebels' bodies to protect them from bullets.[97] Years later, Edward Long, a British colonial administrator and plantation owner, described the Obeah practitioners as "chief in counseling and instigating the credulous herd."[98]

The first legislation against Obeah in the British Caribbean was passed because of Tacky's rebellion.[99] The drafters asserted that the priests who had administered these oaths and ritual protections had "influence over the minds of their fellow slaves"[100] and that because of their influence, "many and Great Dangers have arisen destructive of the Peace and Welfare of this Island."[101] Among other things, the Obeah Act prohibited the possession of grave dirt, rum, and blood—the three items that had been used to administer the oaths in Tacky's rebellion and other insurrections.[102] Many British colonies in the Caribbean implemented similar laws banning Obeah in the following decades, often including these statutes in provisions designed to suppress slave rebellions. The practice of Obeah was often punishable with public whipping, transportation (banishment), or execution.

Despite these prohibitions on "Obeah oaths," the first major planned insurrection in Jamaica in the nineteenth century used methods and ritual ingredients similar to those employed in earlier oaths. Two days before Christmas in 1824, dozens of people gathered at the house of James Thompson.[103] A man referred to as "Obeah Jack" created a mixture of rum, gun powder, blood from one of the rebels, and dirt that a white man had stepped on.[104] Another insurgent, Henry Oliver, gave each person a cup of the mixture and asked them to swear that they would be faithful to one another and stand together in battle.[105] Jack told the rebels that the effects of the oath would kill that person in three days if they failed to keep the rebellion a secret.[106]

Jack also administered other ritual protections. He rubbed the faces of each participant with a wild sage bush and told them that it would make them strong—able to catch a bullet in their hands.[107] He also killed a chicken, boiled it, and then rubbed the participants' faces with the water from the pot.[108] Jack asserted that this would prevent white people from "seeing" them.[109] According to other insurgents, Jack also planned to bury a small coffin with white men's hair in the road on the day of the rebellion. This coffin was a ritual object that he claimed would cause a white person to break their neck if they passed over it.[110]

Jack and his co-conspirators were prosecuted for rebellion, conspiracy, and imagining the death of white people. Jack was also charged with practicing Obeah, possessing instruments of Obeah, administering unlawful oaths, and otherwise "pretending to have supernatural powers."[111] Jack was convicted and sentenced to death.[112] Sacred oaths continued to feature in every major Jamaican rebellion until at least the end of the nineteenth century.

More than a hundred years later, Africans on the continent also employed sacred oaths in their efforts to free themselves of oppressive colonial rule. The best-known example is the Mau Mau rebellion against the colonial government of Kenya. This guerrilla insurgency posed a serious threat to colonial authorities, forcing them to declare a state of emergency in Kenya that lasted most of the 1950s, with the height of the conflict taking place between 1952 and 1959.[113] Although historians have been unable to uncover the details about the process or terms, it is widely known that the Mau Mau administered oaths to their followers.[114] Like their counterparts in the eighteenth- and nineteenth-century Caribbean, colonial officials described the Mau Mau rebellion as coercive and claimed that they used oaths to force others to participate in the rebellion by playing off their "superstitions."[115]

Ironically, to neutralize the influence of these oaths, the colonial government hired "witchdoctors" to administer a counter-oath that would release the oath-taker of his or her commitment to the rebellion.[116]

In addition to administering counter-oaths to contain the Mau Mau influence, the British also passed new legislation in Kenya in 1950 and 1955 related to unlawful oaths.[117] These laws prohibited the administration of oaths to bind a person to commit a felony, to engage in seditious activity, to disturb the public peace, or to obey orders of groups of people that were not "lawfully constituted."[118] By 1960, nearly identical laws were passed in Nigeria, Northern Rhodesia (Zambia), and the Gambia.[119] Some of these were passed due to concerns about the Mau Mau rebellion spreading to other regions, while other laws may have been the result of general concerns that oaths might be used in other anti-colonial activities.[120]

"Anti-Witchcraft Oaths" in West Africa

Another historical practice that provides a great example of the versatile nature of West African sacred oaths and biased European interpretations of them is the "fetish oath" administered by anti-witchcraft movements that arose in British colonies like the Gold Coast (modern-day Ghana), Tanzania, Kenya, Uganda, and Nigeria in the mid-twentieth century, from the 1930s to the 1950s. Before someone could become a member of one of these societies or movements, they often had to take an oath and admit to past crimes. For example, the Aberewa witch-finding society in the Gold Coast (modern-day Ghana) was known to administer a mixture of animal blood, herbs, and water to initiates of the movement.[121] Upon consumption of this mixture, initiates would swear to abide by the rules of the society.[122] Societal rules might have included prohibitions against theft, using violence against others (including domestic violence and community disputes), and practicing witchcraft or sorcery.[123] If a person did not follow the rules of the community, they would become ill and eventually die from the effects of the binding oath they had taken, unless they went to the priest of the shrine to admit what rule they had broken and remedy what they had done, possibly through the payment of a fine.[124]

In addition to the cleansings and protections that they provided for their members, anti-witchcraft societies would also occasionally perform witch-finding functions. After some oracles, or "fetishes" as they were sometimes referred to by the government, were established in a particular area, people who became ill believed that the oracle was causing their sickness, and they would voluntarily go to the shrine and confess to practicing witchcraft, to avoid what they believed would be imminent death.[125] They would ask the priests of the shrine for forgiveness and turn in their witchcraft materials.

The British prohibited these movements, claiming that they accused people of witchcraft simply to increase the wealth of the society or its priests.[126] Naturally, colonial governments were also concerned about the following that these movements could generate. Lots of people flocked to these societies, and since initiates were often given oath mixtures or charms to protect them from illness, disease, witchcraft, and even bullets, officials worried that these movements could create substantial opposition forces who believed themselves to be immune to attack.[127]

For these reasons, these anti-witchcraft movements perhaps provide an even better example of the complex function of sacred oaths in West African societies than those used in rebellion. Like the "voodoo" oaths administered by human traffickers, anti-witchcraft societies employed oaths and ritual practices to implement an alternative form of governance to the official Eurocentric structures. In both instances, community members are asked to swear allegiance to the oath administrators (or the people on whose behalf the oath is administered) and to promise to carry out or forgo certain activities. In the case of anti-witchcraft movements, these oaths were (at least theoretically) sworn for the betterment of the community—to suppress interpersonal violence, including spiritual attacks like witchcraft and sorcery. In the case of the twenty-first-century human trafficking to Europe, these oaths bind the swearers to the traffickers and serve as insurance that debts would be paid, and secrecy maintained. However, in both circumstances, the oath takers and administrators predict that violators would suffer physical harm and/or die.

Conclusion

This chapter has provided just a few examples of the use of sacred oaths in the history of West Africa and the African diaspora. In many cases, the use of these oaths has been productive and community oriented—particularly in protecting insurgents in their fight against slavery and colonization. These human-trafficking oaths that European authorities describe as "voodoo" are likely modern-day evolutions of these historical practices.

For this reason, these oaths should be viewed in their broader context and not just for the harm that they can cause to trafficking victims. It is important to remember that many societies in West Africa do not view spiritual power in the dichotomous way that followers of Abrahamic religions do. Spiritual power or practices are often themselves neither "good" nor "bad"; they are manipulated to serve the ends of the priest or client. Therefore, the oaths that today bind trafficking victims to their madams or other abusers are likely related to the oaths and shrines where insurgents swore to protect one another in battle or community members promised to end interpersonal violence.

It is wrong for authorities to gloss these oaths as "voodoo," "juju," and "witchcraft," and to compound the negative stereotypes about voodoo, Vodou, and Vodun. It is also unethical for authorities to target entire systems of knowledge, spirituality, and governance simply because some choose to abuse it. Experts on human trafficking should ask the women who swear these oaths about the name that they use to describe them, where the oaths occurred, and what function the oaths serve in society. After they have collected more information about these ritual processes, they should develop policies that target those who abuse indigenous religions, and employ spiritual leaders to help combat human trafficking and apprehend the perpetrators.

Conclusion
Voodoo, Obeah, and Macumba

The previous six chapters have explored how "voodoo" has been used in controversies over the civil and human rights of people of African descent. The term has been manipulated to argue that Black people are incapable of ruling themselves and participating in government; to denounce Black men as savages who raped, enslaved, and murdered others for ritual purposes; and to debate the acceptance of Haitian refugees in the United States and African immigrants in Europe. In addition to exploring the relationship between narratives about "voodoo" and the rights of Black people in general, it is important to also interrogate the long-term impact that negative uses of the term "voodoo" has on the rights and freedoms of devotees of African-derived religions.

In the Introduction, I explored how Vodou adepts and devotees of other African diaspora religions have been subjected to extreme acts of discrimination and violence in recent years, particularly following the devastating 2010 earthquake in Haiti and the subsequent cholera outbreak. In several parts of this book, I argue that one can observe the intimate connection between stereotypes of "voodoo" and these acts of intolerance; for example, in the narratives about "voodoo" and devil worship causing the earthquake and the cholera outbreak.[1] Other present-day and historical examples of the persecution of African diaspora religions provide additional proof of the destructive power of these racist labels and why we need to be rid of them.

Haitian Vodou

One does not have to dig deeply in the historical records to realize that the persecution of Haitian Vodou that took place in 2010 and 2011 was not an aberration; it was part of a long history of discrimination and violence against "voodoo" practitioners. For much of the history of Haiti, prejudice against

Vodou has been embedded in law. One will recall that the use of talismans was prohibited in eighteenth-century St. Domingue after rumored Vodou priest Francois Makandal used his herbal knowledge to attempt to poison the water supply in the northern part of the colony. A few decades after they achieved independence from France, in 1835, the government of Haiti replicated, and one could argue expanded, these colonial restrictions. They prohibited the use of "ouangas," "macandals," or other charms and the practice of fortune-telling and "vaudoux."[2] Persons who violated this law could be sentenced to six months' imprisonment as well as a fine.

Perhaps one of the most repressive periods occurred due to the U.S. occupation of Haiti (1915–1934). U.S. marines enforced antiquated laws barring "voodoo," fortune-telling, "sorcery," and charms during this period.[3] They used these laws as an excuse to raid ceremonies, arrest devotees, and confiscate ritual objects. For example, between January 1924 and January 1925, at least 123 people were arrested for violating statutes banning "sorcery" in the district of Jérémie alone.[4]

One will recall that the U.S. media frequently published stories about alleged "voodoo" practices such as cannibalism and human sacrifice leading up to and during the occupation. In the later years of the occupation, marines themselves also published sensationalized accounts of their time stationed in Haiti, including claims about the prevalence of barbaric "voodoo" practices and the marines' efforts to suppress them. Both media accounts and books by former marines typically celebrated U.S. imperialism as a "civilizing" force in Haiti.

Following the U.S. occupation, the persecution of Vodou continued through intermittent periods. The first president following the occupation, Sténio Vincent, introduced a new law that banned "superstitious practices" including medico-religious healing and various kinds of dances, ceremonies, and rituals.[5] Meanwhile, Rafael Trujillo, dictator of the neighboring Dominican Republic, rounded up and executed approximately 20,000–30,000 Haitians who had been working there. In his efforts to justify the massacre, Trujillo cited Vodou as one of the "polluting" influences that Haitians had on the Dominican Republic that were supposedly causing the country to deteriorate.[6]

Shortly thereafter, in 1941, President Elie Lescot joined with the Catholic Church to persecute Vodou devotees in an "anti-superstition" campaign. In addition to arresting Vodou devotees, the government and the Church seized sacred objects and publicly burned them in bonfires in the street.[7] Previous presidents had collaborated with the Catholic Church to carry out similar campaigns in 1864, 1896, and 1912. Studies suggest that they destroyed numerous temples and killed hundreds of people.[8]

Following the Duvalier dictatorships (1957-1986), Vodou devotees were persecuted once more. In complete opposition to his predecessors, Francois Duvalier (1957-1971) had embraced Vodou and made it an integral part of his government. He depicted himself as the personification of Baron Samedi—the *lwa* who governs the cemeteries and guards the border between the world of the living and that of the dead.[9] Duvalier was known for donning the signature top hat, black clothes, and dark glasses of Baron Samedi. He also recruited Vodou priests to serve as part of his personal militia—the Tonton Macoutes.[10]

John Merrill, legal scholar and former deputy director of the Haiti Task Force for the U.S. Department of Defense, asserts that at least 500 Vodou priests were murdered after the fall of the Duvalier government as a backlash against their role in this brutal regime.[11] Merrill reports that this number was confirmed by verifiable data, but that Vodou organizations claimed that the real death toll may have been around 2,000 people. Furthermore, Merrill argues that many of those killed may not have been affiliated with the Tonton Macoutes. Instead, "they were the victims of a zealous Haitian Christian clergy eager to exploit public anger at the Tontons Macoute excesses as an opportunity to resume their long-standing inquisition to eradicate Vodou's power altogether."[12] He contends that the clergy spread all-too-familiar rumors about Vodou priests eating children and engaging in other evil practices to help turn the public against them.

Based on this lengthy history of violence, it is clear that the attacks in 2010 and 2011 are part of a disturbing pattern. Both colonial and post-independence governments restricted Vodou practices, while private citizens and the Catholic church have been permitted, and at times encouraged, to attack devotees. At no time in history have the perpetrators of these offenses been held accountable, nor has the Haitian government taken serious measures to prevent future violence. Nevertheless, there has been little media coverage of this problem and, aside from the UN queries about how Haiti handled the 2010-2011 attacks, virtually no denunciations of these gross human rights violations.

It seems likely that biases about "voodoo" play a key role in the lack of public interest in protecting this vulnerable religious community. As noted briefly in the conclusion of Chapter 5, following the earthquake, there were numerous comments in newspaper editorials or on TV shows where outsiders opined that Haiti had brought this devastating tragedy upon itself by engaging in "superstitions" instead of embracing Christianity. With such pervasive and long-standing stereotypes about "voodoo," it is difficult to generate concern or support for the well-being of devotees, even in the most tragic of circumstances.

Obeah

As noted in the Introduction, "Obeah" is the term that the British used to refer to African religions in their Caribbean territories. Public perceptions of Obeah in the Caribbean are comparable to public perceptions of "voodoo"; it is often regarded as a religion based on devil worship and hexing. As discussed briefly in Chapter 6, after African priests repeatedly led slave rebellions, the British began to prohibit Obeah in their colonies, starting with Jamaica in 1760. Obeah legislation was modeled on British laws that banned the "pretended" practice of witchcraft or sorcery.[13]

The prosecution of "Obeah practitioners" in the Anglophone Caribbean was constant for approximately three hundred years.[14] During slavery, persons convicted of violating Obeah laws could be banished or executed. After emancipation, the penalties for Obeah were reduced to periods of incarceration and whipping at the beginning and end of the sentence. Arrests for "practicing Obeah" became widespread in the mid-nineteenth century and lasted until the mid-twentieth century, when prosecution rates drastically declined. In Jamaica alone, hundreds, perhaps thousands, of people were incarcerated, sentenced to forced labor, and brutally beaten for "practicing Obeah." The majority were engaging in seemingly innocuous rituals like conjuring spirits and performing divination.

Unlike most African religions, which were decriminalized by the mid-twentieth century, the practice of Obeah remains against the law in several countries today.[15] Many of the laws that continue to prohibit Obeah describe it as an "occult" practice or "pretending" to possess supernatural powers.[16] Not surprisingly, when legislators have proposed to decriminalize Obeah, they have received backlash from people who believe that devotees practice witchcraft or devil worship.[17] As I have explored in greater detail elsewhere, this opposition to Obeah is in stark contrast to recent trends to protect the rights of self-proclaimed "witches" or Wiccans.[18]

Even outside the Caribbean, colonial perceptions of Obeah have had a strong negative impact on religious freedom. For instance, in 2007, an inmate in a correctional facility in Connecticut requested some materials—honeysuckle, oils, parchment paper, incense, etc.—for the practice of Obeah.[19] The director of religious services denied his request, arguing that these seemingly harmless materials posed a danger to the prison. During a court hearing evaluating the appropriateness of the denial, a U.S. professor described Obeah to the judges who were unfamiliar with this belief system. Her testimony, which was full of colonial stereotypes, asserted that Obeah was primarily used to poison and murder others and that it was an "inherently dangerous and threatening" belief system based on "dark magic." After the court heard the professor's testimony, they denied the inmate's request.

Two cases from Canada are even more shocking.[20] In each case, the police in Toronto suspected that Jamaican-Canadians were responsible for violent crimes. Lacking evidence to prove their theories, the police manipulated the suspects' spiritual beliefs to obtain confessions. In the first case, they paid a well-known local Obeah practitioner to provide rituals for the young men and then testify about everything that they revealed during the ceremonies. In the second case, the police went even further. One of the officers went undercover and posed as an Obeah practitioner. He initiated contact with the mother of two brothers who he believed were involved in a murder. The officer harassed the mother for months—staging a car accident with her, leaving dead animals on her doorstep, and even having her arrested—to convince the family of his spiritual power. The undercover officer told them that these unfortunate events were caused by a spirit who was harassing their family. The officer arrested the brothers based almost solely on information they shared during a ritual purportedly meant to appease this spirit.

In reviewing both cases, Canadian appellate courts claimed that they recognized Obeah as a religion, but they still allowed evidence of what was said during these fraudulent rituals to be used against the men. While issuing their ruling, the judges acknowledged that the Supreme Court had previously held that police officers could not pretend to be a Catholic priest and take confession to try to obtain evidence. Although the officers went much further than this in staging Obeah rituals, the court did not believe that devotees' rights had been violated.

Macumba

Historical and present-day uses of the term "macumba" and the persecution of "macumbeiros" (people who practice in "macumba") are even more troubling. Like Obeah and voodoo, the word "macumba" is likely of African origin and is used by a small number of people in Brazil to refer to their religion. However, it came into popular use between the late nineteenth and mid-twentieth centuries, when the federal government passed a new penal code criminalizing the use of talismans, practicing "magic" or spiritism, and working as a "faith healer" or a fortune-teller.[21] Devotees of Afro-Brazilian religions such as Candomblé and Umbanda were prosecuted using this statute. "Macumba" became the term used to refer to religious communities who were considered to be violating this law.

In the early twentieth century, police invaded Afro-Brazilian religious communities throughout the country, seized their sacred artifacts, and arrested religious leaders. If one talks to members of Afro-Brazilian temples that have been around since this period, most will have stories of at least one occasion where they had the misfortune of being harassed by the authorities. However, the most severe attack took place in 1912, when Afro-Brazilian religious communities in the greater Maceió region of the state of Alagoas were nearly eradicated in an incident known as Quebra de Xangô or the "Breaking of Xangô."

In the elections of 1911, the governor of Alagoas, Euclides Malta, was defeated by a landslide. Malta was known to frequent some of the Candomblé communities in Maceió, and his opponents claimed that he and his powerful family had gained and held their influence for many years through sorcery.[22] On the evening of February 1, 1912, members of a group of Malta's opponents, known as the League of Republican Combatants (Liga dos Republicanos Combatentes), took to the streets in protest. At approximately 10:30 p.m., the protesters began invading Candomblé temples that were rumored to have supported Malta, violently assaulting devotees and stealing their sacred objects. Some adepts were beaten so badly that they were hospitalized. At least one priestess died from her injuries.[23] Countless ritual items were lost to the rioters, who burned them in giant bonfires, sold the goods that had street value, and kept other items in the League headquarters.

These assaults were so widespread and devastating that Afro-Brazilian religions virtually disappeared from the region for decades. When Gonçalves Fernandes visited Alagoas nearly 30 years later, he wrote of a carefully hidden tradition practiced by devotees who conducted their rituals in small groups and in near silence.[24] He claimed that most dared not sing, clap, or drum for their divinities for fear of persecution.

Although official prosecution of Afro-Brazilian religions virtually ceased by the mid-twentieth century, widespread persecution of these religions has returned in the twenty-first century and has reached levels of frequency and severity that near, if not surpass, those seen in the early twentieth century. In 2022, I compiled a database of 500 cases of intolerance against Afro-Brazilian religious communities since the beginning of the year 2000.[25] These cases ranged from slander and verbal harassment to the arson of temples and murder of priests. In around 20 percent of cases, the perpetrator used the phrase "macumba" or "macumbeiro/a" while carrying out the attack.[26]

For example, Evangelical drug traffickers have recently terrorized Afro-Brazilian religious communities in the state of Rio de Janeiro.[27] Traffickers have prohibited devotees from wearing any symbols of their religions. They have threatened to kill religious leaders who continue to hold ceremonies in their territory. They have invaded communities that refused to shut down, assaulted religious leaders, destroyed sacred objects, and set fire to the temple. In 2017, the traffickers recorded their assaults on the leaders of two Afro-Brazilian religious communities. The traffickers forced the priests to destroy their own temples while the traffickers screamed phrases like "didn't we already tell you that we don't want any macumba here" and "destroy all these things that belong to the devil."

Several teenagers have used similar language when they physically assaulted classmates who are devotees of Candomblé.[28] In the first incident, which took place in 2015, a 14-year-old girl, Agnes, posted a video of herself on social media that had references to her religion. When she went to school the next day, one of her classmates kicked her, knocking Agnes down and causing her to hit her face against a wall. While the assault took place, her classmates encouraged the attacker, yelling "kick that macumba."

The following year, a 16-year-old named Isadora Jaques Leão posted a picture of herself on social media wearing a sacred necklace of Candomblé.[29] Like Agnes, when Isadora went to school the next day, her classmates began to taunt her, calling her a "macumbeira." On several occasions, groups of students plotted to ambush Isadora outside of school. One of these times, the assailants knocked Isadora off the bike that she was trying to use to safely get away from her attackers. A few days later, two students knocked Isadora to the ground, then punched and kicked her repeatedly. During both attacks, the assailants called Isadora a "macumbeira."

Recent years have also brought numerous reports of private individuals attacking Afro-Brazilian religious temples with incendiary devices. For example, in 2017, in Salvador, Bahia, a neighbor repeatedly launched fireworks into an Umbanda temple when the devotees were hosting ceremonies.[30] He claimed that he was trying to get the "macumba" out of his neighborhood. More recently, in February 2020, attackers launched a homemade bomb into an Umbanda temple in Ribeirão Preto, São Paulo. When the devotees tried to flee the space, the attackers stoned, punched, and kicked them. They severely beat a 25-year-old man, knocking out five of his teeth and rendering him unconscious. Like the perpetrator in the 2017 Bahia case, the attackers told devotees that they don't allow "macumba" in their neighborhood.[31]

Moving Forward

In recent years, historians have done an excellent job of reconstructing the African origins of the words that Europeans adopted to describe African religions in their colonies. They have examined how European influence transformed words that typically meant something positive in their original African language and made them into terms that were synonymous with devil worship, black magic, and witchcraft.[32] Scholars have also documented the harassment, prosecution, and systematic destruction of African-derived religious communities in the eighteenth, nineteenth, and early twentieth centuries.[33]

However, despite these scholars' valiant efforts, awareness of the role of racism in constructing public understandings of concepts like Obeah, voodoo, and macumba have remained largely confined to the ivory tower. The public continues to use these words dismissively and derogatorily. Public (mis)understandings of these religions generate fear that legalizing African diaspora religions will invite "witchcraft" into their communities and that the widespread practice of African "superstitions" has led to natural disasters. People who carry out physical assaults on African diaspora religious communities continue to deploy these terms to try to rationalize acts of violence. These attacks, though extremely brutal and pervasive, go largely unnoted in the media.

Prejudices about African religions are among the many stereotypes that slavery, colonization, and segregation relied on for their continued existence. Allegations about African peoples' promiscuity were used to justify the rape of Black women and the lynching of Black men. Claims that the entire race was prone to laziness were used to support enslavement and other coercive labor practices after emancipation. Assertions about Africans' biological inferiority supported the carving up of an entire continent and its placement under European rule. Yet the stereotypes about African-derived religions seem to have been some of the most effective, as they are the only prejudices that continue almost without question.

In the twenty-first century, if someone publicly stated that Black people are lazy, stupid, or promiscuous, it is likely that they would be publicly ridiculed, possibly fired from their job, and, in some countries, prosecuted for racial discrimination. Nevertheless, derogatory comments about someone practicing "voodoo" rarely cause a raised eyebrow or a sideways glance. Yet the preceding chapters have shown the racially charged origins of the term in Civil War–era New Orleans and its use in opposition to extending voting rights and opportunities for political participation to African Americans. It played an integral role in U.S. imperialism in the Caribbean, with journalists and travelers claiming that Haitians and Cubans were unprepared for independence because people of African descent were reverting to barbaric "voodoo" practices. African Americans were the subject of similar claims when they migrated from the South to the North and West seeking jobs and an escape from racism, as well as when they established all-Black towns and religious organizations like the Nation of Islam that centered on the independence and uplift of people of African descent. Debates about Haitian immigration to the United States and African immigration to Europe continue to feature stories about the "voodoo" rituals that smugglers employ before and during the passage.

Biases against voodoo, Obeah, macumba, and related terms are deeply held but can be broken with effort. Courses on African American and African diaspora history need to highlight the importance of religion in anti-slavery and anti-colonial rebellions. Educators need to make knowledge about the origins of the term "voodoo" and the persecution and prosecution of African diaspora religions universal. Films and television shows featuring negative depictions of "voodoo" must stop being produced. Organizations, working groups, and initiatives designed to combat racism need to include the protection of African-derived religious communities as part of their action plans. Finally, perhaps most importantly, governments need to be held accountable for ensuring that African diaspora religious communities enjoy the same rights as other individuals and that persons who commit violence against them are swiftly and consistently prosecuted.

Notes

Introduction

1. Bellegarde-Smith, "Man-Made Disaster," 264–265.
2. See Chapter 5.
3. Paisley Dodds, "Haiti Earthquake Leads to Increased Tensions among Religions," *Associated Press*, February 13, 2010, http://www.nola.com/religion/index.ssf/2010/02/haiti_earthquake_leads_to_increased_tensions_among_religions.html. Germain, "The Earthquake, the Missionaries," 250, 257.
4. Dodds, "Haiti Earthquake Leads to Increased Tensions"; Carelock, *Leaky House*, 47, 94–95.
5. Frerichs, *Deadly River*, 1; Agence France-Presse, "45 People Lynched Amid Haiti Cholera Fears: Officials," December 23, 2010.
6. "45 Lynchings over Cholera," *Sunshine Coast Daily* (Maroochydore, Queensland, Australia), December 24, 2010.
7. "45 People Lynched Amid Haiti Cholera Fears."
8. Frerichs, *Deadly River*, 1.
9. Grimaud and Legagneur, "Community Beliefs and Fears," 27.
10. "Haiti-Cholera-Voodoo Leader Says 45 People Lynched Amid Cholera Fears," *CANANews* (Barbados), December 24, 2010; "45 Lynchings over Cholera," *Sunshine Coast Daily* (Maroochydore, Queensland, Australia), December 24, 2010; Grimaud and Legagneur, "Community Beliefs and Fears," 28. Additional murders took place in other parts of the country. Human Rights Council, "Report of the Independent Expert," ¶ 39. Cornelio Sotelo, "Witch Hunters in Haiti Kill 12 Accused of Spreading Cholera," *El Paso Examiner*, December 4, 2010; Johnathan M. Katz, "Cholera Panic Sparks Haiti Witch-Hunt; 12 Killed," *Associated Press News Service*, December 3, 2010; "45 People Lynched Amid Haiti Cholera Fears."
11. Human Rights Council, "Report of the Independent Expert," ¶ 39.
12. Human Rights Council, "National Report Submitted." Human Rights Committee, "Consideration of Reports," ¶ 98.
13. Human Rights Committee, "Consideration of Reports," ¶ 115.
14. Human Rights Committee, "List of Issues," 4.
15. Átila Nunes, "Pastor evangélico que nega intolerância ao usar a expressão "Macumbeiro", é o quê?," Notícias de Terreiro, August 26, 2019, https://noticiasdeterreiro.com.br/2019/08/26/pastor-evangelico-que-nega-intolerancia-ao-usar-expressao-macumbeiro-e-o-que/ (last visited November 22, 2022).
16. Handler and Bilby, "On the Early Use."
17. Desmangles, *The Faces of the Gods*, xi, 2.

18. Moreau de Saint Méry, *A Civilization That Perished*, 15.
19. Burnham, "Makandal, François," 1362–1363.
20. Paton, "Witchcraft, Poison, Law and Atlantic Slavery," 254–255.
21. Pogue, "Bois Caiman," 130–131.
22. Paton, "Obeah Acts."
23. Handler and Bilby, "On the Early Use"; Paton, "Obeah Acts."
24. Desmangles, *The Faces of the Gods*, 1.
25. For example, see *Law and Order, Criminal Intent: The Healer* (NBC television broadcast, April 23, 2006); *Bones: The Man in the Morgue* (FOX television broadcast, April 19, 2006).
26. See, for example, *Tales of Voodoo* (Videoasia, 2007) (a five-DVD series, released from 2005 to present); *Zombie Nation* (Working Poor Productions, 2004); *The Skeleton Key* (Universal Pictures, 2005); *London Voodoo* (Zen Films, 2004); *Voodoo Dawn* (Bridge Pictures, 2000); *Voodoo Academy* (Full Moon Entertainment, 2000); *Tales from the Hood* (40 Acres and a Mule Filmworks, 1995); *Voodoo* (Planet Productions, 1995); *Serpent and the Rainbow* (Serpent & the Rainbow & Universal Pictures, 1988); *Angel Heart* (Carolco International N.V., 1987); *Curse of the Voodoo* (Galaworld Film Production, Gordon Films, 1965); *I Walked with a Zombie* (RKO Radio Pictures, 1943); *White Zombie* (Edward Halperin Productions, 1932).
27. *The Princess and the Frog* (Disney, 2009).
28. Johnson, *Blood Libel*, 1.
29. Chireau, *Black Magic*, 12.
30. Anderson, *Conjure in African American Society*, xi–xii.
31. Ibid. While root work is usually a part of conjure or hoodoo, root doctors might not all be conjurers or hoodoo practitioners.
32. Anderson, *Conjure in African American Society*, x.
33. Ibid.
34. Chireau, *Black Magic*, 7.
35. Anderson, *Conjure in African American Society*, 3.
36. Ibid., 4–5.
37. Ibid., 16–17.
38. Anderson, *Conjure in African American Society*, 16.
39. Ramsey, "From 'Voodooism' to 'Vodou,'" 14–15.
40. Patrick Bellegarde-Smith, Kaiama Glover, Carolyn Shread, and Kate Ramsey, "Vodou in Translation: A Roundtable on the English-Language Translation of Vodou," H-Net H-Haiti Discussions, February 17, 2018, (last visited February 4, 2023).
41. Ibid.
42. Ibid.

Chapter 1

1. "Misrule in Louisiana," *Defiance Democrat*, June 14, 1873 (emphasis in original).

2. Gaston, "The Case of Voodoo in New Orleans," 129.
3. This distinction is meant to leave room for the possibility that "voodoo" was discussed in French-language presses or other written materials in the Louisiana territory after it was annexed by the United States. Such research is beyond the scope of this book, which instead focuses on the emergence of the interest in "voodoo" in the United States and the rest of the Anglophone world.
4. "Black State Rep. Thanks God for Slavery," *Grio*, March 4, 2018, https://thegrio.com/2018/03/04/black-state-rep-thanks-god-slavery/.
5. "City Intelligence," *Times-Picayune* (New Orleans, LA), July 6, 1850; "City Intelligence," *Times-Picayune* (New Orleans, LA), July 7, 1850.
6. "More of the Voudous," *Times-Picayune* (New Orleans, LA), July 30, 1850.
7. More of the Voudous," *Times-Picayune* (New Orleans, LA), July 31, 1850; "Unlawful Assemblies," *Times-Picayune* (New Orleans, LA), July 31, 1850.
8. "Rites of Voudon," *Alexandria Gazette* (Alexandria, VA), August 16, 1850.
9. "City Intelligence" *Times-Picayune* (New Orleans, LA), July 25, 1851; "City Intelligence" *Times-Picayune* (New Orleans, LA), July 26, 1851.
10. This could have been because of a lack of interest in the story. However, a *Times Picayune* article from 1863 indicated that "This is the first time for years that a Voudou meeting has been interrupted." *Times-Picayune* (New Orleans, LA), July 31, 1863.
11. "The City," *Times-Picayune* (New Orleans, LA), July 31, 1863.
12. I found only one reprint of these voudou stories prior to the 1860s. Ironically, given that this coverage of New Orleans voudou was so negative, the original account of these events was printed in the *New Orleans Era*, a Union newspaper that began circulation in 1863 and ended in 1865.
13. "Heathenism in New Orleans," *Norwich Aurora* (Norwich, CT), August 22, 1863; "Heathenism in New Orleans—Extraordinary Scene," *San Francisco Bulletin*, September 9, 1863.
14. "Superstition in New Orleans," *Weekly Patriot and Union* (Harrisburg, PA), October 22, 1863.
15. Emphasis added. "Heathenism in New Orleans—Extraordinary Scene," *San Francisco Bulletin*, September 9, 1863.
16. Ibid.
17. Emphasis added. "American Pagans of African Descent," *Daily Milwaukee News*, August 19, 1863. This appears to be the only reprint with this section.
18. "Heathenism in New Orleans—Extraordinary Scene," *San Francisco Bulletin*, September 9, 1863. This appears to be the only reprint with this section.
19. "Untitled," *Columbian Register*, August 15, 1863.
20. "Untitled," *Patriot*, October 22, 1863.
21. "The City," *Times-Picayune* (New Orleans, LA), August 2, 1863.
22. Ibid.
23. "Dark Deeds: A Graveyard Violated," *Times-Picayune* (New Orleans, LA), May 1, 1864.
24. "Shocking Recital. Freed Negroes Returning to the Barbarous Bites of Voudouism," *Daily Ohio Statesman* (Columbus, OH), May 25, 1864.

25. "Voodooism: The Native African Paganism Rife among the Freedman," *Washington Review and Examiner* (Washington, PA), December 19, 1866; "Voodooism: The Native African Paganism Rife among the Freedmen," *Daily Eastern Argus* (Portland, ME), December 3, 1866; "African Superstitions in America," *Crisis* (Columbus, OH), December 5, 1866; "African Superstitious in America: The Negro Marching Back," *Macon Daily Telegraph* (Macon, GA), November 20, 1866; "African Superstitions in America: The Negro Marching Back," *Cincinnati Daily Enquirer*, November 21, 1866.
26. "The Black Cloud in the South," *Crisis* (Columbus, OH), July 31, 1867.
27. Ibid.
28. "Untitled," *Crisis* (Columbus, OH), March 24, 1869.
29. Ibid. There were many other one-liner-style insults about African American religion and the right to vote in the 1860s and 1870s. One author argued that Asians were much more suited to citizenship and suffrage than persons of African descent, in part because they "are far better looking than" Black people, and also because their religion was substantially better than "an odd jumble of Christianity and Voudou superstition." "Naturalization," *Patriot*, February 17, 1869. Similarly, an article titled "The Indian and the Ballot," published in 1879, stated, "The Indian, even the sun-dancing brave, is just as ready for the polls as were the field hands of Georgia or the Voodoo-worshippers of Louisiana." "The Indian and the Ballot," *Cherokee Advocate*, July 30, 1879.
30. "Misrule in Louisiana," *Defiance Democrat*, June 14, 1873. The author emphasizes their point by noting that this article first appeared in a Republican paper. The author stated that this made it clear that "[e]ven the Republicans sicken of the prospect in Louisiana."
31. Ibid.
32. Ibid. Emphasis in original.
33. "Sixteenth Amendment," *Mountain Democrat*, June 26, 1869.
34. Ibid.
35. Ibid.
36. Ibid.
37. John Fisher, "Georgia," *Coshocton Democrat*, March 8, 1870.
38. Ibid.
39. "How Wade Hampton Saved His State," *Fort Wayne Daily Gazette* (Fort Wayne, IN), January 26, 1883; "How Wade Hampton Saved His State," *Cedar Rapids Evening Gazette* (Cedar Rapids, IA), January 24, 1883.
40. Ibid.
41. This is consistent with arguments previously made by Kate Ramsey, who said that before the mid-nineteenth century, literature in English referred to "fetishes," "superstition," or the moral regression of Haiti, but did not mention "voodoo" or "vaudoux" as it was usually spelled. Ramsey, *The Spirits and the Law*, 65–66.
42. "From Cape Haytian: Correspondence of the Philadelphia Exchange," *Southern Patriot* (Charleston, SC), April 27, 1846
43. Ramsey, *The Spirits and the Law*, 80; Desmangles, *The Faces of the Gods*, 46–47.

44. "Faustin Soulouque, The Black Emperor of Hayti," *Vermont Journal* (Windsor, VT), November 30, 1849.
45. "Things in Hayti- The Emperor Souslouque- The Negro Religion- Vaudoux and its Pecularities- The Burlesque Empire, & c." *New York Herald*, April 3, 1858; "The Empire of Haiti," *New York Times*, February 14, 1859; "Paganism," *Albany Evening Journal* (Albany, NY), March 19, 1859; "Paganism," *Columbian Register* (New Haven, CT), April 2, 1859.
46. I only found one article about Haitian "voodoo" published between 1860 and 1870. That was an article about serpent worship, which featured a section on "vaudoux" in Haiti. "Serpent-Worship," *Weekly Patriot and Union* (Harrisburg, PA), January 15, 1863.
47. Underhill, *The West Indies*, 160–162.
48. Ibid., 163.
49. Ibid., 175.
50. Ibid.
51. "Souslouque, King of Hayti, and the Snake Worshippers," *Manchester Times*, June 21, 1862; "Souslouque, King of Hayti, and the Snake Worshippers," *Lancaster Gazette* (Lancaster, England), July 18, 1863; "Souslouque, King of Hayti, and the Snake Worshippers," *Wrexham Advertiser*, August 1, 1863.
52. "The Logic of History," *Wisconsin Daily Patriot*, December 15, 1863.
53. For example see Shannon, *Jean Price-Mars*, 14; Desmangles, *The Faces of the Gods*, 1–2.
54. Ramsey, *The Spirits and the Law*, 83–91.
55. "Cannibalism Revived among the Free Negroes of Hayti," *Times-Picayune*, April 3, 1864.
56. "Human Sacrifices and Cannibalism," *East London Advertiser*, April 23, 1864; "Human Sacrifices and Cannibalism," *Englishman*, April 2, 1864; "The 'Vaudoux' in Haiti," *Illustrated Times*, April 30, 1864; "Horrible Superstition and Crime in Hayti," *Miner and Workman's Advocate*, April 2, 1864; "Human Sacrifices and Cannibalism," *London Standard*, March 30, 1864; "Human Sacrifices and Cannibalism," *London South Advertiser*, April 23, 1864; "Superstitious Horrors," *Reynolds's Newspaper*, April 3, 1864; "Human Sacrifices and Cannibalism," *Bucks Herald* (Aylesbury, England) April 16, 1864.
57. "Horrible Superstition and Crime in Hayti," *Miner and Workman's Advocate*, April 2, 1864; "Human Sacrifices and Cannibalism," *Englishman*, April 2, 1864.
58. J. B., "Our Feuileton: The 'Vaudoux' in Haiti," *Illustrated Times*, April 30, 1864.
59. "Human Sacrifices and Cannibalism," *London Magnet*, April 4, 1864; "Horrible Superstition and Crime in Hayti," *Miner and Workman's Advocate*, April 2, 1864.
60. Carribee, "Canniabalism [sic] in Hayti—Negroes Shot for Eating Children—Human Sacrifices," *Dawson's Fort Wayne Daily Times*, March 25, 1864;
61. Ibid.
62. "Cannibalism in Hayti—Negroes Shot for Eating Children," *Sullivan Democrat* (Sullivan, IN), April 7, 1864, p. 1.
63. Ibid.

64. Ibid.
65. Carribee, "Canniabalism [sic] in Hayti—Negroes Shot for Eating Children—Human Sacrifices," *Dawson's Fort Wayne Weekly Times*, March 30, 1864; "Cannibalism in Hayti—Negroes Shot for Eating Children," *Sullivan Democrat*, April 7, 1864.
66. "Canibalism [sic] Revived among the Free Negroes of Haiti," *Times-Picayune* (New Orleans, LA), April 3, 1864. Emphasis added.
67. "Canibalism [sic] in Hayti," *Delphi Times*, April 9, 1864.
68. Ibid.
69. Ibid.
70. "The Popularity of the War," *Dawson's Fort Wayne Weekly Times*, March 30, 1864.
71. "A Capital Hit—The Lincoln Catechism—Questions and Answers." *Sullivan Democrat* (Sullivan, IN), April 7, 1864.
72. "Voudou Superstition," *Aurora Commercial* (Aurora, IN), September 29, 1864.
73. "The St. Domingo Annexation," *Crisis* (Columbus, OH), January 19, 1870; "Political," *Columbian Register* (New Haven, CT), February 5, 1870.
74. "The St. Domingo Commission," *New York Herald*, March 31, 1871.
75. "Nagualism, Voodooism, and Other Forms of Crytopaganism in the United States," 4.
76. Ibid., 9.
77. Ibid.
78. Ibid.
79. Spenser St. John, *Hayti; or the Black Republic*.
80. Ibid., vii.
81. Ibid, ix.
82. Ibid. xi
83. Ibid., 187–231; 232–257.
84. Ibid., 187–189.
85. Ibid., 192.
86. Ibid., 200–201.
87. Ibid., 210–220.
88. Ibid., xii.
89. Pettinger and Milne, "From Vaudoux to Voodoo," 419.
90. Farmer, *The Uses of Haiti*, 190.
91. Ibid.
92. "Vaudoux Worship," *New York Times*, December 14, 1884; "Africa in Hayti," *Burlington Daily Hawkeye Gazette* (Burlington, IA), December 9, 1886; "Voudoo Worship: Revolting Superstitions Prevailing among the Negroes of Hayti," *Hagerstown Herald and Torchlight* (Hagerstown, MD), March 17, 1887.
93. "Voodoo Worship in Haiti," *Algoona Upper Des Moines* (Algoona, IA), April 1, 1885.
94. "Demoralized Hayti: A Land of Cannibalism and Barbarous Voodoo Worship," *World* (New York), December 20, 1885.
95. Ibid.
96. "The Black Republic: The Failure of Civilization in Santo Domingo," *Review* (Decatur, IL), April 25, 1885.
97. "Negro Rule in Haiti," *Aiken Journal*, July 15, 1885.

98. Ibid.
99. "Orgies in Hayti: A Story of Voudou Horrors That [Illegible] Belief," *Times-Picayune* (New Orleans, LA), January 21, 1889.
100. "A Southern View of It," *Newark Daily Advocate*, April 23, 1892.
101. Ibid.
102. Ibid.
103. "Where the Colored Man Hath Sway; The Retrogression of Hayti under Negro Domination; The Heathen Rites of Voudouism as Now Practiced," *Times-Picayune* (New Orleans, LA), January 4, 1895.
104. Prichard, *Where Black Rules White*, 74–101.
105. Ibid., 75
106. Ibid, 75.

Chapter 2

1. "Horrors of Voodooism Break Out Again: Babies Stolen in Cuba and Hayti for Human Sacrifices to Sacred Serpents," *Lexington Herald* (Lexington, KY), October 4, 1908;
2. Such observations began at least as early as 1888. See Newell, "Myths of Voodoo Worship and Child Sacrifice in Haiti," 16–30; Plummer, *Haiti and the Great Powers*, 71–77.
3. Plummer, *Haiti and the Great Powers*, 75.
4. Roman, *Governing Spirits*; De la Fuente, *A Nation for All*; Helg, "Black Men, Racial Stereotyping, and Violence,"
5. "A Worse Lot Than the Voudoos," *Philadelphia Inquirer*, March 16, 1876, p. 1. "Voodooism in Cuba," *Baltimore Sun*, March 16, 1876.
6. "The Voodoo Fetich: How This Degrading Superstition Is Practiced Today," *Olean Weekly Democrat*, January 19, 1894.
7. "For Good Luck in War: Voodoo Incantations Invoked by Cuban Insurgents," *Steubenville Daily Herald*, March 24, 1896; "For Good Luck in War: Voodoo Incantations Invoked by Cuban Insurgents," *Eau Claire Leader*, March 25, 1896; "For Good Luck in War: Voodoo Incantations Invoked by Cuban Insurgents," *Marion Daily Star*, March 23, 1896.
8. "In Cisneros' Camp: Lights and Shadows of Army Life in Battle Scared Cuba," *Steubenville Daily Herald*, September 10, 1896.
9. In 1897, there was only one reference to voodoo in Cuba—a confusing statement that Americans imprisoned in Cuba had been arrested on "trifling" charges such as voodooism. "Untitled," *Goshen Weekly Times*, April 9, 1897, p. 3.
10. Perez, *Cuba and the United States*, 83–89.
11. Ibid., 97–100.
12. Helg, "Black Men, Racial Stereotyping, and Violence," 585–586, noting the vast differences between the status of Black Cubans and Black people in the U.S. at the turn of the twentieth century.

13. Musgrave, *Under Three Flags in Cuba*.
14. Ibid., 4.
15. Ibid., 4–5, note 1.
16. "Fetish Worship in Cuba," *Daily Advocate,* November 10, 1899.
17. Ibid.
18. Perez, *Cuba and the United States*, 109–110.
19. Ibid., 112
20. Guerra, *The Myth of Jose Marti*, 156–158; Perez, *Cuba and the United States*, 153.
21. Perez, *Cuba and the United States*, 178.
22. Ibid.
23. Guerra, *The Myth of Jose Marti,* 180.
24. Perez, *Cuba and the United States*, 153–154.
25. Guerra, *The Myth of Jose Marti,* 183.
26. Ibid., 193.
27. Palmié, *Wizards & Scientists*, 212.
28. Ibid., 211.
29. Helg, "Black Men, Racial Stereotyping, and Violence," 583–584.
30. Bronfman, "En Plena Libertad y Democracia," 549–554.
31. "Ate White Child's Heart: Voodoo Doctor on Trial in Cuba for Murder," *Oregonian* (Portland, OR), March 24, 1905; "Negro Savagery in Cuba Equals Darkest Africa," *Decatur Daily Review*, March 23, 1905.
32. "Child a Victim of Voudoo Doctor: All Cuba Excited over Revelation of Revolting Voudooism in the Island," *Montgomery Advertiser* (Montgomery, AL), March 27, 1905.
33. "Ate White Child's Heart: Voodoo Doctor on Trial in Cuba for Murder," *Oregonian* (Portland, OR), March 24, 1905.
34. "Cuba Excited Over Voodooism: Negro 'Priest' Accused of Inducing 'Patient' to Murder White Child to Regain Health," *Pawtucket Times* (Pawtucket, RI), March 23, 1905; "Child a Victim of Voudoo Doctor: All Cuba Excited over Revelation of Revolting Voudooism in the Island," *Montgomery Advertiser* (Montgomery, AL), March 27, 1905.
35. "Voodooism in the West Indies: Negroes in Cuba and Haiti Condemned to Death for Sacrificing Infants in their Horrid Devil Worship," *News Magazine* (Galveston, TX), May 7, 1905.
36. For example, see "Horrible Rites of Voodooism Practice in the West Indies," *Colorado Springs Gazette*, May 20, 1905; "Rites of Voodoo Carried Out in Hayti," *Duluth News Tribune*, May 21, 1905.
37. Henry Whitehouse, "Voodoo Mysteries: Haytians Returning to the Black Arts of Africa," *Daily Herald*, June 16, 1905.
38. Guerra, *The Myth of Jose Marti*, 197.
39. Ibid., 197.
40. Ibid., 201.
41. Des Voeux. *My Colonial Service*.
42. Ibid., 272–275.

43. "Execution of Adolphe La-Croix," U.K. National Archives, C.O. 321/12/36.
44. Ibid.
45. Udal, "Obeah in the West Indies," 286–287.
46. Ibid., 289.
47. Ibid., 292.
48. Ibid., 293.
49. "Barbarous Superstition," *Dallas Morning News*, October 12, 1904; "Ghastly Crime," *Columbus Enquirer*, October 12, 1904; "Ghastly Crime Committed," *Madison Wisconsin State Journal*, October 12, 1904.
50. "Barbarism in St. Lucia," *Times-Picayune* (New Orleans, LA), October 14, 1904.
51. "What Is Obeah?" *The Gleaner* (Kingston, Jamaica), October 14, 1904.
52. "Ghastly Murder in Saint Lucia," *The Gleaner* (Kingston, Jamaica), October 15, 1904, p. 6.
53. The St. Lucia Obeah Horror," *The Gleaner* (Kingston, Jamaica), December 1904; "The Horror of St. Lucia," *The Gleaner* (Kingston, Jamaica), December 30, 1904.
54. "The Horror of St. Lucia," *The Gleaner* (Kingston, Jamaica), December 30, 1904
55. By 1907, they had announced this new law in the *Journal of Comparative Legislation*. Macdonell & Manson, eds., "Criminal Law: Obeah," 541.
56. Pitman, "Slavery on British West Indies," 652.
57. "Troops Quit Cuba Jan 28," *Galveston Daily News*, September 14, 1908; "To Evacuate Cuba January 28," *Baltimore Sun*, September 6, 1908.
58. "Horrors of Voodooism Break Out Again: Babies Stolen in Cuba and Hayti for Human Sacrifices to Sacred Serpents," *Lexington Herald* (Lexington, KY), October 4, 1908; "Horrors of Voodooism Break Out Again: Babies Stolen in Cuba and Hayti for Human Sacrifices to Sacred Serpents," *San Antonio Light*, October 11, 1908.
59. "Hayti," *Oregonian* (Portland, OR), December 2, 1908.
60. Ibid. Emphasis added.
61. Guerra, *The Myth of Jose Marti*, 203.
62. "Race War Feared in Cuba," *Baltimore Sun*, July 9, 1908; "Voodoo Murder May Cause War," *Detroit Free Press*, July 9, 1908. "Race War in Cuba," *Montgomery Advertiser* (Montgomery, AL), July 9, 1908.
63. "Fear Race War in Cuba: Wizards Who Killed Child in Religious Rite Almost Lynched by Populace," *Plain Dealer* (Cleveland, OH), July 9, 1908
64. Helg, "To Be Black and to Be Cuban," 134.
65. Ibid., 134–135.
66. Guerra, *The Myth of Jose Marti*, 228.
67. Helg, "To Be Black and to Be Cuban," 137.
68. Guerra, *The Myth of Jose Marti*, 229.
69. Ibid., 228.
70. "Cuban Republic Faces a Crisis: Independent Negro Party Foments Trouble," *Colorado Springs Gazette* (Colorado Springs, CO), May 5, 1910.
71. "Cuba Is Facing Political Crisis: Grave Danger of War between the Races," *Colorado Springs Gazette* (Colorado Springs, CO), May 6, 1910; "Trouble in Cuba: II. The Race Question," *Fort Worth Star Telegram* (Fort Worth, TX), May 6, 1910.

72. The third page is not available in any paper that I have been able to locate.
73. "Cuba Is Facing Political Crisis: Grave Danger of War between the Races," *Colorado Springs Gazette* (Colorado Springs, CO), May 6, 1910.
74. Frederic J. Haskin, "Trouble in Cuba: The Problem of Annexation," *Times Picayune*, May 8, 1910.
75. Perez, *Cuba and the United States*, 156.
76. Guerra, *The Myth of Jose Marti*, 229; Helg, "Black Men, Racial Stereotyping, and Violence," 587
77. Guerra, *The Myth of Jose Marti*, 229.
78. Perez, *Cuba and the United States*, 157; Ironically, Lillian Guerra asserts that no U.S. property was damaged during the uprising. Guerra, *The Myth of Jose Marti*, 229.
79. De la Fuente, *A Nation for All*, 74.
80. Guerra, *The Myth of Jose Marti*, 229.
81. Helg, "Black Men, Racial Stereotyping, and Violence," 587.
82. Ibid, 587–587; Guerra, *The Myth of Jose Marti*, 231.
83. Guerra, *The Myth of Jose Marti*, 232.
84. Ibid., 236.
85. Ibid., 199.
86. "Cuba Wars on Voodoo: President Menocal Striving to Stamp Out Orgies," *Washington Post*, December 29, 1913; "Cuban Child Butchered by Voodooists: Government of Cuba Fighting Voodooism," *Galveston Daily News*, December 28, 1913; "Cuba Stops Voodooism," *Los Angeles Times*, April 19, 1914; "Cuba Stops Voodooism," *The Philadelphia Inquirer*, February 15, 1914.
87. "Cuban Child Butchered by Voodooists," *Galveston Daily News*, December 28, 1913.
88. For example, see "Two Negro Sorcerers in Cuba Condemned to Die," *Colorado Springs Gazette*, May 10, 1916; "Death for Three Voodooists," *Washington Post*, May 14, 1916.
89. Guerra, *The Myth of Jose Marti*, 243; Perez, *Cuba and the United States*, 156.
90. Perez, *Cuba and the United States*, 156.
91. Ibid., 157.
92. Guerra, *The Myth of Jose Marti*, 244.
93. Ibid., 246.
94. "Awful Rites of Voodoo: Torture of 7 Year Old Cuban Girl Reveals Witchcraft Cult Is on New Ground," *Lowell Sun*, October 15, 1918; "Beautiful Girl Is Victim of Voodooism in Havana; Father Leads in Torture of Daughter," *Miami District Daily News*, September 25, 1918.
95. Perez, *Cuba and the United States*, 161.
96. Ibid., 161.
97. Ibid., 163.
98. "Cuba Has Outbreak of Cannibalistic Practices," *Baltimore American*, August 10, 1919; "Voodoo Orgies Are Discovered in Cuba," *Dallas Morning News*, August 9, 1919; "Fear Little Ones May Be Offered In Cannibal Rites," *The Ogden Examiner* (Ogden, UT), August 11, 1919; "Cuban Voodoos Slay: Keep Parents on Island in Constant Fear," *Palo Alto Reporter*, August 11, 1919; "Cuban Voodoo Fanatics

Practice Cannibalism," *Fort Wayne News and Sentinel*, August 11, 1919; "Parents Terrorized as Voodoo Worship Is Revived in Cuba," *Bridgeport Standard Telegram*, August 8, 1919; "Voodoo Fanatics in Cuba Offer Innocents as Human Sacrifice," *San Antonio Light*, August 8, 1919; "Voodoos Kill Cuban Babes," *Reno Evening Gazette*, August 8, 1919.

99. Aline Helg compares lynching in the U.S. and Cuba and the role of accusations of the rape of white women in the former compared to allegations of witchcraft in the latter. Helg, "Black Men, Racial Stereotyping, and Violence," 578.
100. Román, *Governing Spirits*, 83.
101. Additionally, another accused individual was found dead in his cell the day before the mob stormed the prison. Palmie does not specify the cause of this man's demise. Palmie, *Wizards & Scientists*, 241–242; "Little Girls Voodoo Victims of Fanatical Cuban Organizations," *Billings Gazette* (Billings, MT), November 9, 1919; "Negros Charged with Death of Girls Killed by Soldiers," *Galveston Daily News* (Galveston, TX), July 1, 1919.
102. "Guards Shoot Negro Voodoo Worshippers," *Syracuse Herald*, June 30, 1919; "Voodoo Worshippers Slain," *Charleston Mail*, June 30, 1919; "Negro Voodoo Worshipers Shot," *Commerce Journal* (Hunt County, TX), July 4, 2019.
103. "Lynching Fighting Voodoo Cannibals," *Macon Telegraph*, August 17, 1919.
104. "Cubans Invoke Lynch Law to Curb Voodoos," *Twin Falls News*, August 7, 1919.
105. "Revival of Voodoo Practices in Cuba Causes Lynchings," *Montgomery Advertiser*, August 10, 1919
106. "Enraged Cubans Apply Lynch Law against Voodoo," *Idaho Statesman*, August 8, 1919.
107. See "Fear Little Ones May Be Offered in Cannibal Rites" and "Chicago Race Rioters Fill Jails," *Ogden Examiner*, August 11, 1919.
108. "Little Girls Voodoo Victims of Fanatical Cuban Organizations," *Billings Gazette* (Billings, MT), November 9, 1919.
109. Ibid.; "The Cult of Human Sacrifices," *Dallas Morning News*, November 23, 1919.
110. "Little Girls Voodoo Victims of Fanatical Cuban Organizations," *Billings Gazette* (Billings, MT), November 9, 1919
111. "The Cult of Human Sacrifices," *Dallas Morning News*, November 23, 1919.
112. "Sorcerers to Die for Voodoo Murder," *Pawtucket Times*, May 10, 1916.
113. "Mexican Method Is Used in Cuba," *Gleaner* (Kingston, Jamaica), July 12, 1919.
114. Helg, "Black Men, Racial Stereotyping and Violence," 581.
115. Ibid., 581–582.
116. Quoted in Bronfman, "En Plena Libertad y Democracia," 585.
117. Quoted in Ibid., 585.
118. "White Child Voodoo Victim," *Victoria Daily Advocate*, December 18, 1922, p. 3 (Victoria, TX); "White Child Voodoo Victim," *Washington Post*, November 17, 1922; "White Child Voodoo Victim," *Victoria Daily Advocate*, December 18, 1922
119. "White Girl Burned on Jungle Altar?" *Moberly-Monitor Index*, December 8, 1922; "Cuba Has Another Voodoo Mystery," *Nevada State Journal*, December 3, 1922; "Probe Voodoo Mystery," *Lexington Herald*, December 8, 1922; "Disappearance of

Child Gives Rise to Voodoo Mystery," *Twin Falls News*, December 3, 1922; "Cuba Has Another Voodoo Mystery," *Nevada State Journal*, December 3, 1922; "Child Sacrificed by Negro Voodoo Doctors, Is Fear," *Janesville Daily Gazette*, December 8, 1922.
120. "Body Is Found in Voodoo Hut," *Reno Evening Gazette*, April 4, 1923; "White Boy Slain in Voodoo Rites," *Oakland Tribune*, April 4, 1923.
121. C. W. Lowther, "Voodooism in Cuba," *Times* (London), October 10, 1919.
122. George Musgrave, "Voodooism in Cuba," *Times* (London), October 14, 1919.
123. De La Fuente, *A Nation for All*, 102
124. Carr, "Identity, Class, and Nation," 94.
125. McLeod, "Undesirable Aliens," 611.
126. Arthur Powell, "Cuban Mystic Voodoo Rites Resemble U.S. Ceremonies: Criminal Aspects Removed," *Syracuse Herald*, January 13, 1929.
127. Ibid.
128. "Girl of 7 Chosen as Sacrifice," *Helena Independent*, April 17, 1927.
129. Arthur Powell, "Cuban Mystic Voodoo Rites Resemble U.S. Ceremonies: Criminal Aspects Removed," *Syracuse Herald*, January 13, 1929; "Cuban Mystic Voodoo Rites Resemble U.S. Ceremonies: Government Wars on Mystic Ceremonies and Cults," *Mason City Globe Gazette*, June 27, 1929.
130. "Cuban Voodoos Behead Child in Rites, Report," *Capital Times*, December 16, 1930; "Probe Activities of Voodoo Worshippers," *Monitor-Index and Democrat* (Moberly, MO), December 16, 1930.
131. "Girl of 7 Chosen as Sacrifice," *Helena Independent*, April 17, 1927.

Chapter 3

1. Lammasniemi, "Anti-White Slavery Legislation," 68.
2. Ibid., 64–65.
3. Ibid., 67.
4. Ibid., 66–67.
5. Morone, *Hellfire Nation*, 260.
6. Donovan, *White Slave Crusades*, 2.
7. Diffee, "Sex and the City," 416.
8. Lammasniemi, "Anti-White Slavery Legislation," 66.
9. Donovan, *White Slave Crusades*, 1.
10. Morone, *Hellfire Nation*, 266.
11. Ibid., 265.
12. Donovan, *White Slave Crusades*, 1.
13. Morone, *Hellfire Nation*, 266.
14. Ibid., 267.
15. Morgan, "Jack Johnson versus the American Racial Hierarchy," 79.
16. Hutchinson, "Framing White Hopes," 25.
17. Morgan, "Jack Johnson versus the American Racial Hierarchy," 80.

18. Hutchinson, "Framing White Hopes," 32.
19. Morgan, "Jack Johnson versus the American Racial Hierarchy," 82.
20. Hutchinson, "Framing White Hopes," 31.
21. Ibid., 36.
22. Ibid., 36.
23. Ibid., 37
24. Ibid., 37
25. Morone, *Hellfire Nation*, 268.
26. Public Broadcasting Service, "Jack Johnson's Arrest," https://www.pbs.org/kenburns/unforgivable-blackness/johnsons-arrest/ (last visited December 14, 2021)
27. "William Johnson Disciple of Jack," *Connersville Evening News*, January 28, 1913.
28. Ibid.
29. Ibid.
30. Ibid.
31. Ibid.
32. "Voodoo Doctor Sentenced," *Bloomfield News* (Bloomfield, IN), January 30, 1913
33. "William Johnson Disciple of Jack," *Connersville Evening News*, January 28, 1913.
34. Ibid.
35. Ibid.
36. 'Voodoo Doctor Sentenced," *Bloomfield News* (Bloomfield, IN), January 30, 1913.
37. Ibid.
38. Ibid.
39. "William Johnson Disciple of Jack," *Connersville Evening News*, January 28, 1913
40. "Voodoo Artist Needs His Spirits' Aid Now," *News-Sentinel* (Fort Wayne, IN), April 2, 1922.
41. Ibid.
42. "White Woman Is Held by Negro," *Lincoln Star* (Lincoln, NE), April 1, 1922
43. "White Woman Held Prisoner Eight Years by Negro Voodoo 'Doctor,'" *San Antonio Evening News* (San Antonio, TX), April 1, 1922
44. Diffee, "The White Slavery Scare," 414.
45. "Voodoo Artist Needs His Spirits' Aid Now," *News-Sentinel* (Fort Wayne, IN), April 2, 1922.
46. Ibid.
47. "White Woman Is Held by Negro," *Lincoln Star* (Lincoln, NE), April 1, 1922.
48. Ibid.
49. "Voodoo Artist Needs His Spirits' Aid Now," *News-Sentinel* (Fort Wayne, IN), April 2, 1922; "White Woman, Eight Years Captive of Negro 'Voodoo' Doctor, Rescued by Police," *Wisconsin State Journal*, April 2, 1922
50. "White Woman Held Prisoner Eight Years by Negro Voodoo 'Doctor,'" *San Antonio Evening News* (San Antonio, TX), April 1, 1922
51. Ibid.
52. Ibid.
53. Morone, *Hellfire Nation*, 269

54. "Voodoo Artist Needs His Spirits' Aid Now," *News-Sentinel* (Fort Wayne, IN), April 2, 1922
55. "White Woman Held Prisoner Eight Years by Negro Voodoo 'Doctor,'" *San Antonio Evening News* (San Antonio, TX), April 1, 1922
56. "White Woman, Eight Years Captive of Negro 'Voodoo' Doctor, Rescued by Police," *Wisconsin State Journal*, April 2, 1922
57. Watson, "Mary Church Terrell," 68.
58. Ibid., 69.
59. Hixson, "Moorfield Storey and the Defense of the Dyer Anti-Lynching Bill," 67.
60. Ibid., 66.
61. Ibid., 67–68.
62. Ibid., 74.
63. Ibid., 68.
64. "Death for Girl's Assailant," *Washington Post*, March 15, 1922.
65. Ibid.
66. Ibid.
67. "Attempt Made to Save Negro," *Evening Review* (East Liverpool, OH), May 3, 1922.
68. Ibid.
69. "Negro Handed at Moundsville," *Evening Review* (East Liverpool, OH), May 5, 1922.
70. "Voodoo Doctor Kills Girl Who Refuse to Pay Sum Demanded," *Fitchburg Sentinel*, October 8, 1923
71. "'Hand of Death' to Feature Trial," *Altoona Mirror* (Altoona, PA), October 9, 1923.
72. "Hauley Held in Nurse Murder Case," *Kingston Daily Freeman* (Kingston, NY), October 9, 1923. "Nurse Killed by Negro with 70-Pound Rock," *Oneonta Daily Star* (Oneonta, NY), October 9, 1923.
73. Ibid.
74. Ibid.
75. "Hauley Held in Nurse Murder Case," *The Kingston Daily Freeman* (Kingston, NY), October 9, 1923.
76. Ibid.
77. "Nurse Killed by Negro with 70-Pound Rock," *Oneonta Daily Star* (Oneonta, NY), October 9, 1923.
78. Ibid. "Murder Charge Made against Negro Butler," *Brownsville Herald*, October 8, 1923
79. "Nurse Killed by Negro with 70-Pound Rock," *Oneonta Daily Star* (Oneonta, NY), October 9, 1923
80. "A Negro Voodoo Doctor a Killer," *Hutchinson News* (Hutchinson, KS), October 8, 1923
81. "Hauley Held in Nurse Murder Case," *Kingston Daily Freeman* (Kingston, NY), October 9, 1923; "Voodoo Man Killed Girl," *Lincoln State Journal*, October 8, 1923
82. This article says that the taxi driver's name was Will Shaw, not Walter Hauley. This appears to be the only news story using this name. "Voodoo Man's Bloody Cards Solve Homicide," *Baltimore Afro-American*, October 12, 1923.

83. "Voodoo Man's Bloody Cards Solve Homicide," *Baltimore Afro-American*, October 12, 1923.
84. Ibid.
85. "'Hand of Death' to Feature Trial," *Altoona Mirror* (Altoona, PA), October 9, 1923; "Murder Charge Made against Negro Butler," *Brownsville Herald*, October 8, 1923.
86. "Voodoo Doctor Kills Girl Who Refuse to Pay Sum Demanded," *Fitchburg Sentinel*, October 8, 1923.
87. "'Voodoo Doctor' Guilty," *Titusville Herald* (Titusville, PA), November 23, 1923
88. "Negro Voodoo Doctor Electrocuted for Murder," *Daily Constitution* (Chillicothe, MO), April 1, 1924
89. "'Voodoo Doctor' to Pay Death Penalty at Moundsville," *Evening Review* (East Liverpool, OH), May 4, 1922; "Voodoo Doctor Hanged," *Gettysburg Times*, May 6, 1922.
90. "'Voodoo' Crime: Pretty Girl Murdered," *Sydney Farmer and Settler* (Sydney, Australia), October 12, 1923. Interestingly, except for a Black newspaper, the *Baltimore Afro-American*, and an article written by H. B. Laufman that circulated in a few newspapers, very few reporters outright specified Barthel's race. H. B. Laufman, "Voodoo Murderer Summons Demons with Wild Tattoo," *Canton Daily News* (Canton, OH), October 11, 1923; "Voodoo Man's Bloody Cards Solve Homicide," *Baltimore Afro-American*, October 12, 1923 However, descriptions of her innocence, youth, and beauty likely suggested her whiteness to readers.
91. "'Voodoo Doctor' Confessed to Murder of Pretty Nurse," *Moberly Evening Democrat* (Moberly, MO), October 8, 1923.
92. "A Negro Voodoo Doctor a Killer," *Hutchinson News* (Hutchinson, KS), October 8, 1923; "'Voodoo Doctor' Confessed to Murder of Pretty Nurse," *Moberly Evening Democrat* (Moberly, MO), October 8, 1923.
93. "Voodoo Doctor Kills Girl Who Refuse to Pay Sum Demanded," *Fitchburg Sentinel*, October 8, 1923; "A Negro Voodoo Doctor a Killer," *Hutchinson News* (Hutchinson, KS), October 8, 1923.
94. "A Negro Voodoo Doctor a Killer," *Hutchinson News* (Hutchinson, KS), October 8, 1923; Nurse Murdered by Voodoo Doctor," *Lowell Sun* (Lowell, MA), October 8, 1923
95. H. B. Laufman, "Voodoo Murderer Summons Demons with Wild Tattoo," *Canton Daily News* (Canton, OH), October 11, 1923.
96. "Negro Voodoo Doctor Goes to His Death," *Mexia Daily News* (Mexia, TX), March 31, 1924; "'Voodoo Doctor' to Pay Death Penalty at Moundsville," *Evening Review* (East Liverpool, OH), May 4, 1922.
97. "Negro Voodoo Doctor Goes to His Death," *Mexia Daily News* (Mexia, TX), March 31, 1924; "'Voodoo Doctor' to Pay Death Penalty at Moundsville," *Evening Review* (East Liverpool, OH), May 4, 1922
98. "Death for Girl's Assailant," *Washington Post*, March 15, 1922.
99. "Went to Death Calmly," *Athens Messenger* (Athens, OH), May 5, 1922.
100. "Negro Handed at Moundsville," *Evening Review* (East Liverpool, OH), May 5, 1922.

101. Laufman, "Voodoo Murderer Summons Demons with Wild Tattoo," *Canton Daily News* (Canton, OH), October 11, 1923.
102. Ibid.
103. Alexander, "The Great Migration in Comparative Perspective," 361.
104. Laufman, "Voodoo Murderer Summons Demons With Wild Tattoo," *Canton Daily News* (Canton, OH), October 11, 1923.
105. Ibid.
106. Ibid.
107. Ibid.
108. Ibid.
109. "Voodoo Doctor Threatens All His Captors," *Baltimore Afro-American*, October 19, 1923; H. B. Laufman, "Slayer Calls Voodoo Sorcery Demons," *Marion Daily Star*, October 12, 1923
110. Slocum, *Black Towns, Black Futures*, 3.
111. Oklahoma Commission to Study the Tulsa Race Riot of 1921, "Tulsa Race Riot," 37–302.
112. Ibid., 12–13.
113. Ibid., 88–89.
114. Jason Romisher, "Lawnside, New Jersey," *Encyclopedia of Greater Philadelphia*, https://philadelphiaencyclopedia.org/archive/lawnside-new-jersey/ (last visited March 4, 2021).
115. Roberts, *Rediscover the Hidden New Jersey*, 3.
116. Borough of Lawnside, New Jersey, "About Us," https://www.lawnside.net/about-us (last visited March 4, 2021).
117. "Find Negro Voodoo Doctor's Victims," *Appleton Post-Crescent* (Appleton, WI), April 10, 1925
118. "Bones Lead to Arrest of Negro Voodoo Doctor," *Titusville Herald*, (Titusville, PA), April 10, 1925.
119. "Alleged Voodoo 'Doctor' Listed Victims, Claimed," *Oil City Derrick* (Oil City, PA), April 11, 1925; "Child Accuses Voodoo Doctor," *Fitchburg Sentinel*, April 10, 1925.
120. "Find Negro Voodoo Doctor's Victims," *Appleton Post-Crescent* (Appleton, WI), April 10, 1925.
121. "Alleged Voodoo 'Doctor' Listed Victims, Claimed," *Oil City Derrick* (Oil City, PA), April 11, 1925.
122. Ibid.; "Find Negro Voodoo Doctor's Victims," *Appleton Post-Crescent* (Appleton, WI), April 10, 1925.
123. "Slates Persons for Murder or 'To Be Ruined,'" *Logansport Morning Press* (Logansport, IN), April 11, 1925
124. "Bones Lead to Arrest of Negro Voodoo Doctor," *Titusville Herald*, (Titusville, PA), April 10, 1925.
125. "Voodoo Doctor Is Murder Suspect," *Des Moines Capital* (Des Moines, IA), April 10, 1925; "Voodoo Doctor's List of Murders," *Helena Independent* (Helena, MT), April 11, 1925; "Police Raze Voodoo House Labyrinths," *Waterloo Evening Courier* (Waterloo, IA), April 13, 1925.

126. "Police Raze Voodoo House Labyrinths," *Waterloo Evening Courier* (Waterloo, IA), April 13, 1925.
127. "Still Believe in 'Witches,' 'Spells' and 'Evil Spirits,'" *San Antonio Light* (San Antonio, TX), January 27, 1929.
128. "Horrors of New Voodoo Love Cult Terrorize Negroes in South Jersey," *Abilene Daily Reporter* (Abilene, TX), August 12, 1926.
129. "Secrets of Vicious 'Voodoo Doctors' Who Victimize Gullible Girls," *Hamilton Evening Journal* (Hamilton, OH), October 9, 1926.
130. Ibid.
131. Ibid.
132. "Secrets of Vicious 'Voodoo Doctors' Who Victimize Gullible Girls," *Hamilton Evening Journal* (Hamilton, OH), October 9, 1926..
133. Ibid.
134. "Voodoo Seer Languishes in Jail at Tulsa," *Amarillo Sunday News and Globe*, January 8, 1928.
135. "Woman's Story Lands Negro Mystic in Jail," *Miami News Record*, January 8, 1928.
136. "Awarded Small Damages," *Ada Evening News* (Ada, OK), May 11, 1928; "Negro Seer on Trial for Attacking Woman," *Miami News Record*, January 24, 1928.
137. "Voodoo Seer Languishes in Jail at Tulsa," *Amarillo Sunday News and Globe*, January 8, 1928.
138. "Woman's Story Lands Negro Mystic in Jail," *Miami News Record*, January 8, 2020; "Voodoo Seer Languishes in Jail at Tulsa," *Amarillo Sunday News and Globe*, January 8, 1928; "Tulsa Violinist Is Awarded $750 Damages," *Admore Daily Admoreite*, May 11, 1929.
139. "Woman's Story Lands Negro Mystic in Jail," *Miami News Record*, January 8, 1928.
140. "Voodoo Seer Languishes in Jail at Tulsa," *Amarillo Sunday News and Globe*, January 8, 1928.
141. "Negro Seer on Trial for Attacking Woman," *Miami News Record*, January 24, 1928.
142. Ibid.
143. "Voodoo Seer Languishes in Jail at Tulsa," *Amarillo Sunday News and Globe*, January 8, 1928
144. Ibid.; "Woman's Story Lands Negro Mystic in Jail," *Miami News Record*, January 8, 2020
145. "Voodoo Seer Languishes in Jail at Tulsa," *Amarillo Sunday News and Globe*, January 8, 1928.
146. Ibid.
147. "Awarded Small Damages," *Ada Evening News* (Ada, OK), May 11, 1928.

Chapter 4

1. "Headless Body Found in Ohio; 'Doctor' Held," *Sheboygan Press*, December 21, 1928, p. 1 (Sheboygan, WI).

2. Ibid.; "Voodoo Doctor Admits Slaying; No Victim Found," *Billings Gazette*, December 22, 1928.
3. "Voodoo Doctor Admits Slaying; No Victim Found," *Billings Gazette*, December 22, 1928, p. 2.
4. "Voodoo Rite Blamed for Beheading," *Davenport Democrat*, December 21, 1928, p. 1 (Democrat, IA). Similarly, a reporter for the *Billings Gazette* wrote that the detective "could advance no motive other than some ghastly rite for the slaying." "Voodoo Doctor Admits Slaying; No Victim Found," *Billings Gazette*, December 22, 1928.
5. "Headless Body of Man and Story of 'Voodoo' Mystify," *Messenger*, December 31, 1928, p. 3 (Athens, OH).
6. "Voodoo Doctor Held in Headless Body Case," *Amarillo Globe* (Amarillo, TX), December 21, 1928, p. 2; "'Voodoo Healer' Admits Murder," *Port Arthur News*, December 21, 1928, p. 9.
7. "Headless Body of Man and Story of 'Voodoo' Mystify," *Messenger* (Athens, OH), December 31, 1928, p. 3; "Headless Body Found in Ohio; 'Doctor' Held," *Sheboygan Press* (Sheboygan, WI), December 21, 1928, p. 1.
8. *Adams v. State*, 114 Tex. Crim. 494, November 20, 1929 (Court of Criminal Appeals of Texas) at 495.
9. "Hold Voodoo Doctor in Killing," *San Antonio Light*, February 14, 1929, p. 10A; *Adams v. State*, 114 Tex. Crim. 494, November 20, 1929 (Court of Criminal Appeals of Texas) at 496.
10. "Negro Voodoo Doctor Given Death Penalty," *Galveston Daily News*, March 16, 1929, p. 6.
11. "Court Affirms Sentence Given to Voodoo Doctor," *Galveston Daily News*, November 21, 1929, p. 2.
12. "Voodoo Doctor Executed for Murder of Grocer in Austin Store Robbery," *San Antonio Express*, March 13, 1929, p. 1.
13. Interestingly, one reporter describing the execution said, "Adams, who forsook his voodoo charms, first for the Baptist faith, later—today—reaffirmed his allegiance to Catholicism, his childhood faith." "Voodoo Doctor Executed for Murder of Grocer in Austin Store Robbery," *San Antonio Express*, March 13, 1929, p. 1.
14. "Voodoo Doctor Expects Life to Be Saved," *Amarillo Globe*, March 11, 1930.
15. "Negro Voodoo Doctor Given Death Penalty," *Galveston Daily News*, March 16, 1929, p. 6; "Texas Voodoo Doctor Sentenced to Death," *Fresno Bee*, March 16, 1929, p. 2.
16. "Axe Used to Kill Parents and Kiddies," *Border Cities Star*, July 3, 1929; "Arrest in Cult Murder," *Evening Independent*, July 4, 1929.
17. "Exposing the 'Evil Eye' in Civilized America," *Spokesman-Review*, August 2, 1929.
18. Nance, "Mystery of the Moorish Science Temple," 126, 127.
19. Lincoln, *The Black Muslims in America*, 51.
20. Turner, *Islam in the African American Experience*, 92–93; Lincoln, *The Black Muslims in America*, 51.
21. Turner, *Islam in the African American Experience*, 93; Nance, "Mystery of the Moorish Science Temple," 134–135.
22. Lincoln, *The Black Muslims in America*, 52.

23. "Guard Patrols Scene of Negro 'Cult' Battle," *Sheboygan Press*, September 26, 1929, p. 24; "Police Patrol Black Belt to Prevent Riots," *Decatur Evening Herald*, September 26, 1929, p. 1; "'Black Belt' of Chicago Is Being Guarded," *Delphos Daily Herald* (Delphos, OH), September 26, 1929, p. 1; "A Secret Negro Cult Revealed," *Marshall Evening Chronicle* (Marshall, MI), September 26, 1929, p. 1; "Cops, Militia on Guard in Black Belt," *Wisconsin State Journal*, September 26, 1929, pp. 1, 6.
24. "Guard Patrols Scene of Negro 'Cult' Battle," *Sheboygan Press*, September 26, 1929, p. 24; "Police Patrol Black Belt to Prevent Riots," *Decatur Evening Herald*, September 26, 1929, p. 1.
25. "Guard Patrols Scene of Negro 'Cult' Battle," *Sheboygan Press*, September 26, 1929, p. 24; "Police Patrol Black Belt to Prevent Riots," *Decatur Evening Herald*, September 26, 1929, p. 1.
26. "Called by Allah to Kill, Negro Slays Neighbor," *Nevada State Journal*, November 22, 1932.
27. "Cult Leader Says Victim Gave Consent," *Daily Mail*, November 22, 1932 (Hagerstown, MD); "Head of Cult Admits Killing," *Detroit News*, November 21, 1932; "Negro Slain in Voodoo Rites," *Escanaba Daily Press* (Escanaba, MI), November 22, 1932, p. 1.
28. "Negro Slain in Voodoo Rites," *Escanaba Daily Press*, November 22, 1932, p. 1.
29. Marsh, *From Black Muslims to Muslims*, 37.
30. White Jr., *Inside the Nation of Islam*, 7–9.
31. Ibid., 15–16.
32. Marsh, *From Black Muslims to Muslims*, 37.
33. "Negro Cult Leader Held after Making Sacrifice," *Circleville Herald* (Circleville, OH), November 21, 1932, p. 1.
34. "Negro Confesses Killing Another in Cult Sacrifice," *Sarasota Herald-Tribune*, November 21, 1932. Other newspapers reported similar suspicions: "Tells of Killing Negro on Altar," *Spokesman-Review*, November 21, 1932.
35. "Negro Slain in Voodoo Rites," *Escanaba Daily Press*, November 22, 1932, p. 1.
36. "Called by Allah to Kill, Negro Slays Neighbor," *Nevada State Journal*, November 22, 1932.
37. Ibid.
38. "Negro Slain in Voodoo Rites," *Escanaba Daily Press*, November 22, 1932, p. 1.
39. Ibid.
40. "'Cult' Crime in Detroit," *Lowell Sun* (Lowell, MA), November 21, 1932; "Negro Cult Leader Admits Killing Man in Voodoo Worship," *Komoko Tribune* (Komoko, IN), November 25, 1932.
41. "Leader of Cult Called Insane," *Detroit News*, November 22, 1932.
42. Ibid.
43. "Leader of Cult to Be Quizzed" *Detroit News*, November 23, 1932.
44. Evanzz, *The Messenger*, 85. Gladys Smith was no relation to the victim, James Smith, and she had no connection to the Black Islamic community.
45. "Leader of Cult to Be Quizzed," *Detroit News*, November 23, 1932.
46. Ibid.

47. Ibid.
48. "Harris, Cult Slayer, Faces Court Friday," *Detroit News*, November 24, 1932.
49. "Cult Members Move to Free Their Leaders, *Morning Herald* (Hagerstown, MD), November 25, 1932.
50. "Cult Slayer Pleads Guilty," *Detroit Free Press*, November 25, 1932.
51. Ibid.
52. Ibid.
53. "Negro Cult Leader Admits Killing Man in Voodoo Worship," *Komoko Tribune* (Komoko, IN), November 25, 1932. Correlation Summary: Wallace D. Fard, January 15, 1958, FBI Files: Wallace D. Fard, Part 2, p. 63, http://foia.fbi.gov/fard/fard2.pdf.
54. "Negro Cult Leader Admits Killing Man in Voodoo Worship," *Komoko Tribune*, November 25, 1932; "Cult Chief Admits He Killed Victim," *Ironwood Daily Globe* (Ironwood, MI), November 25, 1932.
55. Spenser St. John, *Hayti; or the Black Republic* (London: Smith, Elder, 1889) xii. First published in 1884.
56. For example, see "Cuban Child Butchered by Voodooists," *Galveston Daily News* (Galveston, TX), December 28, 1913; "Fear Little Ones May Be Offered in Cannibal Rites," *Ogden Examiner* (Ogden, UT), August 11, 1919; Cuba Has Another Voodoo Mystery," *Nevada State Journal*, December 3, 1922.
57. Turner, *Islam in the African American Experience*, 159.
58. Marsh, *From Black Muslims to Muslims*, 39; "Background Information on Wallace Fard," Letter, October 4, 1957, FBI Files: Wallace D. Ford, Part 1, p. 13, http://foia.fbi.gov/fard/fard1.pdf.
59. Wallace Fard Muhammad, FBI Files, Part 2 of 7, p. 42.
60. "Police Guard Woman, Girl," *Daily Hawk-Eye Gazette*, January 19, 1937.
61. Marsh, *From Black Muslims to Muslims*, 39.
62. Beynon, "The Voodoo Cult among Negro Migrants in Detroit," 902.
63. Ibid.; Clegg, *An Original Man*, 29.
64. Marsh, *From Black Muslims to Muslims*, 43.
65. One paper suggested that "prominent negroes, alarmed at the rate of withdrawal of colored students from the public schools and the teachings of the cult, complained to police." "Close Negro Cult School in Detroit," *Marshall Evening Chronicle* (Marshall, MI), April 17, 1934, pp. 1, 5.
66. "Close Negro Cult School in Detroit," *Marshall Evening Chronicle*, April 17, 1934, pp. 1, 5.
67. Ibid.
68. Central Research Section, Federal Bureau of Investigation, "The Muslim Cult of Islam," Monograph, June 26, 1955, FBI files: Nation of Islam, Part I, p. 33, http://foia.fbi.gov/nation_of_islam/nation_of_islam_part01.pdf.
69. "Nation of Islam: Cult of the Black Muslims," Monograph, May 1965, FBI files, Nation of Islam, Part 3, pp. 36–37, http://foia.fbi.gov/nation_of_islam/nation_of_islam_part03.pdf.
70. "Mob of Negroes Attack Policemen," *Daily Ardmoreite* (Ardmore, OK), April 18, 1934, p. 1.

71. "Six Policemen Beaten by Mob: Negro 'Voodoo' Worshippers Tear Coats of Detroit's Finest," *Jefferson City Post-Tribune*, April 14, 1934, p. 2.
72. "Cops Battle Negro Cult; Score Hurt," *Ottumwa Daily Courier* (Ottumwa, IO), April 18, 1934, p. 1.
73. "Detroit Mob Beats Police," *Santa Fe New Mexican*, April 18, 1934.
74. "Closing of Negro 'University of Islam' in Detroit Starts Riots in Which 500 Battle Police with Knives and Bricks," *San Antonio Express*, April 19, 1934.
75. These reports are cited in Clegg, *An Original Man*, 37. FBI files note only the charge for contributing to the delinquency of a minor. See: Inspection Report, May 16, 1957, FBI Files: Wallace D. Fard, Part 5, p. 3, http://foia.fbi.gov/filelink.html?file=/fard/fard5.pdf. Additionally, another document in the FBI files says that this arrest was due to the fact that they were not letting the children from the "University of Islam" attend public schools. Office Memorandum Re: Wallace Fard, July 3, 1957, FBI Files: Wallace D. Fard, Part 5, p. 20, http://foia.fbi.gov/filelink.html?file=/fard/fard5.pdf.
76. "Close Negro Cult School in Detroit," *Marshall Evening Chronicle* (Marshall, MI), pp. 1, 5.
77. "University of Islam," *Helena Daily Independent*, April 23, 1934, p. 4.
78. Ibid.
79. "Voodoo Leader Scares Couple into Collapse," *Daily Courier* (Connellsville, PA), January 20, 1937.
80. "Save Mother and Daughter from Sacrifice," *Morning Herald* (Uniontown, PA), January 20, 1937.
81. "Voodoo Leader Scares Couple into Collapse," *Daily Courier* (Connellsville, PA), January 20, 1937.
82. "Police Guard Woman, Girl: Negress Says Husband Threatened to 'Sacrifice Her to Allah,'" *Daily Hawk-eye Gazette* (Burlington, IO), January 19, 1937; "Voodoo Cult's Sacrifice to Allah Failed," *Lima News* (Lima, OH), January 20, 1937.
83. "Voodoo Leader Scares Couple into Collapse," *Daily Courier* (Connellsville, PA), January 20, 1937 However, aside from this initial flurry of articles in the days immediately following McQueen's arrest, little is known about these events. It is unclear if McQueen was actually a member of the Nation of Islam or whether he had ever met Robert Harris, Wallace Fard, or Elijah Muhammad. It is also unknown whether McQueen was ultimately charged for the threats he made to his wife and if so, the disposition of McQueen's case.
84. Beynon, "The Voodoo Cult among Negro Migrants in Detroit," 894–907.
85. Ibid., 894.
86. Edward Curtis, a scholar writing on the Nation of Islam in 2002, noted that almost every work on the history of Black Islam relies on "a seminal article by sociologist Erdmann Beynon." Curtis, *Black Muslim Religion in the Nation of Islam*, 69.
87. Beynon, "The Voodoo Cult among Negro Migrants in Detroit," 903–904.
88. Ibid., 903–904.
89. Ibid., 904.
90. Allen, "When Japan Was 'Champion of the Darker Races,'" 28.
91. Ibid., 29.

92. Ibid.
93. Ibid.
94. Ibid., 31.
95. Ibid. 32.
96. Ibid. 32–33.
97. Ibid. 34–36; Wallace Fard Muhammad, FBI Files, Part 2 of 7, p. 53.
98. "Negro Woman's Fear Leads to Cult Activity," *Mexia Weekly Herald*, January 22, 1937, p. 4; "Cult Sacrifice Plot Is Bared," *Ogden Standard Examiner* (Ogden City, UT), January 20, 1937, p. 1; "Practice Voodoo Cult Revealed in N.Y., Chicago, Can." *Brainerd Daily Dispatch* (Brainerd, MN), January 20, 1937, p. 1.
99. "Negro Woman's Fear Leads to Cult Activity," *Mexia Weekly Herald*, January 22, 1937, p. 4;
100. Marsh, *From Black Muslims to Muslims*, 44; Allen, "When Japan Was 'Champion of the Darker Races,'" 23.
101. Turner, *Islam in the African American Experience*, 168–169.
102. "FBI Arrests Members of Three Negro Religious Cults," *Freeport Journal Standard* (Freeport, IL), September 21, 1942, p. 11.
103. Ibid.
104. "Murphy on Negro Cult's Sacrifice List," *Waterloo Daily Courier* (Waterloo, IA), September 23, 1942, p. 14.
105. Wallace Fard Muhammad, FBI Files, Part 2 of 7, p. 54.
106. "Background Information on Wallace Fard," Office Memorandum, March 4, 1965, FBI Files: Wallace D. Ford, Part 1, p. 8, http://foia.fbi.gov/fard/fard1.pdf.
107. Lincoln, *The Black Muslims in America*, 13.
108. Ibid. Later Lincoln merely says, "The Detroit Muslims of the 1930s had a number of bizarre excesses charged against them, including, as we have seen, human sacrifice." After quoting a newspaper account of the Harris trial, Lincoln continued, "Other reports of sacrifices or attempted sacrifices were current in Detroit as late as 1937." Ibid., 204.
109. George Sokolsky, "U.S. Negro Cult Preaches Hate, Claims ¼ Million Membership," *Ogden Standard Examiner* (Ogden, UT), February 28, 1961; George Sokolsky, "Islam Cult in UN Riot," *Sunday Light* (San Antonio, TX), February 26, 1961.
110. "Black Muslim Founder Exposed as a White," *Herald Examiner* (Los Angeles, CA), July 28, 1963.
111. Ibid.
112. Elijah Muhammad famously responded by declaring the entire article to be a fabrication and offering to pay $100,000 if someone could prove these claims.
113. Brown, "Black Muslims and the Police," 119–126.
114. Ibid., 120.
115. Ibid., 125–126.
116. Merv Block, "Muslims Gain Strength under Paradoxical Leader," *Daily Review* (Hayword, CA), March 26, 1972 ; Merv Block, "The Black Muslims: Leaders Teach Austerity but Live Stylishly, Prosperously," *The Register* (Danville, VA), March 30,

1972 ; Merv Block, "The Black Muslims Messengers of Allah," *Stars and Stripes*, March 29, 1972.
117. Clegg, *An Original Man*, 31–32. Clegg argued that "Robert Harris, in his own distorted way, was trying to carry out the literal essence of this [Fard's] teaching," However, Elijah Muhammad's son argued in 1975 that Fard's teachings about the "white devils" were not meant to be literal. Turner, *Islam in the African American Experience*, 225. Other researchers repeated Clegg's angle in various recounts of the 1930s events. One scholar, Martha Lee, completely omitted Smith's race and Harris's insanity in her analysis of this crime. Lee stated that although Fard's support of human sacrifice "appears to have been temporary, at least one sacrifice was offered," again treating Smith's murder as an act fulfilling the purported teachings of Fard that followers of Islam must sacrifice four "white devils." Lee, *The Nation of Islam*, 24.
118. Evanzz, *The Messenger*, 83–84. Evanzz relies exclusively on newspaper archives to establish the purported connection between Fard and Harris. Ibid., 355–356.

Chapter 5

1. Allan Woods, "Fleeing to Canada, Asylum Seekers' Old Lies Revealed in the Scraps Found along New York's Roxham Rd.," *Toronto Star*, August 18, 2017, https://www.thestar.com/news/canada/2017/08/18/fleeing-to-canada-asylum-seekers-old-lives-revealed-in-the-scraps-found-along-new-yorks-roxham-rd.html.
2. Miller, *The Plight of Haitian Refugees*, 90.
3. Ibid.
4. Loyd and Mountz, *Boats, Borders, and Bases*, 45.
5. Ibid.
6. Laguerre, *American Odyssey*, 24; Miller, *The Plight of Haitian Refugees*, 62.
7. Ibid.
8. Ralph, "Haitian Interdiction on the High Seas," 232; Loyd and Mountz, *Boats, Borders, and Bases*, 43.
9. Ralph, "Haitian Interdiction on the High Seas," 232–233. Another source reports that out of 40,000 cases, only 100 were not dismissed as "frivolous." Loyd and Mountz, *Boats, Borders, and Bases*, 43.
10. Ralph, "Haitian Interdiction on the High Seas," 232–233.
11. Loyd and Mountz, *Boats, Borders, and Bases*, 46.
12. *Haitian Refugee Center et al. v. Benjamin Civiletti*, 517, 520, 524.
13. Ibid., 524.
14. Ralph, "Haitian Interdiction on the High Seas," 233; Loyd and Mountz, *Boats, Borders, and Bases*, 47; *Haitian Refugee Center et al. v. Benjamin Civiletti*, 524.
15. Loyd and Mountz, *Boats, Borders, and Bases*, 47.
16. Ibid.
17. Ralph, "Haitian Interdiction on the High Seas," 233; *Haitian Refugee Center et al. v. Benjamin Civiletti*, 451.

18. Refugee Act of 1980.
19. Ibid.
20. Ralph, "Haitian Interdiction on the High Seas," 229.
21. Ibid., 229–230.
22. LaGuerre, *American Odyssey*, 24–25.
23. Fjellman and Gladwin, "Haitian Family Patterns of Migration to South Florida," 302.
24. Laguerre, *American Odyssey*, 28.
25. "Haitians: Brother Murdered," *Times-Picayune*, August 3, 1980, Sect. 1, p. 34.
26. Ibid.; "Haitians Helpless in Brother's Death," *Colorado Springs Gazette Telegraph*, August 2, 1980, p. 47.
27. Miller, "International Concern for Haitians," 35–36.
28. Ibid., 36.
29. *Haitian Refugee Center et al. v. Benjamin Civiletti*.
30. Ibid., 451. Emphasis in original.
31. Ibid., 519.
32. Ibid., 477–493.
33. Ibid., 532.
34. Miller, *The Plight of Haitian Refugees*, 69; Loyd and Mountz, *Boats, Borders, and Bases*, 31.
35. Miller, *The Plight of Haitian Refugees*, 70; Loyd and Mountz, *Boats, Borders, and Bases*, 32.
36. Loyd and Mountz, *Boats, Borders, and Bases*, 31–32.
37. "Bahamians Back Police Action," *Colorado Springs Gazette Telegraph*, November 21, 1980, p. 8A.
38. Marc Charney, "Hungry Refugees Return to Haiti," *Cumberland News*, November 17, 1980, p. 2.
39. *United States v. Saintil and Tacius*, 753 F.2d 984, 1–2.
40. Ibid., 7.
41. Ibid., 3–4. "Haitian Refugee Deaths on a 2d Boat Reported," *New York Times*, October 24, 1981, Sect. 1, p. 7.
42. *United States v. Saintil and Tacius*, 753 F.2d 984, 3–4.
43. Miller, *The Plight of Haitian Refugees*, 72.
44. Ralph, "Haitian Interdiction on the High Seas," 235–236.
45. Ibid., 236.
46. Ronald Reagan, "Proclamation 4865—High Seas Interdiction of Illegal Aliens," September 29, 1981, available at https://www.archives.gov/federal-register/codification/proclamations/04865.html (last visited May 29, 2021).
47. Ibid.
48. Ronald Reagan, "Executive Order 12324—Interdiction of Illegal Aliens," September 29, 1981, https://www.archives.gov/federal-register/codification/executive-order/12324.html (last visited May 30, 2021).
49. Ralph, "Haitian Interdiction on the High Seas," 227.
50. Miller, *The Plight of Haitian Refugees*, 127.

51. Ibid., 128.
52. Ibid., 128.
53. Ibid., 129.
54. "Haitian Slayings Probed," *Brownsville Herald* (Brownsville, TX), October 16, 1981, p. 12A.
55. "U.S. Probes Abuse, Killings on Haitian Refugee Boat," *Madison Wisconsin State Journal*, October 16, 1981, p. 2.
56. "Haitian Slayings Probed," *Brownsville Herald*, October 16, 1981, p. 12A.
57. "U.S. Officials Check Haitian Murder Reports," *Medicine Hat News* (Medicine Hat, Alberta, Canada), October 17, 1981, p. 19.
58. *United States v. Belony Saintil and Kersazan Tacius*, 705 F.2d 415, 2.
59. William Safire, "Last Gasp for the 1960's Felt through Nation," *Alton Telegraph*, October 27, 1981, p. A-5.
60. William Safire, "Terrorists Try to Destroy U.S." *Times-Standard* (Eureka, CA), November 5, 1981, p. 4.
61. "State Department Says No U.S. Burials for Drowned Haitians," *Clearfield Progress* (Clearfield, PA), October 29, 1981, p. 24.
62. George Stelon, "Seeking New Life, Many Find Death," *Colorado Springs Gazette*, October 27, 1981, p. 5B.
63. "Flight for New Life to Florida Has Meant Death for Many Haitians," *Panama City News Herald* [Florida], April 1, 1982, p. 3E.
64. *United States v. Reme and Pierrot*, 738 F.2d 1156, 1–2.
65. "Human-Sacrifice Voodoo Deaths of Haitians Probed," *Madison Wisconsin State Journal*, November 11, 1981, p. 15; "Escape Boat Voodoo Deaths Report Probed," *Times-Picayune*, November 11, 1981, Sect. 3, p. 5; "Refugee Voodoo Killings Target of U.S. Probe," *Cedar Rapids Gazette* (Cedar Rapids, IA), November 15, 1981, p. 11A.
66. *United States v. Reme and Pierrot*, 738 F.2d 1156, 3.
67. Ibid., 4–5.
68. "Witness: Crew Feared Spirits Threw 2 Refugees Overboard," *Playground Daily News* (Fort Walton Beach, FL), November 12, 1982, p. 4B.
69. Ibid.
70. "Escape Boat Voodoo Deaths Report Probed," *Times-Picayune*, November 11, 1981, Sect. 3, p. 5; Karen Payne, "Tales of Voodoo Surface," *Santa Ana County Register*, November 11, 1981, p. A2.
71. "Escape Boat Voodoo Deaths Report Probed," *Times-Picayune*, November 11, 1981, Sect. 3, p. 5; "Feds Probe Claims of Human Sacrifice," *Lawrence World Journal* (Lawrence, KS), November 11, 1981, p. 30.
72. "Escape Boat Voodoo Deaths Report Probed," *Times-Picayune*, November 11, 1981, Sect. 3, p. 5; "Feds Probe Claims of Human Sacrifice," *Lawrence World Journal*, November 11, 1981, p. 30.

73. "Escape Boat Voodoo Deaths Report Probed," *Times-Picayune*, November 11, 1981, Sect. 3, p. 5; "Haitians Say 2 Sacrificed for Voodoo," *Charlotte Observer*, November 11, 1981, p. 4a
74. "Escape Boat Voodoo Deaths Report Probed," *Times-Picayune*, November 11, 1981, Sect. 3, p. 5.
75. Ibid.
76. "Voodoo Gods Are Satisfied," *Burlington Daily Times News* (Burlington, NC), November 14, 1981, p. 6; "Escape Boat Voodoo Deaths Report Probed," *Times-Picayune*, November 11, 1981, Sect. 3, p. 5; Karen Payne, "Tales of Voodoo Surface," *Santa Ana County Register*, November 11, 1981, p. A2; "Feds Probe Claims of Human Sacrifice," *Lawrence World Journal*, November 11, 1981, p. 30.
77. Ibid.
78. Ibid.
79. *United States v. Belony Saintil and Kersazan Tacius*, 705 F.2d 415, 4.
80. "Judge Dismisses Conspiracy Charges against 2 Haitians," *Fort Walton Beach Playground Daily News*, July 8, 1982, p. 5B.
81. Ibid.; "'Voodoo' Crew Indicted," *Colorado Springs Gazette Telegraph*, July 11, 1982, p. A10.
82. "10 on Voodoo Ship Indicted on Smuggling Charges," *Galveston Daily News* (Galveston, TX), July 11, 1982, p. 28; "'Voodoo' Crew Indicted," *Colorado Springs Gazette Telegraph*, July 11, 1982, p. A10.
83. "Haitian Detainees Now in Despair," *Kokomo Tribune* (Kokomo, IN), July 11, 1982, p. 7; "Freedom Has a Loophole," *Galveston Daily News*, July 11, 1982, p. 28.
84. "Haitian Detainees Now in Despair," *Kokomo Tribune*, July 11, 1982, p. 7; "Freedom Has a Loophole," *Galveston Daily News*, July 11, 1982, p. 28.
85. "Haitian Detainees Now in Despair," *Kokomo Tribune*, July 11, 1982, p. 7; "Freedom Has a Loophole," *Galveston Daily News*, July 11, 1982, p. 28.
86. "Haitian Detainees Now in Despair," *Kokomo Tribune*, July. 11, 1982, p. 7; "Freedom Has a Loophole," *Galveston Daily News*, July 11, 1982, p. 28.
87. *United States v. Reme and Pierrot*, 738 F.2d 1156, 3.
88. Ibid., 10–11.
89. Ibid., 29.
90. Ibid., 31.
91. Ibid., 20.
92. Ibid., 9.
93. Ibid.
94. Ibid., 36–37.
95. "A Haitian Boat Captain Accused of Killing Two Men . . . ," *United Press International*, January 11, 1983, https://www.upi.com/Archives/1983/01/11/A-Haitian-boat-captain-accused-of-killing-two-men/3516411109200/.
96. Ibid.
97. *United States v. Belony Saintil and Kersazan Tacius*, 705 F.2d 415, 9–10.
98. *United States v. Saintil and Tacius*, 753 F.2d 984, 17.

99. Doralisa Pilarte, "Illegal Florida Haitians Struggle to Survive," *Clovis News Journal* (Clovis, NM), December 24, 1985, p. 35.
100. Ibid.
101. Ibid.
102. Doralisa Pilarte, "Haitians Struggle toward Dream of Better Life," *Doylestown Intelligencer* (Doylestown, PA), December 29, 1985, p. 10; "Immigrant's Dream: A Better Life in America," *Northwest Arkansas Times* (Fayetteville, AK), December 22, 1985, p. 11A; Doralisa Pilarte, "Thousands of Haitians Fight to Stay in the City of Foreign Tongues," *Playground Daily News* (Fort Walton Beach, FL), December 22, 1985, p. 8B.
103. Doralisa Pilarte, "Florida Haitians: 'Last of the Unwanted Refugees,'" *European Stars and Stripes*, December 23, 1985, p. 13 (Darmstadt, Hesse); Doralisa Pilarte, "Haitian Immigrants Fight U.S. Policies to Stay in America," *Frederick Post* (Frederick, MD), January 9, 1986, p. E-4; Doralisa Pilarte, "Illegal Florida Haitians Struggle to Survive," *Clovis News Journal*, December 24, 1985, p. 35.
104. *United States v. Fritz Pierrot*, 861 F.2d 266 (1988).
105. "South Florida Schools Prepare for Haitian Influx," *Americans for Legal Immigration*, January 15, 2010, https://www.sun-sentinel.com/2010/01/15/south-florida-schools-prepare-for-haitian-influx/.
106. Ibid.
107. Elliot Spagat, Ashley Matthews, and Samantha Tatro, "US Toughens Stance on Haitians Seeing Entry from Brazil," *NBC 7 San Diego*, September 22, 2016, https://www.nbcsandiego.com/news/local/us-toughens-stance-on-haitians-seeking-entry-from-brazil/93858/.
108. Ibid.
109. Makini Brice and Sarah Marsh, "Hurricane Matthew Pummels Haiti and Cuba, Prepares to Strike US," *Charisma News*, October 5, 2016, https://www.charismanews.com/world/60363-hurricane-matthew-pummels-haiti-and-cuba-prepares-to-strike-us.
110. Ibid.
111. Jackie Littleford, "Matthew's Path," Letters to the Editor, *Orlando Sentinel*, October 28, 2016.
112. "Voodoo Haiti and Hurricane Matthew: Letter Writers Push Back," *Orlando Sentinel*, October 29, 2016, https://www.orlandosentinel.com/2016/10/29/voodoo-haiti-and-hurricane-matthew-letter-writers-push-back/.
113. Ibid.

Chapter 6

1. Van Dijk, "'Voodoo' on the Doorstep," 563.
2. Protocol to Prevent, Suppress and Punish Trafficking in Persons, art. 3.
3. Baarda, "Human Trafficking for Sexual Exploitation," 258.

4. Mrs. Halima Embarek Warzazi, Report of the Working Group on Contemporary Forms of Slavery on its twenty-seventh session, Economic and Social Council, UN Doc. E/CN.4/Sub.2/2002/33, June 17, 2002, at paragraph 16.
5. Cole, "Reducing the Damage," 217.
6. Dunkerley, "Exploring the Use of Juju," 84–85.
7. Cole, "Reducing the Damage," 219–221.
8. "Spanish Police Arrest 23 People for 'Using Voodoo Curses,'" *Telegraph*, May 22, 2009.
9. Cole, "Reducing the Damage," 223.
10. Cole, "Reducing the Damage," 220.
11. "Spanish Police Arrest 23 People for 'Using Voodoo Curses,'" *Telegraph*, May 22, 2009; Emma Anderson, "Busted: Gang That Used Voodoo to Exploit Women," *Local* (Stockholm, Sweden), June 8, 2015.
12. "Italian Police Break Up Prostitution Ring," *NewsBank*, October 5, 2012.
13. Cole, "Reducing the Damage," 221; Van Dijk, "'Voodoo' on the Doorstep," 565.
14. Dunkerley, "Exploring the Use of Juju," 84.
15. Van Dijk, "'Voodoo' on the Doorstep," 565; Cole, Reducing the Damage, 222.
16. Baarda, "Human Trafficking for Sexual Exploitation," 265; Taliani, "Coercion, Fetishes and Suffering, 591, 594; Watt and Kruger, "Exploring 'Juju' and Human Trafficking," 75–76; Dunkerley, "Exploring the Use of Juju," 90.
17. Paul Peachey, "Jailed: The Slave Trader in Britain Who Sold Women around Europe for Sex under the Spell of His 'Juju' Witchcraft," *Independent Online*, October 26, 2012; Dunkerley, "Exploring the Use of Juju," 90; Watt and Kruger, "Exploring 'Juju' and Human Trafficking," 75–76.
18. Nagle and Owasanoye, "Fearing the Dark," 584–585; Peachey, "Jailed: The Slave Trader in Britain Who Sold Women around Europe for Sex under the Spell of His 'Juju' Witchcraft," *Independent Online*, October 26, 2012; Dunkerley, "Exploring the Use of Juju," 90.
19. Van Dijk, "'Voodoo' on the Doorstep," 569–570; Dunkerley, "Exploring the Use of Juju," 90; Taliani, "Coercion, Fetishes and Suffering," 594.
20. Baarda, "Human Trafficking for Sexual Exploitation," 266–267.
21. Cole, "Reducing the Damage," 222; Anderson, "Busted: Gang That Used Voodoo to Exploit Women," *The Local*, June 8, 2015; Ikeora, "The Role of African Traditional Religion," 7.
22. Van Dijk, "'Voodoo' on the Doorstep," 571.
23. Van Dijk, "'Voodoo' on the Doorstep," 571.
24. Ibid.
25. Cole, "Reducing the Damage," 222
26. Dunkerley, "Exploring the Use of Juju," 91; Ikeora, "The Role of African Traditional Religion," 9.
27. "Spanish Police Arrest 23 People for 'Using Voodoo Curses,'" *Telegraph*, May 22, 2009, https://www.telegraph.co.uk/news/worldnews/europe/spain/5364373/Spanish-police-arrest-23-people-for-using-voodoo-curses.html.

28. UPI NewsTrack, "Italian Police Break Up Prostitution Ring," *NewsBank*, October 5, 2012, https://www.upi.com/Top_News/World-News/2012/10/05/Italian-police-break-up-prostitution-ring/28081349462830/.
29. Associated Press Archive, "Spanish Police Arrest 17 Suspected Pimps," *NewsBank*, December 30, 2012, https://www.police1.com/archive/articles/spanish-police-arrest-17-suspected-pimps-NWnunov7OwjBJA16/
30. Ibid.
31. Anderson, "Busted: Gang That Used Voodoo to Exploit Women," *Local*, June 8, 2015, https://www.thelocal.es/20150608/police-catch-voodoo-human-trafficking-group-prostitution.
32. Commission on Human Rights, "Addendum to Report of the Special Rapporteur on the sale of children, child prostitution and child pornography, Ms. Ofelia Calcetas-Santos: Report on the mission of the Special Rapporteur to Belgium and the Netherlands: 30 November–4 December 1998," E/CN.4/2000/73/Add.1, December 22, 1999, at paragraph 26.
33. Mrs. Halima Embarek Warzazi, Report of the Working Group on Contemporary Forms of Slavery on its twenty-seventh session, Economic and Social Council, UN Doc. E/CN.4/Sub.2/2002/33, June 17, 2002, at paragraph 16.
34. Garcia, "Voodoo, Witchcraft and Human Trafficking in Europe," 1.
35. Joy Ezeilo, Report of the Special Rapporteur on trafficking in persons, especially women and children, on her mission to Italy, April 1, 2014 A/HRC/26/37/Add.4, p. 4.
36. Office to Monitor and Combat Trafficking in Persons, U.S. Department of State, "Nigeria," https://www.state.gov/j/tip/rls/tiprpt/2014/index.htm.
37. Van Dijk, " 'Voodoo' on the Doorstep," 564.
38. Ibid., 564.
39. Ibid., 572.
40. Cole, "Reducing the Damage," 222.
41. Ibid.
42. Taliani, "Coercion, Fetishes and Suffering," 589.
43. Ikeora, "The Role of African Traditional Religion," 6.
44. Ibid., 2.
45. Ibid., 10.
46. Ibid., 13.
47. Bokhari, "Falling Through the Gaps."
48. Ibid., 206.
49. Baarda, "Human Trafficking," 258.
50. Ibid., 258.
51. Nagle and Owasanoye, "Fearing the Dark," 567.
52. Van der Watt and Kruger, "Exploring 'Juju' and Human Trafficking," 75.
53. Ironically, after calling Eshu an "evil god" in the text of their article, Van de Watt and Kruger clarify in a footnote that concepts like "juju" and "witchcraft" and "voodoo" are "fraught with nuances and complexities" in Africa and that "[u]nlike the Eurocentric meaning of 'witchcraft,' practitioners in African societies use magic or supernatural

powers for either evil or beneficial purposes." Van der Watt and Kruger, "Exploring 'Juju' and Human Trafficking," 83.
54. Nagle and Owasanoye, "Fearing the Dark," 569.
55. Ibid., 591–592.
56. Baarda, "Human Trafficking," 270.
57. Joy Ezeilo, Report of the Special Rapporteur on trafficking in persons, especially women and children, on her mission to Italy, April 1, 2014 A/HRC/26/37/Add.4, p. 4.
58. Cited in Adepitan, *Decolonizing Human Trafficking*, 38–39.
59. Van Dijk, "'Voodoo' on the Doorstep," 568–569.
60. Taliani, "Coercion, Fetishes and Suffering," 583–584, 591.
61. Baarda, "Human Trafficking for Sexual Exploitation," 269.
62. Ibid., 264–265.
63. Don, "The Resurgence of Ayelala."
64. Ibid.
65. Ibid.
66. Ibid.
67. Ojo, "Incorporation of Ayelala," 997.
68. Ibid., 998.
69. Ibid., 998.
70. Idumwonyia and Ikhidero, "Resurgence of the Traditional Justice System," 129.
71. Ibid.
72. Don, "The Resurgence of Ayelala."
73. Ibid.
74. Ibid.
75. Idumwonyia and Ikhidero "Resurgence of the Traditional Justice System," 132–133.
76. Ibid.
77. Ibid.
78. Ibid.
79. Ibid.
80. Ojo, "Incorporation of Ayelala," 1002.
81. Ibid., 1002.
82. Ibid., 996.
83. Ikeora, "The Role of African Traditional Religion," 14.
84. Ibid., 12.
85. Ibid., 6.
86. McManus, *Black Bondage in the North*, 127–128.
87. Harris, *In the Shadow of Slavery*, 45.
88. Rucker, *The River Flows On*, 83–84.
89. Konadu, *The Akan Diaspora in the Americas*, 131.
90. Craton, *Testing the Chains*, 121.
91. Ibid., 121.
92. Ibid., 122; *A Genuine Narrative of the Intended Conspiracy*, 12.
93. Lazarus-Black, *Legitimate Acts and Illegal Encounters*, 42.
94. Rucker, *The River Flows On*, 44.

95. Ibid., 129, 137–138.
96. Ibid., 127, 138. Konadu, *The Akan Diaspora*, 155; Brown, "Spiritual Terror and Sacred Authority," 37.
97. Brown, "Spiritual Terror and Sacred Authority," 45; Brown, *The Reaper's Garden*, 149; Craton, *Testing the Chains*, 131.
98. Long, *The History of Jamaica*, 451.
99. Jamaica, "Act 24 of 1760," 52.
100. Ibid.
101. Ibid.
102. Jamaica, "An Act for the protection, subsisting, clothing, and for the better order, regulation, and government of Slaves; and for other purposes of 1809," in House of Commons, *Miscellaneous Papers*, February 1, 1816–July 2, 1816. vol. 19, p. 125.
103. "Trial of Obeah Jack and Prince," *Courier* (London), June 7, 1824.
104. Corberand's own testimony only includes that mixture of rum, blood, and gunpowder, used as "a solemn oath to be faithful to each other." "Examination of J. B. Corberand," in *Hamel, the Obeah Man*, ed. Candace Ward and Tim Watson (Toronto: Broadview Editions, 2010), 469. Another informer named Mack confirmed this oath mixture, but stated that it may have included either powder or grave dirt. Hart, *Slaves Who Abolished Slavery*, 236. This last ingredient was, according to Jack's confession, provided by Corberand himself. "Trial of Obeah Jack and Prince," *Courier* (London), June 7, 1824.
105. "Trial of the Conspirators at Buff Bay," *Courier* (London), March 15, 1824.
106. "Trial of Obeah Jack and Prince," *Courier* (London), June 7, 1824.
107. Ibid. See also "Confession of Jack," in *Hamel, the Obeah Man*, ed. Candace Ward and Tim Watson (Toronto: Broadview Editions, 2010), 471; "Trial of Obeah Jack and Prince," *Courier* (London), June 7, 1824; Hart, *Slaves Who Abolished Slavery*, 234–235.
108. "Trial of Obeah Jack and Prince," *Courier* (London), June 7, 1824; Hart, *Slaves Who Abolished Slavery*, 234–235.
109. Hart, *Slaves Who Abolished Slavery*, 234–235.
110. "Trial of Obeah Jack and Prince," *Courier* (London), June 7, 1824.
111. Ibid.
112. "Execution and Trial of Rebel Negroes," *Courier* (London), April 24, 1824; see also Ward and Watson, *Hamel the Obeah Man*, 460.
113. Luongo, *Witchcraft and Colonial Rule in Kenya*, 159.
114. Katherine Luongo reports that she also was unable to convince any of the Mau Mau rebellion participants whom she interviewed to divulge information about the oath because they were sworn to secrecy. Ibid., 167–168.
115. Ibid., 161, 169–171.
116. Luongo, "Polling Places and 'Slow Punctured Provocation,'" 580.
117. Luongo, *Witchcraft and Colonial Rule in Kenya*, 181.

118. Kenya, "Penal Code of 1930," in *The Laws of Kenya in force on the 21st Day of September, 1948*, ed. Donald Kingdon (Nairobi, Kenya: The Government Printer, 1948), 1:200–201, 210.
119. Gambia, "Criminal Code of 1934," in *The Laws of The Gambia in force on the 1st Day of January, 1955*, ed. Donald Kingdon (London: Waterlow & Sons, 1955) 1:181–182; Nigeria, "Chapter 42 of the Criminal Code of Nigeria," in *The Laws of the Federation of Nigeria and Lagos in force on the 1st day of June, 1958*, ed. Donald Kingdon (London: Eyre and Spottiswoode, 1959), 2:625–626.
120. Ranger, "The Reception of the Mau Mau," 66.
121. Gray, "Independent Spirits," 141–145; Gray, *The Legal History of Witchcraft*, 59.
122. Olsen, "Children for Death," 531; Gray, "Independent Spirits," 141–144; Gray, *The Legal History of Witchcraft*, 59; Luongo, *Witchcraft and Colonial Rule in Kenya*, 68.
123. Parker, "Witchcraft, Anti-Witchcraft and Trans-Regional Ritual," 407; Gray, *The Legal History of Witchcraft*, 9, 59. Gray, "Independent Spirits," 141–144; Luongo, *Witchcraft and Colonial Rule in Kenya*, 70.
124. Olsen, "Children for Death," 532; Gray, *The Legal History of Witchcraft*, 59; Gray, "Independent Spirits," 141–144; Luongo, *Witchcraft and Colonial Rule in Kenya*, 68.
125. Rattray, *Religion and Art in Ashanti*, 32.
126. Parker, "Witchcraft, Anti-Witchcraft and Trans-Regional Ritual," 414.
127. Gray, "Independent Spirits," 145–146.

Conclusion

1. See the Introduction and Chapter 5.
2. Ramsey, *Spirits and the Law*, 58–67.
3. Ibid., 121.
4. Ibid., 153.
5. Ibid., 184.
6. Johnson, "Secretism and the Apotheosis of Duvalier," 428; Farmer, *The Uses of Haiti*, 89.
7. Murrell, *Afro-Caribbean Religions*, 66; Ramsey, *Spirits and the Law*, 200–202.
8. Murrell, *Afro-Caribbean Religions*, 66.
9. Johnson, "Secretism and the Apotheosis of Duvalier," 438.
10. Lewis, "Language, Culture and Power," 46; Merrill, *Vodou and Political Reform in Haiti*, 43.
11. Merrill, *Vodou and Political Reform in Haiti*, 46.
12. Ibid.
13. Paton, "Obeah Acts."
14. For more information about the prosecution of Obeah, see Paton, "Obeah Acts"; Boaz, "Obeah, Vagrancy, and the Boundaries"; Paton, *The Cultural Politics of Obeah*; Boaz, "Fraud, Vagrancy and the 'Pretended' Exercise of Supernatural Powers."
15. Paton, "Obeah Acts," 5–7; Boaz, "Obeah, Vagrancy, and the Boundaries," 423.

16. For example, see Jamaica, The Obeah Act, January 1, 1898, available at https://moj.gov.jm/laws/obeah-act (last visited December 22, 2021).
17. Boaz, "Obeah, Vagrancy, and the Boundaries," 436–438.
18. Boaz, *Banning Black Gods*, 141–159.
19. Ibid., 161–162.
20. Boaz, "Religion or Ruse?" 17–31.
21. Rafael and Maggie, "Sorcery Objects," 282; Johnson, "Law, Religion and Public Health," 19.
22. Rafael and Maggie, "Sorcery Objects," 292; Maggie, *Medo do feitiço*, 252.
23. Maggie, *Medo do feitiço*, 252–253; Rafael, *Muito Barulho*, para. 51–64.
24. Gonçalves, *O sincretismo religioso no Brasil*, 17–18.
25. Danielle Boaz, "Religious Racism in Brazil," www.religiousracism.org/brazil.
26. This high percentage is particularly striking because the perpetrators were never identified in many cases.
27. Boaz, "Exoticizing Terrorism," 1–16.
28. Boaz, "Twenty Years of Religious Racism in Brazil," 20; "Jovem de 14 anos praticante de candomblé denuncia ter sido agredida por intolerância religiosa em Curitiba," October 1, 2015, https://www.geledes.org.br/jovem-de-14-anos-praticante-de-candomble-denuncia-ter-sido-agredida-por-intolerancia-religiosa-em-curitiba/ (last visited December 24, 2021).
29. Boaz, "Twenty Years of Religious Racism in Brazil," 20; Ariana Lobo, "Violencia em Nome de Deus," April 8, 2017, http://intoleranciareligiosadossie.blogspot.com/2016/04/violencia-em-nome-de-deus.html (last visited December 24, 2021).
30. Dossiê Intolerância Religiosa, Centro de Umbanda em Piatã é Atacado Durante Festa e Três Pessoas Ficam Feridas, February 13, 2017, http://intoleranciareligiosadossie.blogspot.com/2017/02/centro-de-umbanda-em-piata-e-atacado.html (last visited December 24, 2021).
31. Eduardo Schiavoni, "Terreiro de Umbanda é Alvo de Bomba e Praticantes São Espancados em SP," February 6, 2020, https://noticias.uol.com.br/cotidiano/ultimas-noticias/2020/02/06/terreiro-de-umbanda-e-alvo-de-bomba-e-praticantes-sao-espancados-em-sp.htm (last visited December 24, 2021).
32. For example, see Handler and Bilby, "On the Early Uses"; Paton, "Witchcraft, Poison, Law, and Atlantic Slavery."
33. For example, see Roman, *Governing Spirits*; Paton, *Cultural Politics of Obeah*; Ramsey, *Spirits and the Law*.

Bibliography

Court Cases

Haitian Refugee Center et al. v. Benjamin Civiletti, Attorney General of the United States, et al., 503 F.Supp. 442 (1980).
United States v. Fritz Pierrot, 861 F.2d 266 (1988).
United States v. Reme and Pierrot, 738 F.2d 1156; 1984 U.S. App. LEXIS 19708 (1984).
United States v. Saintil and Tacius, 705 F.2d 415; 1983 U.S. App. LEXIS 27984 (May 16, 1983).
United States v. Saintil and Tacius, 753 F.2d 984; 1985 U.S. App. LEXIS 28173 (1985).

Human Rights Reports

Human Rights Committee. "Consideration of Reports Submitted by States Parties under Article 40 of the Covenant, Initial Reports of States Parties: Haiti." UN Doc. CCPR/C/HTI/1 (January 23, 2013).
Human Rights Committee. "List of Issues in Relation to the Initial Report of Haiti." UN Doc. CCPR/C/HTI/Q/1 (April 23, 2014).
Human Rights Council. "National Report Submitted in Accordance with Paragraph 15 (a) of the Annex to the Human Rights Council Resolution 5/1: Haiti." UN Doc. A/HRC/WG.6/12/HTI/1 (July 19, 2011).
Human Rights Council. "Report of the Independent Expert on the Situation of Human Rights in Haiti, Michel Forst." UN Doc. A/HRC/17/42 (April 4, 2011).

Laws

Protocol to Prevent, Suppress and Punish Trafficking in Persons, Especially Women and Children, supplementing the United Nations Convention against Transnational Organized Crime (2000), available at https://www.unodc.org/res/human-trafficking/2021the-protocol-tip_html/TIP.pdf (last visited December 22, 2021).
The Refugee Act of 1980, Public Law 96–212 (March 17, 1980).

Secondary Sources

Adepitan, Oyinkansola. *Decolonizing Human Trafficking: A Case Study of Human Trafficking in Edo State Nigeria*. M.A. thesis, University of South Florida, 2000.

A Genuine Narrative of the Intended Conspiracy of the Negroes at Antigua. 1737; repr., New York: Arno Press, 1972.

Alexander, J. Trent. "The Great Migration in Comparative Perspective: Interpreting the Urban Origins of Southern Black Migrants to Depression-Era Pittsburgh." *Social Science History* 22, no. 3, Special Issue: Migration and the Labor Markets (Autumn 1998): 349–376.

Allen, Ernest, Jr. "When Japan Was 'Champion of the Darker Races': Satokata Takahashi and the Flowering of Black Messianic Nationalism." *The Black Scholar* 24, no. 1 (1994): 23–46.

Anderson, Jeffrey. *Conjure in African American Society.* Baton Rouge: Louisiana State University Press, 2005.

Apter, Andrew. "Atinga Revisited: Yoruba Witchcraft and the Cocoa Economy, 1950–1951." In Jean Comaroff and John L. Comaroff, eds. *Modernity and Its Malcontents: Ritual and Power in Post-Colonial Africa.* Chicago: University of Chicago Press, 1993, 111–128.

Baarda, C. S. "Human Trafficking for Sexual Exploitation from Nigeria into Western Europe." *European Journal of Criminology* 13, no. 2 (2016): 257–273.

Bellegarde-Smith, Patrick. "A Man-Made Disaster: The Earthquake of January 12, 2010—A Haitian Perspective." *Journal of Black Studies* 42, no. 2 (2011): 264–275.

Beynon, Erdmann Doane Beynon. "The Voodoo Cult among Negro Migrants in Detroit." *The American Journal of Sociology* 43, no. 6 (May 1938): 894–907.

Boaz, Danielle. *Banning Black Gods: Law and Religions of the African Diaspora.* University Park: Penn State University Press, Africana Religions Book Series, 2021.

Boaz, Danielle. "Exoticizing Terrorism: Religious Bias and the Unchecked Threat of Evangelical Extremism in Brazil." *Journal of Religion & Society* 23 (2021): 1–20.

Boaz, Danielle. "Fraud, Vagrancy and the 'Pretended' Exercise of Supernatural Powers in England, South Africa and Jamaica." *Law and History* 5, no. 1 (2018): 54–84.

Boaz, Danielle. "Obeah, Vagrancy, and the Boundaries of Religious Freedom: Analyzing the Proscription of 'Pretending to Possess Supernatural Powers' in the Anglophone Caribbean." *Journal of Law and Religion* 32, no. 3 (2017): 423–448.

Boaz, Danielle. "Religion or Ruse? African Jamaican Spiritual Practices and Police Deception in Canada." *Alternation* 22 (2018): 11–34.

Bokhari, Farrah. "Falling Through the Gaps: Safeguarding Children Trafficked into the UK." *Children & Society* 22 (2008): 201–211.

Bronfman, Alejandra. "'En Plena Libertad y Democracia': Negros Brujos and the Social Question, 1904–1919." *Hispanic American Historical Review* 82, no. 3 (2002): 549–587.

Brown, Lee P. "Black Muslims and the Police." *The Journal of Criminal Law, Criminology, and Police Science* 56, no. 1 (March 1965): 119–126.

Brown, Vincent. "Spiritual Terror and Sacred Authority in Jamaican Slave Society." *Slavery and Abolition* 24, no. 1 (2003): 24–53.

Brown, Vincent. *The Reaper's Garden: Death and Power in the World of Atlantic Slavery.* Cambridge, MA: Harvard University Press, 2008.

Burnham, Thorald. "Makandal, François." In Colin Palmer, ed., *Encyclopedia of African-American Culture and History.* Detroit, MI: Macmillan Reference, 2006, 1362–1363.

Carelock, Nicole Payne. *A Leaky House: Haiti in the Religious Aftershock of the 2010 Earthquake.* Ph.D. dissertation, Rice University, 2012.

Carr, Barry. "Identity, Class, and Nation: Black Immigrant Workers, Cuban Communism, and the Sugar Insurgency, 1925–1934." *The Hispanic American Historical Review* 78, no. 1 (February 1998): 83–116.

Chireau, Yvonne. *Black Magic: Religion and the African American Conjuring Tradition*. Berkeley and Los Angeles: University of California Press, 2006.

Clegg, Claude. *An Original Man: The Life and Times of Elijah Muhammad*. New York: St. Martin's Press, 1997.

Cole, Jeffrey. "Reducing the Damage: Dilemmas of Anti-Trafficking Efforts among Nigerian Prostitutes in Palermo." *Anthropologica* 48, no. 2 (2006): 217–228.

Craton, Michael. *Testing the Chains: Resistance to Slavery in the British West Indies*. Ithaca, NY: Cornell University Press, 1982.

Curtis, Edward. *Black Muslim Religion in the Nation of Islam*. Chapel Hill: University of North Carolina Press, 2006.

De la Fuente, Alejandro. *A Nation for All: Race, Inequality, and Politics in Twentieth-Century Cuba*. Chapel Hill: University of North Carolina Press, 2001.

Desmangles, Leslie. *The Faces of the Gods: Vodou and Roman Catholicism in Haiti*. Chapel Hill: University of North Carolina Press, 1992.

Des Voeux, William. *My Colonial Service in British Guiana, St. Lucia, Trinidad, Fiji, Australia, Newfoundland and Hong Kong with Interludes*. London: John Murray, 1903.

Diffee, Christopher. "Sex and the City: The White Slavery Scare and Social Governance in the Progressive Era." *American Quarterly* 57, no. 2 (2005): 411–437.

Don, Akhilomen. "The Resurgence of Ayelala in Benin Kingdom: An Indictment of the Conventional Dispensation of Justice in Nigeria." (2006) http://magazine.biafranigeriaworld.com/akhilomen_don/2006/10/15/the_resurgence_of_ayelala_in_benin_kingdom_an_indictment_of_the_conventional_dispensation_of_justice_in_nigeria.php (last visited January 1, 2022).

Donovan, Brian. *White Slave Crusades: Race, Gender, and Anti-vice Activism, 1887–1917*. Urbana: University of Illinois Press, 2006.

Dunkerley, Anthony W. "Exploring the Use of Juju in Nigerian Human Trafficking Networks: Considerations for Criminal Investigators." *Police Practice and Research* 19, no. 1 (2018): 83–100.

Evanzz, Karl. *The Messenger: The Rise and Fall of Elijah Muhammad*. New York: Vintage Books, 1999.

Farmer, Paul. *The Uses of Haiti*. Monroe, ME: Common Courage Press, 2006.

Fjellman, Stephen M., and Hugh Gladwin. "Haitian Family Patterns of Migration to South Florida." *Human Organization* 44, no. 4 (1985): 301–312.

Garcia, Ana Dols. "Voodoo, Witchcraft and Human Trafficking in Europe." New Issues in Refugee Research, Research Paper No. 263, UNHCR, 2013.

Gaston, Jessie Ruth. "The Case of Voodoo in New Orleans." In Joseph Holloway, ed., *Africanisms in American Culture*. Bloomington & Indianapolis: Indiana University Press, 2005, 111–151.

Germain, Felix. "The Earthquake, the Missionaries, and the Future of Vodou." *Journal of Black Studies* 42 (2011): 247–263.

Gonçalves Fernandes, Albino. *O sincretismo religioso no Brasil*. Curitiba: Editora Guaíra limitada, 1941.

Gray, Natasha. "Independent Spirits: The Politics of Policing Anti-Witchcraft Movements in Colonial Ghana, 1908–1927." *Journal of Religion in Africa* 35, no. 2 (2005): 139–158.

Gray, Natasha. *The Legal History of Witchcraft in Colonial Ghana: Akyem Abuakwa, 1913–1943*. Ph.D. dissertation, Columbia University, 2000.

Grimaud, Jérôme, and Fedia Legagneur. "Community Beliefs and Fears During a Cholera Outbreak in Haiti." *Intervention* 9, no. 1 (2011): 26–34.

Guerra, Lillian. *The Myth of Jose Marti: Conflicting Nationalisms in Early Twentieth-Century Cuba*. Chapel Hill: University of North Carolina Press, 2006.

Handler, Jerome S., and Kenneth Bilby. "On the Early Use and Origin of the Term 'Obeah' in Barbados and the Anglophone Caribbean." *Slavery and Abolition* 22, no. 2 (2001): 87–100.

Harris, Leslie. *In the Shadow of Slavery: African Americans in New York City, 1626–1863*. Chicago: University of Chicago Press, 2003.

Hart, Richard. *Slaves Who Abolished Slavery: Blacks in Rebellion*. Kingston: University of the West Indies Press, 2002.

Helg, Aline. "Black Men, Racial Stereotyping, and Violence in the U.S. South and Cuba at the Turn of the Century." *Comparative Studies in Society and History* 42, no. 3 (2000): 576–604.

Helg, Aline. "To Be Black and to Be Cuban: The Dilemma of Afro-Cubans in Post-Independence Politics." In Darién J. Davis, ed., *Beyond Slavery: The Multilayered Legacy of Africans in Latin America*. Lanham, MD: Rowman & Littlefield, 2007, 123–142.

Hixson, William B., Jr. "Moorfield Storey and the Defense of the Dyer Anti-Lynching Bill." *The New England Quarterly* 42, no. 1 (March 1969): 65–81.

Hutchinson, Phillip J. "Framing White Hopes: The Press, Social Drama, and the Era of Jack Johnson, 1908–1915." In Chris Lamb, ed., *From Jack Johnson to LeBron James: Sports, Media, and the Color Line*. Lincoln: University of Nebraska Press, 2016, 19–51.

Idumwonyia, Itohan Mercy, and Solomon Ijeweimen Ikhidero. "Resurgence of the Traditional Justice System in Postcolonial Benin (Nigeria) Society." *African Journal of Legal Studies* 6 (2013): 123–135.

Ikeora, May. "The Role of African Traditional Religion and 'Juju' in Human Trafficking: Implications for Anti-trafficking." *Journal of International Women's Studies* 17, no. 1 (2016): 1–18.

Johnson, Paul C. "Secretism and the Apotheosis of Duvalier." *Journal of the American Academy of Religion* 74, No. 2 (2006): 420–445.

Johnson, Paul C. "Law, Religion and 'Public Health' in the Republic of Brazil." *Law and Social Inquiry* 26 (2001): 9–33.

Johnson, Hannah. *Blood Libel: The Ritual Murder Accusation at the Limit of Jewish History*. Ann Arbor: University of Michigan Press, 2012.

Konadu, Kwasi. *The Akan Diaspora in the Americas*. New York: Oxford University Press, 2010.

Laguerre, Michel S. *American Odyssey: Haitians in New York City*. Ithaca, NY: Cornell University Press, 1984.

Lammasniemi, Laura. "Anti-White Slavery Legislation and Its Legacies in England." *Anti-Trafficking Review* 9 (2017): 64–76.

Lazarus-Black, Mindie. *Legitimate Acts and Illegal Encounters: Law and Society in Antigua and Barbuda*. Washington, DC: Smithsonian Institution Press, 1994.

Lee, Martha. *The Nation of Islam: An American Millenarian Movement*. Syracuse, NY: Syracuse University Press, 1996.

Lewis, R. Anthony. "Language, Culture and Power: Haiti under the Duvaliers." *Caribbean Quarterly* 50, no. 4 (2004): 42–51.

Lincoln, C. Eric. *The Black Muslims in America*. Boston: Beacon Press, 1961.

Long, Edward. *The History of Jamaica*. London: T. Lowndes, 1774.

Loyd, Jenna M., and Alison Mountz. *Boats, Borders, and Bases: Race, the Cold War, and the Rise of Migration Detention in the United States*. Berkeley: University of California Press, 2018.

Luongo, Katherine. "Polling Places and 'Slow Punctured Provocation': Occult-Driven Cases in Postcolonial Kenya's High Courts." *Journal of Eastern African Studies* 4, no. 3 (2010): 577–591.

Luongo, Katherine. *Witchcraft and Colonial Rule in Kenya, 1900–1955*. New York: Cambridge University Press, 2011.

Macdonell, John, and Edward Manson, eds. "Criminal Law: Obeah." *Journal of the Society of Comparative Legislation*. London: John Murrary, 1907, 541.

Maggie, Yvonne. *Medo do feitiço: Relações Entre Magia e Poder no Brasil*. Rio de Janeiro: Arquivo Nacional, Orgão do Ministério da Justiça, 1992.

Marsh, Clifton. *From Black Muslims to Muslims: The Resurrection, Transformation, and Change of the Lost-Found Nation of Islam in America, 1930–1995*. Lanham, MD: Scarecrow Press, 1996.

McLeod, Marc. "Undesirable Aliens: Race, Ethnicity, and Nationalism in the Comparison of Haitian and British West Indian Immigrant Workers in Cuba, 1912–1939." *Journal of Social History* 31, no. 3 (Spring 1998): 599–623.

McManus, Edgar J. *Black Bondage in the North*. Syracuse, NY: Syracuse University Press, 1973.

Merrill, John. "Vodou and Political Reform in Haiti: Some Lessons for the International Community." *The Fletcher Forum of World Affairs* 20, no. 1 (1996): 31–52.

Miller, Jake C. "International Concern for Haitians in the Diaspora." *Western Journal of Black Studies* 30, no. 1 (2006): 35–45.

Miller, Jake C. *The Plight of Haitian Refugees*. New York: Praeger, 1984.

Moreau de Saint Méry, Mederic-Louis-Elie. *A Civilization That Perished: The Last Years of White Colonial Rule in Haiti*. Translated by Ivor D. Spencer. Lanham, MD: University Press of America, 1985. First published in 1797 by the author.

Morgan, Denise C. "Jack Johnson versus the American Racial Hierarchy." In Annette Gordon-Reed, ed., *Race on Trial: Law and Justice in American History*. Oxford: Oxford University Press, 2002, 77–102.

Morone, James. *Hellfire Nation: The Politics of Sin in American History* (Yale University Press, 2004)

Musgrave, George Clark. *Under Three Flags in Cuba: A Personal Account of the Cuban Insurrection and Spanish-American War*. Boston: Little, Brown, 1899.

Ojo, Matthias Olufemi Dada. "Incorporation of Ayelala Traditional Religion into Nigerian Criminal Justice System: An Opinion Survey of Igbesa Community People in Ogun State, Nigeria." *Issues in Ethnology and Anthropology* 9, no. 4 (2014): 1025–1044.

Nagle, Luz, and Bolaji Owasanoye. "Fearing the Dark: The Use of Witchcraft to Control Human Trafficking Victims and Sustain Vulnerability." *Southwestern Law Review* 45 (2016): 561–593.

"Nagualism, Voodooism, and Other Forms of Crytopaganism in the United States." *The Catholic World: A Monthly Magazine of General Literature and Science* 25 (1877): 1–11.

Nance, Susan. "Mystery of the Moorish Science Temple: Southern Blacks and American Alternative Spirituality in 1920s Chicago." *Religion and American Culture: A Journal of Interpretation* 12, no. 2 (2002): 123–166.

Newell, William. "Myths of Voodoo Worship and Child Sacrifice in Haiti." *The Journal of American Folklore* 1, no. 1 (April–June 1888): 16–30.

Oklahoma Commission to Study the Tulsa Race Riot of 1921. "Tulsa Race Riot." February 28, 2001.

Olsen, William C. "Children for Death: Money, Wealth, and Witchcraft Suspicion in Colonial Asante." *Cahiers d'Études Africaines* 42 (2002): 521–550.

Palmié, Stephen. *Wizards & Scientists: Explorations in Afro-Cuban Modernity & Tradition*. Durham, NC, and London: Duke University Press, 2002.

Parker, John. "Witchcraft, Anti-Witchcraft and Trans-Regional Ritual Innovation in Early Colonial Ghana: Sakrabundi and Aberewa, 1889–1910." *The Journal of African History* 45, no. 3 (2004): 393–420.

Paton, Diana. *The Cultural Politics of Obeah: Religion, Colonialism and Modernity in the Caribbean World*. Cambridge: Cambridge University Press, 2015.

Paton, Diana. "Obeah Acts: Producing and Policing the Boundaries of Religion in the Caribbean." *Small Axe* 28 (2009): 1–18.

Paton, Diana. "Witchcraft, Poison, Law, and Atlantic Slavery." *William and Mary Quarterly* 69, no. 2 (2012): 235–264.

Perez, Louis. *Cuba and the United States: Ties of Singular Intimacy*. Athens: University of Georgia Press, 1990.

Pettinger, Alasdair, and Lorna Milne. "From Vaudoux to Voodoo." *Forum for Modern Language* 40, no. 4 (2004): 415–425.

Pitman, Frank W. "Fetishism, Witchcraft, and Christianity Among the Slaves." *Journal of Negro History*, 11, no. 4 (1926): 650–668.

Plummer, Brenda. *Haiti and the Great Powers 1902–1915*. Baton Rouge: Louisiana State University Press, 1988.

Pogue, Tiffany. "Bois Caiman." In Molefi Kete Asante and Ama Mazama, eds., *Encyclopedia of African Religion*. Thousand Oaks: Sage Publications, 2009, 130–131.

Prichard, Hesketh. *Where Black Rules White: A Journey across and about Hayti*. New York: Charles Scribner's Sons, 1900.

Rafael, Ulisses Neves. "Muito barulho por nada ou o "xangô rezado baixo": uma etnografia do 'Quebra de 1912' em Alagoas, Brasil." *Etnográfica* 14, no. 2 (2010): 289–310.

Rafael, Ulisses N., and Yvonne Maggie. "Sorcery Objects under Institutional Tutelage: Magic and Power in Ethnographic Collections." *Vibrant* 10, no 1 (2013): 281.

Ralph, David. "Haitian Interdiction on the High Seas: The Continuing Saga of the Rights of Aliens Outside United States Territory." *Maryland Journal of International Law* 7, no. 2 (1993): 227–251.

Ramsey, Kate. "From 'Voodooism' to 'Vodou': Changing a US Library of Congress Subject Heading." *Journal of Haitian Studies* 18, no. 2, Special Issue on Vodou and Créolité (Fall 2012): 14–25.

Ramsey, Kate. *The Spirits and the Law: Vodou and Power in Haiti*. Chicago: University of Chicago Press, 2011.

Ranger, Terence. "The Reception of the Mau Mau in Southern Rhodesia, 1952–1961." In Piet Konings, Wim van Binsbergen, and Gerti Hesseling, eds., *Trajectoires de libération en Afrique contemporaine*. Paris: Karthala, 2000, 49–68.

Rattray, R. S. *Religion and Art in Ashanti*. Oxford: Clarendon Press, 1969; first published in 1927.

Roberts, Russell. *Rediscover the Hidden New Jersey*. New Brunswick, NJ: Rutgers University Press, 2015.

Roman, Reinaldo. *Governing Spirits: Religion, Miracles and Spectacles in Cuba and Puerto Rico, 1898–1956*. Chapel Hill: University of North Carolina Press, 2007.

Rucker, Walter C. *The River Flows On: Black Resistance, Culture, and Identity Formation in Early America*. Baton Rouge: Louisiana State University Press, 2006

Shannon, Magdaline W. *Jean Price-Mars, the Haitian Elite and the American Occupation, 1915–1935*. New York: St. Martin's Press, 1996.

Slocum, Karla. *Black Towns, Black Futures: The Enduring Allure of a Black Place in the American West*. Chapel Hill: The University of North Carolina Press, 2019.

Taliani, Simona. "Coercion, Fetishes and Suffering in the Daily Lives of Young Nigeria Women in Italy." *Africa: Journal of the International African Institute* 82, no. 4 (2012): 579–608.

Tamuno, Tekena. *The Police in Modern Nigeria, 1861–1965: Origins, Development, and Role*. Ibadan: Ibadan University Press, 1970.

Turner, Richard. *Islam in the African American Experience*. Bloomington and Indianapolis: Indiana University Press, 1997.

Udal, J. S. "Obeah in the West Indies." *Folklore* 26, no. 3 (1915): 286–287.

Underhill, Edward. *The West Indies: Their Social and Religious Condition*. London: Jackson, Walford, and Hodder, 1862.

Van der Watt, Marcel, and Beatri Kruger. "Exploring 'Juju' and Human Trafficking: Towards a Demystified Perspective and Response." *South African Review of Sociology* 48, no. 2 (2017): 70–86.

Van Dijk, Rijk. "'Voodoo' on the Doorstep: Young Nigerian Prostitutes and Magic Policing in the Netherlands." *Africa: Journal of the International African Institute* 71, no. 4 (2001): 558–586.

Watson, Martha Solomon. "Mary Church Terrell vs. Thomas Nelson Page: Gender, Race, and Class in Anti-Lynching Rhetoric." *Rhetoric & Public Affairs* 12, no. 1 (2009),: 65–90.

White, Vibert L., Jr. *Inside the Nation of Islam: A Historical and Personal Testimony of a Black Muslim*. Gainesville: University Press of Florida, 2001.

Index

For the benefit of digital users, indexed terms that span two pages (e.g., 52–53) may, on occasion, appear on only one of those pages.

Bizoton affair, 16–18, 19, 20, 22
Bois Caiman, x, 13
Britain (also British), ix, 4, 14, 15–16, 17–18, 19, 21–22, 25, 35–39, 41, 52, 127, 129–30, 132, 133, 138. *See also* England
brujeria (also brujo/bruja), xiv, 33, 35, 39, 40, 41–42, 46–47, 50–51, 52

Candomblé, viii, 123, 140, 141–42
cannibals (also cannibalism), viii, 26, 27, 55, 94
    Cuba, 28, 29, 30–31, 33–35, 41, 47–48, 50–51, 94
    Haiti, 17–18, 19, 20, 21, 22–23, 25, 36, 77, 84–85, 94, 136
Christians (also Christianity), vii, 2, 5, 11, 21, 82, 97, 114–15, 116, 123, 137–38
Civil War (U.S.), xiii–xiv, xvi, 2, 5–13, 15, 16, 19, 24, 26, 56–57, 63, 75
conjure, xii

Democrats (also Democratic Party), 10, 11–12, 19, 28–29, 34–35
Duvalier, Francois, 98, 99, 137
Duvalier, Jean Claude, 98, 99, 104, 137

emancipation, xi, 1–26, 55, 79–80, 138, 143
England, 15–17, 19, 22, 50, 56, 118, 123. *See also* Britain
evangelicals, viii, 109, 141
Evangelista, Benny, 79, 80, 82

Fard, Wallace (also W.D. Fard), 81, 82–83, 85, 87–88, 89, 91, 92, 93–95

Federal Bureau of Investigation (FBI), 57, 62, 85, 86, 88–89, 90, 91, 100–1

Greenwood, Oklahoma, 69–71, 74–75

Haiti, vii–viii, x–xi, xiii–xiv, xvii, 1, 12–25, 26, 27–53, 55, 70–71, 76, 77–78, 79–80, 82–83, 84–85, 88, 94, 95–96, 97–116, 117, 135–39, 143
Haitian Vodou. *See* Vodou
Harris, Robert, 77–78, 81–95, 114
hoodoo, xv, 123

imperialism, xiv, 26, 27–53, 55, 77–78, 85, 98, 136, 143

Jamaica, 4, 14, 16, 28–29, 37–38, 48–49, 50–51, 68, 85, 130, 131, 138

Krome Detention Center, 104–5, 107, 110–11

Lawnside, New Jersey, 70–73
lynching, 46–49, 50, 52–53, 62–69, 70, 75–76, 81, 143

macumba, xv, 140–42
Makandal, Francois, x, 135–36
Monchy murder, 36–38
Moorish Science Temple, xix, 80–81
Muhammad, Elijah, 85, 86–87, 88, 89, 90, 91, 94, 95–96

nanigos, xiv–xv, 28–29, 33, 52
Nation of Islam, xix, 77–96, 114, 143
New Orleans, xii, 1, 2–4, 5–9, 10, 12, 13–14, 15, 18, 20–21, 24, 26, 27, 55, 59–60, 117, 143

Niña Zoila, 32–35, 39

Obeah, viii, 4, 14, 17–18, 35–39, 51, 52, 130, 131, 138–39, 140, 142, 143–44
occupation
    Cuba, xix , 53, 55 , 80
    Haiti, xvii, 5, 27–28, 51, 77–78, 79–80, 98, 136
    New Orleans, 8, 12, 26

Platt Amendment, 31, 32, 34–35, 43–44, 45

race riots, 46, 47–48, 52–53, 63, 70, 75, 86–87
rebellions, x, 4, 13, 17–18, 31–32, 44, 45, 129–32, 138, 143–44
Reconstruction, 8–13, 15, 63
Red Summer, 46, 47, 55
Republicans (also Republican Party), 6–7, 11–12

Santeria, viii, 123
slavery, viii–ix, xiii, 2–4, 15, 16, 19, 26, 43, 56–62, 75, 118, 129, 133, 138, 143–44
Soulouque, Faustin, 14–16, 17–18
St. John's Eve, 3, 4, 5
St. Lucia, 35–39
Spencer St. John, 21–23, 27, 36, 84–85

Takahashi, Satokata, 88–90
Tonton Macoutes, 98, 99, 137

United Kingdom. *See* Britain

Vagrancy, xi
Vodou, vii, 13, 14–15, 50–51, 117, 134, 135–39
vote (also voting), xi, 1, 2, 9–10, 11, 12–13, 20–21, 24, 31–32, 75, 96, 143